!

A

AMERICAN CRISIS BIOGRAPHIES

Edited by

Ellis Paxson Oberholtzer, Ph. D.

The American Crisis Biographies

Edited by Ellis Paxson Oberholtzer, Ph.D. With the counsel and advice of Professor John B. McMaster, of the University of Pennsylvania.

Each 12mo, cloth, with frontispiece portrait. Price $1.25 net; by mail, $1.37.

These biographies will constitute a complete and comprehensive history of the great American sectional struggle in the form of readable and authoritative biography. The editor has enlisted the co-operation of many competent writers, as will be noted from the list given below. An interesting feature of the undertaking is that the series is to be impartial, Southern writers having been assigned to Southern subjects and Northern writers to Northern subjects, but all will belong to the younger generation of writers, thus assuring freedom from any suspicion of wartime prejudice. The Civil War will not be treated as a rebellion, but as the great event in the history of our nation, which, after forty years, it is now clearly recognized to have been.

Now ready:

Abraham Lincoln. By Ellis Paxson Oberholtzer.
Thomas H. Benton. By Joseph M. Rogers.
David G. Farragut. By John R. Spears.
William T. Sherman. By Edward Robins.
Frederick Douglass. By Booker T. Washington.
Judah P. Benjamin. By Pierce Butler.
Robert E. Lee. By Philip Alexander Bruce.
Jefferson Davis. By Prof. W. E. Dodd.

In preparation:

John C. Calhoun. By Gaillard Hunt.
Daniel Webster. By Prof. C. H. Van Tyne.
Alexander H. Stephens. By Louis Pendleton.
John Quincy Adams. By Brooks Adams.
John Brown. By W. E. Burghardt Dubois.
William Lloyd Garrison. By Lindsay Swift.
Charles Sumner. By Prof. George H. Haynes.
William H. Seward. By Edward Everett Hale, Jr.
Stephen A. Douglas. By Prof. Ulrich B. Phillips.
Thaddeus Stevens. By Prof. J. A. Woodburn.
Andrew Johnson. By Waddy Thompson.
Henry Clay. By Thomas H. Clay.
Ulysses S. Grant. By Prof. Franklin S. Edmonds.
Edwin M. Stanton. By Edwin S. Corwin.
"Stonewall" Jackson. By Henry Alexander White.
Jay Cooke. By Ellis Paxson Oberholtzer.

Jeff Davis

AMERICAN CRISIS BIOGRAPHIES

JEFFERSON DAVIS

by

WILLIAM E. DODD, Ph. D.

Author of "Life of Nathaniel Macon," etc.

PHILADELPHIA

GEORGE W. JACOBS & COMPANY

PUBLISHERS

To my Mother

PREFACE

The purpose of this short biography of Jefferson Davis is not to justify or even defend the course of the foremost leader of the Confederate cause ; but simply to relate the story of that remarkably tragic life and, in so far as the limitations of time and space permit, correlate his career to the main current of American history.   If ardent admirers of the Confederate President find reason to complain, I have only to say that I have kept as close to the " sources " as possible ; if on the other hand extreme advocates of nationalism are displeased, I must say that it is extremely doubtful whether there was a real and vital nation within the limits of our republic before the issues for which Davis gave his life were settled.

Whether the American public as a whole is ready for a "life" of Davis is a question which may be debated ; that interest in him is steadily growing is shown by the fact that since the writer began his labors three other students of Southern history have entered the field.   Jefferson Davis and his work will then certainly be discussed anew in the near future, and with less acrimony than in the past.   Let us hope that a juster estimate of his services may be the result.

In the preparation of these pages I have been greatly aided by the authorities of the Confederate Museum in Richmond, of the Virginia State Library, of the Library of Congress, of the Carnegie Institution and of the Charleston City Library. Mr. Thomas M. Owens, of the Alabama Department of History and Archives, and Mr. Dunbar Rowland, of the Mississippi Department of Archives and History, very kindly placed at my disposal the resources of their valuable collections. Dr. Ellis P. Oberholtzer and the publishers have also been unfailing in attention and courtesy while the book was going through the press. To all these and to others who have "lent a hand" I wish here to make hearty acknowledgment.

WM. E. DODD.

Randolph Macon College,
October 21, 1907.

CONTENTS

CHRONOLOGY

1808—June 3, born in Christian County, Ky., the tenth child of Samuel Davis and Jane Cook, one of Georgia, the other of South Carolina origin.

1811—The Davis family settles in Wilkinson County in south-western Mississippi.

1813—Put to school under local teachers in a "log cabin school-house."

1815—Sent to St. Thomas's College, a Dominican school in Washington County, Ky.

1818—Attends Jefferson College in Adams County, Miss., which is soon exchanged for the new Wilkinson County Academy, where he comes under the instruction of John A. Shaw of Boston.

1821—Enters Transylvania University, Lexington, Ky.

1824—Appointed a cadet at West Point.

1828—July, graduates with his class and is promoted to the rank of Second Lieutenant in the Army.

1828-9—Stationed at Fort Crawford, now in Illinois.

1829-31—Stationed at Fort Winnebago, now in Wisconsin.

1831—Superintendent of a government sawmill on the Yellow River in northern Wisconsin.

1832—At Galena, Ill., among the lead mines.

1833—Again at Fort Crawford. Participates in the closing scenes of the Black Hawk War.

1834—Promoted to the rank of First Lieutenant and appointed Adjutant of the First Dragoons. Stationed at Fort Gibson, Ark.

1835—June 30, resigns his commission in the Army, soon to marry Miss Knox Taylor, daughter of Colonel Zachary Taylor. September 15, his wife dies at the home of his sister, Mrs. Smith, Bayou Sara, La. Visits Havana, New York and Washington.

1836—A cotton planter in Warren County, Miss.

1843—Becomes the candidate of the Democratic party for a seat in the legislature ; discusses, in a notable debate at Vicksburg, the issues of the day with S. S. Prentiss.

1844—Polk and Dallas elector. Canvasses the state, making a decided impression.

1845—February 26, married to Miss Varina Howell, Natchez, Miss. Elected to United States House of Representatives. In November, introduces Calhoun to a great assemblage in Vicksburg.

1846—June, resigns his seat in the House to accept command of the Mississippi Rifles, a regiment of volunteers for the Mexican War. September 21–23, bears a distinguished part in the battle of Monterey.

1847—February 23, Taylor's chief assistant in the battle of Buena Vista. December, takes his seat for the first time in the United States Senate.

1851—September, resigns seat in the Senate to become candidate of the Democratic party for the governorship ; defeated by Henry S. Foote.

1852—Takes active part in the Pierce campaign.

1853—March, becomes Secretary of War.

1857—March 4, reënters the Senate.

1858—July 4, makes a speech on board a ship off Boston, in which he deprecates disunion sentiment North as well as South. October 12, speech in Faneuil Hall, urging obedience to the Constitution.

1860—February 2, submits a series of seven resolutions embodying the demands of the Southern Democrats. May 16–17, debate with Douglas.

1861—January 21, withdrawal from the Senate. February 9, elected Provisional President of the Southern Confederacy. February 18, delivers his inaugural address in Montgomery. April 17, proclamation in reply to Lincoln's call for troops. May 29, takes up his residence in Richmond. July 21, battle of First Manassas. October 6, elected President of the Confederate States of America.

1862—February 22, formally inaugurated in front of the Washington monument in Richmond. June 28–July 6, first
siege of Richmond raised. December 10–31, visits the
Southwest in the hope of arousing the people and putting
an end to army difficulties in that region.

1863—April. Battle of Chancellorsville. July 1–3, battles of
Gettysburg and Vicksburg. September 19–20, Chicka-
mauga. November 23–25, Missionary Ridge. December 3,
Pius IX recognizes the Confederacy.

1864—August 17, removes Joseph E. Johnston from the command of the Army of the West. October to November,
visits Georgia to rally the people to the failing Confederacy.

1865—January 1-12, Confederate Congress plans to proclaim Lee
dictator, to supersede President Davis. January 12, Davis
appoints Hampton Roads commissioners. February 9, Lee
made generalissimo. February 22, Lee restores Joseph E.
Johnston to the command of the army in front of Sherman.
April 2, Davis leaves Richmond. April 9, Lee surren-
ders at Appomattox. April 10, Davis flees from Danville,
Va., toward Greensboro, N. C. April 24, leaves Charlotte,
N. C. May 10, captured near Irwinsville, in southern
Georgia and sent to Fort Monroe as a state prisoner.

1865-7—From May, 1865, to May, 1867, in prison at Fort Monroe.

1868—Travels in England and France.

1869—Becomes president of a life insurance company with headquarters in Memphis, Tenn.

1874—Failure of the insurance company.

1877—Visits England a second time, endeavoring to interest British capitalists in a scheme for building up the commerce of
New Orleans and Mobile with South America.

1878—Settles at "Beauvoir," Mississippi, on the Gulf coast.

1881—Publishes his *Rise and Fall of the Confederate Government.*

1889—December 6, dies after a short illness in New Orleans.

JEFFERSON DAVIS

CHAPTER I

EARLY YEARS AND TRAINING

IT is not an easy thing to think and speak dispassionately of Jefferson Davis. His career recalls to the Northern man the long and agonizing struggle of 1861 to 1865; and to the Southerner, it suggests anew the separate nationality once so fondly dreamed of, and the consequent disappointment which bore so heavily upon good and noble men now living. The portrait of Davis as displayed in a show-window in Washington, serves as a barometer to the patriotic feelings of the lingering passer-by : one rails at this inanimate symbol of the past; another stops to pay his tribute to one of its tragic and heroic figures.

Between these extremes, it is the author's aim to steer a middle course, in the hope that the ardent nationalist may be induced to pause while a great career unfolds before him ; in the hope also that the follower of "Jeff" Davis may forget the woes of the past to contemplate blessings of the present which could hardly have been possible had the "lost cause" prevailed.

The grandfather of Jefferson Davis came to Philadelphia from Wales in the early years of the eighteenth century. But, unlike the tendency of our day, the tide of emigration flowed southward through Virginia and the Carolinas to northeastern Georgia. Germans from the wasted Palatinate; Scotchmen and Irish peasants, who thought to better their lots in the new world, moved along the foothills of the Blue Ridge Mountains and spread out to the eastward, wherever the pressure from the tidewater settlements was not too great. Evan Davis joined one of these southern parties. He found a home in Georgia and soon married a Mrs. Williams, formerly Miss Emory, of the same colony. One child sprang from this union, Samuel Davis, who was early left fatherless and on whom fell the responsibility of providing for his mother.

In the year 1778, when the Revolutionary War had been waged with varying fortunes for two long years, an English expedition, sent to the Southern colonies to hold in check the insurgent forces there, threatened to subjugate South Carolina and Georgia. Young Davis, now approaching his majority, raised a company of militia and marched to the relief of Savannah, the point of attack. The British made short work of whatever defenses the city and the surrounding country had set up, and Georgia fell at a single blow into the hands of the enemy. The imperfect records of the time do not show what became of Davis and his troop. A grant of a thousand acres of land by the state of South Carolina when the war had ended is the foundation for the belief that he and his men took service under one of the guerrilla chieftains of the Palmetto State, and that he was an able and patriotic officer.[1]

[1] Original patent now in Confederate Museum, Richmond, Va.

At the close of the struggle, Samuel Davis married
Miss Jane Cook, a South Carolina lady, of Scotch-
Irish descent, and settled near Augusta, Ga., where he
was later made clerk of the county court. About the
turn of the eighteenth century, he moved, with a large
family of children, to Christian County, in central Kentucky, there becoming a tobacco planter and stock
raiser. Here Jefferson was born on June 3, 1808, the
youngest of nine. It is suggestive of the strange
vicissitudes of human destiny to recall the fact that
Abraham Lincoln first saw the light some hundred miles
away in the same state of Kentucky, and only eight
months later. And the circumstances of their births
were not so widely different as has been assumed, for
the parents of each were far removed from the high
circle of "first families" which distinguished Southern society for half a century to come. The Lincolns
were poor, even destitute; the Davises belonged to
the middle class of Southerners whose members owned
few slaves and whose children often did much of the
daily labor of the farm or small plantation.

Samuel Davis could not have been very successful
in Kentucky, for we find him on the road again about
1809. This time he directs his way to Bayou Têche in
Louisiana—a distance of a thousand miles; but the
change of climate being too radical for the health of
his family, he "moves" once more, now settling three
hundred miles to the northeastward in Wilkinson
County in lower Mississippi Territory. It was here,
on a medium-sized plantation about one mile east of
Woodville, the county seat, and some forty miles from
the Mississippi River, that Jefferson spent his early
boyhood. His father could hardly have been wealthy,

having "moved" twenty-five hundred miles in the last
few years and at a time of life when most men have
become firmly rooted in their communities. Besides,
there were many children and agriculture in the South
was anything but profitable at that period.

Samuel Davis was a Baptist and a Democrat, terms
which indicate the character of the man and his social
standing, the small circle of Southern aristocrats of
that day being almost exclusively Episcopalian in religion and Federalist in politics. The new Davis
home was unpretentious and plainly furnished ; the
fields were cultivated by members of the family and
the few negro slaves, under the personal supervision
of the master himself. The oldest son, Joseph Emory
Davis, had been left behind at Hopkinsville, Ky.,
"reading law." He seems to have been unusually
successful, for in a few years we find him settled in
Warren County, Mississippi, the owner of a large
plantation and many slaves. When his father died,
in 1824, he became the head of the family and assumed
the guardianship of the younger children. At the
outbreak of the Civil War, he was rated as "worth" a
million dollars.

The first we know of young Jefferson is that he was
sent to one of the neighborhood schools in company
with an older sister, and that he was a sensitive, proud-
hearted boy who considered himself her "guardian
and protector." It was a "log schoolhouse" and he
was then only six years old. At seven he was sent on
horseback a distance of nearly a thousand miles, to a
Catholic academy for boys in Washington County,
Kentucky, in the very community which young Abraham Lincoln's father was leaving because "it was no

country for a poor man." He was entrusted to a
company of north-bound travelers led by Major Hinds,
the commander of the Mississippi dragoons in the
recent New Orleans campaign against the English.
Jefferson and young Howell, a seven-year-old son of
Major Hinds, rode their ponies day after day on this
journey through the limitless swamps and forests.
The party camped by the wayside at night when
there was no house near by, and to this end a negro
servant with tents, blankets, supplies, and cooking
utensils had been provided. This was just at the close
of the War of 1812, when General Jackson was the
hero of the day. Major Hinds could not fail to
halt at Nashville to stay some time with the idolized
victor of New Orleans. They spent a few days at
the "Hermitage," a roomy log-house in the midst of
large oak-trees and flanked by cotton and grain
fields. The master of the estate, it would seem, made
a decided impression on the mind of the Mississippi
boy.

In the so-called college of St. Thomas, a school of
the Dominican friars, young Davis fell under the particular attention of Father Wallace, who was afterward to become prominent in the South as Bishop
of Nashville. Of his studies and his manner of life
there, we know only what he has preserved for us in
the fragment of an autobiography which Mrs. Davis
has published in her *Memoir*.[1] That he was about to
become a Catholic and was restrained by one of the
teachers ; that he joined in the mischief-making of the
boys who liked practical jokes ; and that he was dis-
ciplined somewhat in the rudiments of an education,

[1] *A Memoir of Jefferson Davis*, by his wife, early chapters of Vol. I.

we learn from the same authority. At nine years of age, he accompanied his guardian, Charles B. Green, back to Mississippi, going on a steamboat by way of the Ohio and Mississippi Rivers. He was then sent to another school with a high-sounding name, Jefferson College, in Adams County, Mississippi; his roommate here was John H. Harmanson, later a member of Congress from Louisiana and a stanch adherent of Davis in the crisis of 1850. From his tenth to his thirteenth year, he attended the new Wilkinson County Academy at Woodville, where he made much progress under the efficient tutelage of John A. Shaw of Boston, later superintendent of schools in the city of New Orleans, and a pioneer in the cause of public education in this far off region.

In the summer of 1821, young Davis, now just entering his fourteenth year, became a student in Transylvania University at Lexington, Ky., then the most important institution of learning west of the Alleghanies. He was probably none too well prepared to join the freshman class, but, as he tells us in his bit of autobiography, above referred to, he declined to associate with younger and smaller boys than himself, and hence matriculated as a sophomore and undertook to "make up" his deficiencies, especially in mathematics, by outside effort. In this he obtained the assistance of one of the professors ; but at the end of his third session we find him only becoming a senior. As this class was expected to be graduated in 1825, it shows that he did not keep up with the one he had joined and perhaps is proof that he was not in all respects a satisfactory student, notwithstanding the assertion that he won "honors" in the examinations of July or August, 1824. Since the records of the college have been entirely destroyed, we are left without adequate information as to his standing. One of his admirers [1] says "he was the first scholar, ahead of all his classes and the bravest, handsomest of all the college boys." Another adds: "He was a good student, always prepared with his lessons, very respectful and polite to the president and professors. I never heard him reprimanded for neglecting his studies or for misconduct of any sort. . . . He was rather taciturn in disposition, attractive in appearance, had a well-shaped head, and of manly bearing." [2] But these estimates must be taken, naturally, *cum grano salis.*

While at college he boarded with a Mrs. Ficklin, who lived on East High Street and whose husband was the postmaster in the town. Here his relations were most cordial and he seems to have entered somewhat into the social life of the place. He was of a lively, mischievous disposition, as is evidenced by a practical joke played on a transient fellow boarder whose self-esteem was all too evident. Davis inserted an announcement in the local paper, signed "Many Voters," calling on the sojourner to become a candidate for the office of sheriff. The subject of the hoax took the matter quite seriously and was the innocent source of much amusement in the neighborhood.

Transylvania University was a high-sounding name; it was not so misleading as some others of later origin. There were departments of law, medicine and theology, besides the regular academic work; and the institution

[1] Geo. W. Jones, of Iowa, see *Memoir*, Vol. I, p. 27.
[2] Judge Peters, Mount Sterling, Ky., to Mrs. Davis. See *Memoir*, Vol. I, p. 29.

had well-known men on its list of professors, among
whom were Holly, the president; Caldwell, of the
University of Pennsylvania; Bishop, of Dublin, later
president of Kenyon College, Ohio; and Jesse Bledsoe.
Davis was unquestionably influenced by Holly and
Bishop, the teacher of ancient languages, of whom he
tells some ludicrous stories suggestive of the nature of
college instruction in the early decades of the nine-
teenth century. As a sort of summing up of the progress made at Transylvania, the student's own words
may be given: "There I completed my studies in
Greek and Latin, and learned a little of algebra,
geometry, trigonometry, surveying, profane and sacred
history, and natural philosophy." His friends at college were David Atchison of Missouri, the later Governor Dodge of Wisconsin, George W. Jones of Iowa,
S. W. Downs, and E. A. Hannegan, all of whom were
members of the United States Senate during the decade just prior to 1860. With Jones the relationship
was intimate and remained so throughout the vicissitudes of the war down to the death of the Confederate chieftain in 1889. During this residence at
Lexington, Davis became known to Henry Clay and
from some remarks of the former in the debates
on the crisis of 1850 one is led to believe that the
great statesman showed the young student special attentions.

Toward the middle of July of this year, Davis received the news of the death of his father, whom he
had not seen since he entered college and indeed had
never known very well. A letter of his, dated Lexington, Ky., August 2, 1824, to his sister-in-law, Mrs.
Susannah Davis, gives us something of the spirit and

mind of this boy, whose life was to play so fatal a part
in the history of our republic :

" DEAR SISTER :

"It is gratifying to hear from a friend, especially one whom I had not heard from so long as yourself ; but the intelligence contained in yours was more
than sufficient to mar the satisfaction of hearing from
any one. You must imagine, I cannot describe, the
shock my feelings sustained at the sad intelligence.
In my father I lost a parent ever dear to me, but
rendered more so (if possible) by the disasters that
attended his declining years. When I saw him last he
told me that we would probably never see each other
again. Yet I still hoped to meet him once more ;
Heaven has refused my wish. This is the second time
I have been doomed to receive the heart-rending intelligence of the death of a friend. God only knows
whether or not it will be the last. If all the dear
friends of my childhood are to be torn from me I care
not how soon I follow. I leave in a short time for
West Point, State of New York, where it will always
give me pleasure to hear from you. Kiss the children
for Uncle Jeff. Present me affectionately to brother
Isaac ; tell him I would be happy to hear from him ;
and to yourself the sincere regard of
                              " Your brother,
                                    " JEFFERSON."

The Davis family took an unusual interest in the
education and training of the youngest son. That he
was especially promising there is no substantial evidence ; that he was quick, alert, and affectionate,
proof enough. He was one of a family of nine
brothers and sisters of equal claims on the attention
and care of the father ; yet he was the only one who
had been sent to the best of schools. Of him alone do

we hear in the plans of the elder Davis, though in all probability the other children received a fair education. And now on the death of the father, the oldest brother, Joseph E. Davis, a man of wealth and influence on his own account, takes particular pains to complete the schooling of young Jefferson. The first plan had been to let him finish his course at Lexington, and then enter the University of Virginia, just opening its doors to the expectant South. This scheme was changed by an appointment to West Point from Congressman Rankin of the lower district of Mississippi, probably because of the influence of Joseph Davis, although there could hardly be any question of the fitness of the proposed candidate.

Davis entered the national military academy on September 1, 1824. Here he was brought into immediate association with a remarkable group of men, including Robert E. Lee, Albert Sidney Johnston, Joseph E. Johnston, as well as many others rendered famous by the great events of the Civil War. Davis did not take a high place in his classes and at the end of the course he stood only number twenty among thirty-three students. Mathematics gave him much difficulty, and his conduct was not the most exemplary. Once, at least, he came near being expelled along with other cadets, since he was suspected of having a share in a student riot in which his roommate was a leader. Refusing to answer questions about his colleague, he paid the penalty of many weeks' close confinement. This conduct, as well as his general demeanor, made him popular with his fellows, a relationship which he prized more highly than the esteem of the authorities. It is needless to add that he was not promoted from the ranks, and he graduated as a private. From the beginning of his career at the academy, he was on bad terms with one of the professors, and the two, according to the report of Davis's friends, were constantly nagging each other. Who the professor was is not stated; but both were popular with the students, which only added interest to the long warfare. On one occasion, when the class to which he belonged was experimenting with some explosives, one of the fuses became ignited. Everybody hastened from the building, the instructor following. Davis, however, quickly seized the dangerous instrument and threw it out of the window.

Notwithstanding the rather untoward events of his cadet life, he was lastingly influenced by the strict soldierly régime; and his close attachment to the fortunes of his *alma mater* was manifested in a hundred ways during the remainder of his life, the intimate friendships of these days becoming a part of his very existence. There was hardly a member of his class whom he did not render some signal service at a later time, and certainly no one of his "set" failed to be advanced by him, either when he was a high official in the United States government or during the short career of the Southern Confederacy. Indeed, one of the permanent traits of Davis's character now appears well defined,—that of absolute and sometimes mistaken loyalty to all whom he regarded as his friends. His devotion to his family took the form of forwarding to his mother the savings from his small salary while at West Point—a touching testimonial of the sacrifices which they had made for him during the whole of his life.

What kind of a young man was this, now leaving the national military academy? In appearance he was fair, delicate of feature, with high forehead, large blue eyes and rather prominent cheek-bones. He was thin and more than six feet tall. His step was light and springy—perhaps a result of his West Point training. His presence, conduct, and manner indicated self-esteem, pride, determination, personal mastery. There was, too, something of the martinet about him, a fearlessness that amounted to temerity at times, if we may judge from the stories of his friends and comrades. He was every whit an officer, the "West Pointer" of Southern origin in almost perfect type—and up to that time the South had seemed to set the tone and make the traditions of our famous military training-school. That this young man had political convictions aside from those of the average army officer—which is to fight for the flag under all circumstances—is very doubtful. His absence from home during the larger portion of his life had precluded any active interest in the politics of his region. He undoubtedly had some recollection of the last year of the War of 1812, when two of his brothers volunteered for the defense of New Orleans under Jackson; and at a very early age he had heard the story of that war from the brave leader of the Mississippi dragoons. He had spent a week or two at the home of the General, whom he says he venerated as one of Nature's noblemen; and he had also been brought under the spell of Henry Clay, so that it is needless to argue that he was anything more than one of the country's devoted young defenders against every enemy. That he had imbibed states' rights views of the Constitution from text-books or teachers at West Point is probably only a theory of later years ; for text-books seldom impress so indelibly the minds of their weary readers, and in 1828 the teaching of governmental science had hardly made a beginning. It is safe to say that Davis accepted his commission without any serious question as to the nature of the government which gave it.[1]

[1] D. H. Maury (So. Hist. Soc. papers VI, 249) says Calhoun ordered Rawle's *View of the Constitution of the United States* to be used as a text-book at West Point in 1822, and that it remained in use there until 1861. The book was first published in 1825 ; but the superintendent writes that there is no reason to suppose that it was ever prescribed for the classes at the Academy.

CHAPTER II

ON THE WESTERN BORDER

FROM West Point Davis journeyed, in July, 1828, to his brother's home, in Warren County, Mississippi, to enjoy his first vacation since 1821. In these years the old homestead in Wilkinson County had been in part broken up. The older brothers and sisters had received their portions of the estate and had settled in the counties along the Mississippi, one going as far south as Bayou Sara in Louisiana. The mother still lived at the old home, but spent a large part of her time at "Hurricane," Joseph Davis's estate. Here Jefferson stayed during the summer and early autumn. How much property he received from his father cannot very well be determined, since it remained in the hands of the older brother as guardian and administrator. One thing is known ; late in the fall, he carried with him to his new post of duty in southwestern Wisconsin, a sturdy, promising young negro slave, who was to become widely known as James Pemberton, long his personal servant.

The two took passage at the beginning of cold weather on a Mississippi River steamer for St. Louis. There Davis received orders to proceed to Fort Crawford, at Prairie du Chien, in the southwest corner of the present state of Wisconsin, near the junction of the Wisconsin and Mississippi Rivers. But he remained in the metropolis of Missouri some days, renewing

acquaintance with his old school-fellows, Albert
Sidney Johnston and Thomas F. Drayton. Johnston
had been a Transylvania student who had preceded
Davis at West Point by two years; Drayton was a
cadet classmate and a scion of Revolutionary stock in
lower South Carolina.

The next we hear of Davis he is at Fort Crawford,
spending his " off hours " with George W. Jones, another Transylvania graduate, who now lived at Sinsinawa, some twenty-five miles south of Prairie du
Chien. The fort was under command of Colonel
Willoughby Morgan, who died three years later and
who was succeeded by Colonel Zachary Taylor, a
Southern planter-soldier, of whom the country was to
hear much in later years. This new region, into which
Davis had come for his initial service as an officer of
the national government, was a typical border land.
Northern Illinois, western Michigan, Wisconsin, and
Minnesota then constituted a vast wilderness, with
here and there a few prairie tracts on which the
buffalo had not ceased to graze. The northern part
was a sort of amphibious section like central Prussia,
lake, river and bog, relieved now and then by thick-
grown land. Here John Jacob Astor had established
his trading posts, whence he received a part of his vast
harvest of furs. At these centres there dwelt a motley
sort of people—Indians, and American and French-
Canadian trappers. The language and civilization of
these isolated settlements were unique—a mixture of
French-English-Indian symbols and ideas. There
were no churches, schools or other meeting-places. The
expanding wilderness, the rough experience of the
wild woods, the occasional struggle with rival trap-

per or with jealous Indian, were their teachers. They lived in single-room log huts built for protection against an enemy as well as the severe winter weather. Superstition and belief in witchcraft were general. If a cock crowed at sunset some member of the family was expected to die; a rabbit that crossed the hunter's path from right to left invariably brought bad luck; the cows were bewitched in spring by Indian squaws belonging to unfriendly tribes. It was a state of culture close akin to that of the Middle Ages of England, as well as that to be found in the mountain fastnesses of the South to-day.

In the early months of 1829, Davis was detailed to superintend the cutting of timber on the banks of the Red Cedar River, a tributary of the Chippewa. The party camped near the site of the present town of Menomonee. Owing to the proximity of unfriendly Indians, it was necessary to fortify the camp and maintain guards or small outposts. A large part of Davis's duty was to protect his men against the savages. Notwithstanding precautions, on one occasion they were attacked, and Davis, it seems, having become isolated from his party, escaped being scalped only by hiding in the dense underbrush. The main business of the detail was to cut logs on the banks of the river, drag them into the water, and fasten them together in large rafts, which were then guided down the stream to the Chippewa, thence to the Mississippi and finally landed at Prairie du Chien, where they were hewn or sawed into the proper shapes, and used in the construction of the fortifications or other buildings which the government was erecting. It was sometimes hazardous work to direct the rafts over the rapids of the smaller streams ; but no fatalities were reported. What the young West Pointer, still under twenty-one years of age, reared in school, and utterly unused to the lumber business, could do in such a place as this we are at a loss to know. But his mission was successful and two years later he was sent to the Yellow River camp to superintend the building and management of a sawmill,—proof, perhaps, of his adaptability and talent, certainly of the confidence of his superiors.

Fort Winnebago, on the shore of the lake of the same name, was in 1830 an important point on the northwestern border. It commanded the portage between the Fox and Wisconsin Rivers and was besides a strategic centre of operations in case of any concerted attack by the many tribes of Indians living between the Wisconsin and the Mississippi. John Jacob Astor had indicated its significance to the national government years before, and had succeeded in having it made a garrisoned stronghold. Davis was sent there in the fall of 1829 ; he remained one year and gained for himself something of a reputation as an adept in improvising comforts for the inmates of the post. He had some furniture made of the heavy timbers of the region, pieces of which have been preserved and are still highly valued by the antiquarians of Wisconsin. The clumsy wardrobes of his manufacture were the source of some amusement to the wives of the officers ; they gave them the name " Davis," which they have borne ever since. W. S. Harney was then in command of the fort, and Saterlee Clarke was also stationed there. Harney afterward played a rôle in the Civil War, being kept in Richmond under arrest for some time at the opening of the struggle. He was released on the order of the Confederate President and went to St. Louis to serve the Union cause. He had been a member of the United States Senate with Davis during the crisis of 1850. There were other West Pointers at Winnebago, and they seem to have formed a very pleasant and friendly group. Theatricals were improvised by the ladies and young officers ; some of the older men cultivated gardens in season; others were fond of hunting deer, then plentiful enough in the neighborhood. Excursions and reconnaissances were made in every direction, Davis recognizing and pointing out for the first time, perhaps, the surpassing beauty of the site of the present city of Madison and its environs. His spare hours were not altogether devoted to these outings or to card playing, the popular diversion of the inmates of the place, but to reading. What was the nature of the literature of this far-off point cannot now be ascertained. The significant fact is that he was a student and won the reputation of being chary of losing time from his books. From hints given out by his friend Jones and others, it had been this fondness for literature that had retarded his progress at Transylvania and caused him to graduate below the middle of his class at West Point. The same habit, it will be recalled, characterized Emerson at Harvard and Poe at the University of Virginia. Notwithstanding his love of the quiet corner, Davis was well liked at the fort and his transfer to another post next year was much regretted.

As already noted, he was sent to the upper waters of the Yellow River to continue the work of cutting timber for use in the rebuilding and enlarging of Fort

Crawford, which was still going on. Here it was a repetition of the experiences of the first winter at Red Cedar River, except that now he was to superintend a sawmill and protect it against Indian invasions. It required something of the diplomat to keep on good terms with the natives, and Davis learned that flattery and management were much cheaper than cold lead, and much easier to apply. He made himself so popular with his dusky neighbors that they installed him as titular head of one of their tribes, being afterward known among them as the "Little Chief."

The young Mississippian fell a victim to the severe weather of that winter, known ever since in the West and Northwest as "the winter of the deep snow." Beginning to fall about Christmas, it continued until three feet deep. Then it rained, the temperature going down to some degrees below zero, and in a short time a thick, almost impenetrable, crust of ice was formed. The extreme cold lasted for many weeks the snow remaining on the ground until spring. The isolation of the Yellow River lumber camp can hardly be imagined. Nicolay and Hay describe the conditions in central Illinois during this winter [1] as almost unbearable. What must it have been in upper Wisconsin, above Chippewa Falls, some three hundred miles from Fort Crawford and nearly as far from Winnebago, with Indians of uncertain friendliness for neighbors and only the few comforts of a lumber camp? It is not surprising that Davis contracted pneumonia ; the wonder is that he did not succumb. But he was tenderly nursed by his faithful servant, James Pemberton, and recovered after a long illness, though it is doubtful if he ever again

[1] See chapter on Illinois in the Life of Lincoln.

was as strong as he had been. From this time forward he was very susceptible to colds, which invariably developed into acute neuralgia, frequently rendering him almost totally blind for several days. While Davis's work at this place was entirely successful, he was not returned to it the following autumn. His next post was nearer Prairie du Chien, and it was much more agreeable, since he was not so far from the borders of civilization.

In the neighborhood of Galena, Ill., valuable deposits of lead ore had been found several years before. About 1825 the region attracted much attention; hundreds, even thousands, of adventurers hastened to the spot in the hope of preëmpting lands which might prove rich in minerals. Meanwhile the Indian claims had not been extinguished; consequently the newcomers were soon in conflict with the original owners of the soil. A state of war ensued and it became the duty of the United States troops to intervene. The government, following its well-known policy of safeguarding the redskins, ordered a regiment to Rock Island, near the seat of the difficulty. The natives, being more timid than their opponents, retreated to the western side of the Mississippi, and the prospective miners at once occupied the lands so recently vacated. Naturally the Indians protested and began to threaten the peace of the neighborhood. A small body of troops was ordered by Colonel Zachary Taylor, now the commandant at Fort Crawford, to march to the lead mines and eject the interlopers, keeping the place clear of all parties until the rights of the natives could be bought off by some general treaty agreement. In the meantime, General Gaines, operating from

St. Louis, had charge of the soldiers at Rock Island and superintended the movements of the Indians. The miners at once complained that their government was favoring the red men at the cost of its own people and refused to move when the troops appeared on the scene. Feeling ran high and whiskey flowed freely. The situation became critical. A second detachment was sent, with Lieutenant Davis in command. Having somehow made a favorable impression, perhaps through the influence of his friend Jones, now a prominent resident near by, he was able to bring about an understanding by which the prospective miners were to give up their claims, each one filing a record of his own case with Davis, until the government could determine its policy. This step having been taken, he then received the complainants day by day until the place was entirely vacated. The affair was deftly managed and the young lieutenant won the just thanks of his superiors for his share in it.

The treaty which followed, June 30, 1831, though for the moment it satisfied the objections of the Indians, did not appease Black Hawk, their most influential chief. Indeed, he had never been a friend of the white man since the battle of the Thames, in which he played a distinguished but a losing part. From the close of the War of 1812, the western boundary of the United States had been steadily expanding, and each new enclosure of unoccupied lands pushed him farther westward until now he was forbidden to come on the eastern side of the Mississippi;—even the burying-ground of his race near Rock Island was not to be visited by him. The reason for this strict limitation of his freedom was the presence, on the upper waters

of the Rock and Wisconsin Rivers, of the Winnebagoes
and Pottawatamies, who might be encouraged by the
persuasions of such a powerful leader to join in hostile
expeditions against the isolated settlements along the
border.

But paper treaties had no terror for so old a warrior;
he crossed the Mississippi with a group of "young
men" in the spring of 1832, and marched up the
Rock River, with the aim of effecting a union with his
former allies of that region. Governor Reynolds, of
Illinois, issued a proclamation, calling out the militia;
and the United States authorities ordered Colonel
Atkinson to move with a strong force in the direction
of Dixon, Ill., on Rock River, twenty miles from its
mouth. The militiamen, under command of Colonel
Whiteside, had reached the designated ground first,
on May 6, 1832. At this rendezvous there appeared
also two battalions of horsemen led by Majors Still-
man and Bailey, who were restless for the fray. Per-
mission was given them to proceed. Finding Black
Hawk and his forces at Old Man's Creek, near by, they
advanced with no order or concerted plan, and soon
met the enemy, killing two or three of them without
difficulty. By this time the party was much scattered
and as jubilant as though they were on a fox chase.
Black Hawk suddenly rallied his men and struck a
blow that brought consternation to the volunteers;
the Illinoisians began to run. The run became a rout,
and there was no halting them until they reached
Whiteside's camp, whence they had come so expect-
antly a few hours before. Eleven of their number had
been killed and but for their fleet-footed horses, it
would have been a wholesale massacre. Black Hawk

and his followers then drew off to avoid the larger white force, and began raiding and scalping wherever unprotected settlements were found. By this time both the Illinois volunteers and the United States regulars saw that there was serious work ahead.

Black Hawk was followed up later in the summer and defeated, on July 21st, near the falls of the Wisconsin. From here the broken ranks of the Indians retreated in disorder toward the Mississippi. They were attacked near the great river, in what is called the battle of the Bad Axe, on August 3d, and utterly routed. Their chief escaped; but being reported as still roaming about the border, Lieutenant Davis was sent with a detachment of troops to an island in the Mississippi, a few miles above Fort Crawford, to capture the remnant of the savages. From his own account,[1] a band of Indians was discovered on the eastern side of the island and they approached their pursuers under cover of a white flag. They proved to be friendly Winnebagoes, and said that they had captured Black Hawk, whom they now proposed to surrender. Davis accepted the offer and led the old chieftain to Colonel Taylor's headquarters, the Winnebagoes following to claim a reward from the United States for their services. Black Hawk was willing that they should enjoy the honor of his capture and receive whatever might be awarded them. Davis then conducted the fallen hero with about sixty of his braves to Jefferson barracks at St. Louis. Cholera broke out among the captives on their way down the river and some of the victims begged to be put off to die together on land. Davis yielded and two poor fellows were left ashore in a

[1] Letter of his in *Memoir*, Vol. I, p. 141.

dying condition, the stronger trying to minister to the needs of his weaker companion. The lieutenant delivered his prisoners and returned to his post.

It was at this time that Davis was first brought face to face with the problem of state *versus* national loyalty. He says in a speech on the Compromise of 1850 [1] and Mrs. Davis repeats the statement in her book, [2] that the rumor of the conflict with South Carolina on the question of nullification reached the army and that the regiment to which he belonged would probably be sent to Charleston, in the event of open hostilities. His own words will best set forth his position, as he viewed it in 1850: "Then, much as I valued my commission, much as I desired to remain in the army, and disapproving as much as I did the remedy resorted to, that commission would have been torn to tatters before it would have been used in civil war with the state of South Carolina." He then goes on to add that the circle of officers in which he moved had the same conception of their duty. How much of this is the sentiment of 1850 cannot be ascertained. One of his friends, Thomas F. Drayton, of South Carolina, would certainly have resigned his commission, and it is not unlikely that all had the same feeling on the burning question of 1832–33. The probability is that Davis remembered and correctly reported the views of himself and his fellows ; but there were other reasons than those of states' rights, *per se*, which may have unconsciously played a part at that time. While Davis had been brought up to honor Jackson, he and his friends of West Point were none too fond

---

[1] *Congressional Globe*, 31st Cong., 1st sess., July 13, 1850.
[2] *Memoir*, Vol. I, pp. 89–90.

of the sturdy backwoods President, whose popularity had not become universal, and whose appeal to the "gallery" was not taken as the *vox Dei*—certainly not with high-bred officialdom.

Soon after the close of the Black Hawk war, a regiment of dragoons was formed and added to the regular service. Henry Dodge of Iowa was made the colonel of the new organization. Davis was promoted to the position of first lieutenant of one of the companies and still further honored by being appointed immediately thereafter adjutant of the regiment—a choice that indicates better than anything else what manner of man he was. The office of adjutant of a corps of troops or regiment is generally filled by one who is proud of the service, punctilious as to the performance of the details of military duty, and careful of his own appearance as well as that of the officers and men. He is besides usually possessed of a clear, ringing voice, able to read the long evening reports before the regiment in such a way that every one may understand them. The promotion from second to first lieutenant was indication enough of the success of Davis's life of four years as a soldier; the assignment to the new regiment of horse with the adjutancy was a signal honor and was so regarded by his fellow officers.

A short time afterward, he was detailed as a recruiting officer and sent to Kentucky to collect horsemen to fill the ranks of the new organization. He remained a little while in Louisville and Lexington, renewing the acquaintances of former days. When engaged on this mission his fibre was tried rather severely by a cholera epidemic. He did not take to flight; and on one occasion it became his duty to bury the remains of two victims of the disease, which he did with the help of a carpenter. His return to the garrison at Fort Crawford brought him again to the neighborhood of Galena, Ill., and Dubuque, Ia., at which latter place he was stationed a large portion of his time. Being conveniently located, he paid frequent visits to his friend Jones at Sinsinawa. It was a pleasant year, that of 1833, with its joy in successful work and its occasional relaxation from military duty in a neighborhood already grown dear to him for its associations.

It was during this year, too, that there sprang up a devoted attachment to Miss Knox Taylor, daughter of Colonel Taylor at the fort, and the twenty-five-year-old lieutenant began to dream of the felicities of married life, and to think of becoming the head of a household. His advances were returned by the young woman, and their plans were beginning to mature, when for some cause or other the stern father interposed his authority and forbade his house to the ardent lover.

Colonel Dodge, with a select company of his dragoons, was sent in 1834 to Fort Gibson on the borders of Arkansas and the Indian Territory near Red River, Davis accompanying the detachment. The policy of the government to collect the remnants of the many tribes of Indians, both southern and northern, in this far-off portion of the country, had been developing since the transfer of the Cherokees and Creeks from western Georgia, upper Alabama, and Mississippi to that reservation. Whether Davis desired to join the commander of his regiment, or whether his superior, Colonel Taylor, caused him to be selected for this duty has not come out in the controversies that have waged concerning him and his love affairs. It would have been only natural for the father of Miss Taylor to think that a long stay at this far distant post might cool the ardor of her suitor. Whether or not it was by design that he was sent on this mission, it is most likely that Davis regarded it in this wise and began to lay his plans to defeat the parental scheme. At any rate, it was here that the young man passed his last years in the United States Army. However he may have felt, a long confinement to this remote post was, to one who had become soundly attached to the Fort Crawford neighborhood, cause enough to suggest the idea of a resignation. There was no longer any prospect of war, and he had served more than the term of years required to repay the government for his training at the academy. After a year and a half at Fort Gibson, he tendered his resignation on June 30, 1835, and thus, in what seemed to outsiders rather hasty action, severed his connection with the army whose service he had certainly loved. His experiences had been very varied. He had manifested decided capacity for successful military command; and his talent for management, and for ready decision in emergencies, had been clearly developed. His habits had been temperate and self-restrained, with a tendency to books and the scholarly life.

Miss Taylor was as much displeased at her father's decision as the young man himself; and after his transfer to Fort Gibson, she spent most of her time near Lexington, Ky., at the home of Colonel Taylor's sister, who, judging from subsequent events, was more favorably inclined to the suit. In all probability,

Davis saw his fiancée when occasion offered; for, when he resigned, they were married at once, leaving time to heal the breach with the father. The young couple traveled by way of the Ohio and Mississippi boats to his brother's plantation in Warren County, where arrangements were speedily made for them to establish a home of their own. In lieu of the negroes his father had left him, Joseph Davis gave Jefferson a tract of a thousand acres adjoining his own estate. A house was built and land cleared for the coming cotton season. Here a new life begins for Davis,—that of the cotton planter of the far South.

Many stories of his marriage have been told and one cannot be sure that the statement given above is absolutely correct. It is the account which the majority of reliable evidence supports. Mrs. Davis, in the *Memoir* of her husband,[1] offers his own version, which is substantially the same as mine. But there are some slightly contradictory statements in the chapter which she devotes to the subject, and we are left a little uncertain about the whole matter. All accounts but one, that of George W. Jones, agree that the father was never reconciled to the match; that he never saw his daughter again; and that he never met Davis after his transfer until the battle of Buena Vista in 1846. Why he felt so incorrigible an aversion to the young man cannot now be ascertained. The reason which the son-in-law gave was that the colonel was inveterate in his likes and dislikes and that antagonism for any one once acquired was never eradicated from his mind. We know that Taylor was positive and decided enough in his way of thinking. But this hardly

[1] Vol. I, p. 162.

accounts for his persistent attitude. Davis also says,[1] that a disagreement over a trivial matter coming up in a court-martial of which both were members, was the beginning of the trouble. The explanation is at the expense of Taylor's good sense and cannot be accepted. Mrs. Davis states that it was Taylor's objection to his daughter's becoming a soldier's wife—likewise a rather poor excuse, since we find a little further on that they were not reconciled when Davis was no longer in the army. So leaving his relations with his father-in-law thus unsatisfactorily touched upon, let us follow the fortunes of the exceedingly interesting young couple.

The husband and wife began life together resolutely. They bought ten negro slaves with money lent them by the ever kindly brother and in the spring of 1836 a crop of cotton was planted on the rough new land "cleared up" during the preceding winter. Davis worked with his own hands and directed personally and through his trusty foreman, James Pemberton, the labor of the fields. A promising harvest was approaching when the "chill and fever" season came on. Not being acclimated and to escape the added dangers of living on a freshly-cleared plantation, he left the responsibility of the estate to Joseph Davis and moved down the river with his wife to the home of a sister, Mrs. Luther Smith, near Bayou Sara in southeastern Louisiana.

Both fell seriously ill and could not be informed of each other's condition. A few days later, September 15, 1836, Mrs. Davis died, singing a favorite air. Suspecting a fatal result, the husband had crept unob-

[1] See J. W. Jones's memorial volume on Davis.

served from his bed to that of his wife and there witnessed the inexpressibly sad scene. They laid away her remains in the Smith burying ground, where she awaits the last summons in a lonely grave. There is nowhere a record of Colonel Taylor's feelings on this trying occasion. The greatest bereavement, however, was that of the young army officer, whom she had accompanied to this far-off region. Davis slowly recovered and returned in mid-October to the deserted plantation, only to leave it again in search of health and oblivion of his sorrow.

He visited New Orleans in the early winter; whence he sailed to Havana and the island of Cuba, the resort of the invalid and grief-stricken of that day. Three weeks were spent in the balmy southern seas, with saltwater baths daily; and he was much improved at the end of his visit. Without acquaintance or companion, except his faithful James, he wandered about ancient Havana, strolled through the suburban plantations with their mediæval ways, and watched the drilling of the Spanish garrison, recalling as it did his own chosen vocation. His bearing, combined with the fact that he had been seen sketching with pencil these refreshing scenes, suggested to the jealous authorities that the slender but military form of the invalid was none other than that of a spy from the neighboring republic whose covetous eye had so long sought a means of getting possession of the Pearl of the Antilles. He was forbidden to approach the fortifications of the city and his footsteps were henceforth carefully followed day by day.

A little later, still an invalid, with none too bright an outlook upon the world, he sailed for New York,

whence he took up his journey to Washington to re-
new his acquaintance with his boyhood friend, George
W. Jones, now a member of Congress from Michigan.
He was heartily welcomed to a Congressional "mess"
near East Capitol Street, at that time a favorite portion
of the city with our national lawmakers. Thomas H.
Benton, then in the prime of his power and influence,
Franklin Pierce, an unassuming Representative from
New Hampshire, Senator William Allen of Ohio, and
John J. Crittenden of Kentucky, were members of the
group. Davis entered at once into the spirit of this
interesting coterie of historic figures. With them he attended the sessions of Congress, took part in their recre-
ations, and not seldom appeared at social gatherings in
the homes of important members of the administration.

Pierce and Davis became friends, together called on
Van Buren, the new President, and later breakfasted
at the White House. No decided impression was made
on the mind of the ardent Mississippian, for we find
him attributing to Van Buren only the arts and tricks
of the politician, which we now know was not a correct
estimate. The President understood the weakness of
his guest well enough, however, to pay a delicate
compliment to his dress. Both were punctilious in
such matters. The impression which Davis records in
his later writings was due to the events of 1844 to 1848
rather than to the present visit. What the President on
his side thought of the young soldier-planter does not
appear.

Crittenden and Allen took Davis to a reception
given by Joel R. Poinsett, the new Secretary of War.
Poinsett was a South Carolina unionist, in bitter opposition to the recent nullification schemes of Robert

Barnwell Rhett and Calhoun. It would have been natural for Davis to have declined this invitation, had he been in 1833 such a states' rights man as he was later represented. The company at Secretary Poinsett's was jovial. Wine flowed freely and, in accordance with the custom of the time, most of the guests drank too much for their own safe home-going. George W. Jones, who was also present, left Davis, Crittenden, and Allen at their cups at a late hour, with the assurance that they would follow later. Probably two hours afterward a great noise in the "mess" aroused him and a Dr. Linn, who resided in the house. Davis was found to be severely wounded on the head. He was unconscious and bleeding profusely, but after receiving the attention of the physician, he seemed not to be in a dangerous condition. He had fallen with Allen into the Tiber, an uncovered stream which used to wash the foundations of the American Capitol as its namesake encircled the walls of government in ancient Rome. The senator had proven a bad guide and, reeling off the narrow bridge, had pulled his companion after him. On the following morning Davis was again found unconscious ; and it was only after much effort that he was restored. In his weakened state, the excitement and accident of the previous evening had proven well-nigh fatal. After another season of nursing, the invalid was once more on his feet and ready to return overland to his home.

This story,[1] which has been preserved by Mrs. Davis

---

[1] Given in Mrs. Davis's *Memoir* of her husband, Vol. I, pp. 167–168; also in *Life and Reminiscences of Joseph E. Johnston and Jefferson Davis* by Bradley T. Johnson ; and in an address by George W. Jones delivered in Richmond, 1893.

and was repeated on the solemn occasion of the reinter-
ment of Davis's remains in Hollywood Cemetery,
Richmond, is retold to show how men lived in Washington in 1837, and also to give the reader a possible
clue to his political opinions at that time.   There is no
mention of Calhoun by any of the Davis circle.   Benton
was certainly most hostile to him ; Crittenden was
hardly more friendly, and all were making merry in
the house of Calhoun's ablest political rival in South
Carolina.   Indeed, Poinsett had received the war
portfolio as an express recognition of his opposition to
the great nullifier.   As to the silent impeachment for
drunkenness, not too much need be said.   There was
scarcely a statesman in Washington in those days who
did not occasionally require assistance on his way
home after a night's carousal, or an evening with some
fashionable family, where the wine-cup was the chief
feature of the entertainment.   Calhoun himself was as
conspicuous for his abstinence and sobriety in matters
of drink as for his masterful speeches ; but he was perhaps the only really prominent figure in the social and
political life of the capital who was never known to
drink to excess.

With the opening of the warm spring weather, Davis
returned to his home on the Mississippi, somewhat
restored in health and peace of mind.   He took up
anew the work of a planter and, with the unfailing aid
of his brother, and in the most secluded retirement,
began to lay the foundations of a great fortune and a
greater political career.   Silently he went about his
estate, which now begins to be known as "Brierfield,"
clearing new lands, building houses for the negro
tenants and growing cotton, the unfailing source of

wealth to the industrious Southern planter. But, following the classic example of the master of " Monticello," the affairs of outdoor life alone did not suffice for the maturing mind of the retired army officer ; the old love for books came back afresh and many hours of the passing days, as well as the quiet evening-time, were spent in close study.

CHAPTER III

LAYING THE FOUNDATIONS

DAVIS'S reading was done in the library of his brother Joseph, where the best English magazines were always at hand; where the great American newspapers of the day, the *National Intelligencer*, the Richmond *Enquirer*, and the Charleston *Mercury*, together with the *Congressional Globe* and the local journals, were regularly on the table; where also the current literature of the time was to be found. Joseph Davis was the leading philosopher of his state, the ablest member of the first Mississippi constitutional convention which had met in 1817, a gentleman of the highest integrity, and an arbiter in "affairs of honor" throughout the region.[1] He was probably, too, the wealthiest planter in his state, a master of many slaves and thousands of acres of rich river lands. Samuel Davis, the father, had been a follower of Thomas Jefferson in the conflict of 1800. His sons succeeded to this trend of thought, which was tempered by the ripe Republicanism of Monroe, and rendered conservative by the steady acquisition of wealth. They were aristocratic Democrats in 1837, while their neighbors were mainly Whigs or supporters of Henry Clay, in the long contest which had been waged between this ready orator and sturdy "Old Hickory." The counties around Vicksburg, the market town of the Davises, were dominated by the

[1] Reuben Davis, *Recollections of Mississippi*, p. 79.

Whigs before 1840 ; but the state, as a whole, was overwhelmingly Democratic, though not quite of the Jackson type.

With these surroundings and with this outlook on the larger life of the nation, Jefferson Davis took up, with his learned brother, the study of John Locke, Adam Smith, Jefferson's writings, *The Federalist*, Elliot's *Debates*, and the resolutions and debates of Congress and the Virginia legislature during the controversy over the Alien and Sedition laws.[1] During a period of eight years, this unremitting study of events and of the great Democratic and states' rights authorities continued. The picturesque yet bitter contest of 1840 did not force either of the brothers from his retirement or cause them to give up their wonted places by the fireside of the "Hurricane" library.

Young Davis found time also for Byron, Burns and Scott ; for Shakespeare, Addison, Steele, and Swift ; and for the historical works of those prolific years. It was indeed an admirable combination of contemporary discussion, the heavy constitutional learning of the late eighteenth century, and the English classics, which he brought to realization in his course of self-culture. That he used these years well and drank deep from the fountains of literature is abundantly shown in his speeches in Congress and before his constituents. There was a fulness and maturity in his oratory from the beginning of his political career which impressed every one, and demanded the applause of such discriminating critics as John Quincy Adams.[2] Though the documentary proof of these

[1] Letter of Mrs. Davis to the author, March, 1905.

[2] *Memoir*, Vol. I, p. 245.

years of quiet study perished in the great war of the sixties, there can be no doubt in the minds of the well-informed that Davis was equipping himself for the gathering battle. He became, like his brother, a conservative Democrat, a stanch protagonist of states' rights, an unconfessed opponent of the Nestor of Democracy, Jackson, and an admirer of Calhoun. The Richmond *Enquirer* and the Charleston *Mercury*, taken together, interpreted events more to his fancy than did the stately *Intelligencer*. Unconsciously he was shaping his views toward radicalism in national affairs and conservatism in the South, contradictory as this assertion may appear.

His daily round of life was not unlike that of other Southern planters of means. His acres were broad and the number of slave-laborers increased annually. It was not difficult to "make money" in those "flush times"; but the income was mainly spent in improvements, new houses, and thoroughbred horses. No Southern gentleman was content with less than a half-dozen of the most expensive thoroughbreds; Davis kept a dozen. Carriages, too, must be provided and negro coachmen trained.

"Davis Bend" was a peninsula in the Mississippi, belonging in its entirety to the brothers. To ride over these magnificent estates was no easy task; to repeat this day after day was a training which, since it was universal in the South, told in the effectiveness of the Confederate cavalry twenty years later. The houses in which these planters lived were not very large nor were they planned on any extravagant basis. Simple one-and-a-half or two-story buildings with four or six rooms on the first floor and two or four on the second, there was enough accommodation for any family and also for a few guests. Spacious halls and high ceilings with wide-spreading verandas gave these homesteads an air of comfort and easy-going contentment for their owners, which was often delusive. Industry, enterprise, and thrift, befitting an Anglo-Saxon community, were far from being rare traits in young and old on these cotton plantations. The planter knew how to manage his labor, to market his products, and invest his savings so that these lower Southern states increased their wealth by leaps and bounds. Between 1810 and 1840 Joseph Davis built up a fortune from practically nothing to an estate approaching a million dollars in value. At the same time he spent money freely in travel, in horses, and for other luxuries. The one sin of these *ante bellum* slave-owners was the incorrigible habit of ruining the soil, though in this the Davises were exceptions. Their lands lay along the river banks and were so level that they could not well be "washed away" except by the river nor could their fertility easily be exhausted.

On such a plantation as "Brierfield" or the "Hurricane," everything needful for the maintenance of the families of master and slaves was produced except the broadcloth, linen, and silks, used in making the clothing of the owner's family; carriages, machinery, and silverware. Otherwise the plantation was a self-sustaining social unit whose director and law-giver was always the head of the household. As master of such an estate and associate with his brother on a much larger one, Jefferson Davis emerged from this period of retirement a tried executive, which, added to his

scholarly attainments and military training, made him
an unusual character, one to whom people would
readily turn for leadership.

Mississippi Territory had gradually grown into the
state of Mississippi ; Adams County with the old
Spanish town of Natchez had been the nucleus. In
1817, when the first constitutional convention assembled, the total population was less than seventy
thousand, exclusive of Indians.   Forty thousand
square miles of prospective territory belonged to the
Choctaw and Chickasaw tribes ; the slave-holding
citizens of the United States, who looked to Washington for the maintenance of their rights, held only a
narrow triangular strip along the river, beginning at
Vicksburg on the north and extending to the Louisiana
boundary on the south.   Adams, Wilkinson, and
Amitie were the dominating counties when the territory became a state.

The Missouri contest of 1820 quickened the slave-
holding South into a realization of its peculiar position in the Union.   The growing of cotton was a
stronger economic bond than the political ties which
held the states together.   And social forms, always
greater forces than they have been allowed to be, drew
all the outlying districts of this unique region nearer
to one another.   Close-fisted and yet far-seeing Southern leaders sketched, as early as 1820, the boundaries
of the coming Confederacy and predicted that cotton-
growing, slave-labor, and common social customs would
be the basis of the new state.[1]   All that was necessary
for the South of 1820 was to fill up the rich and vast
lands which stretched from the James to the Sabine,

[1] Dodd, *Life of Nathaniel Macon*, pp. 319–320, 367.

from Charleston, the philosophical centre of slavery, to northwest Missouri.

Both consciously and unconsciously this work was entered upon. It was stimulated by the sharp and oppressive industrial and financial crisis of 1819 to 1822 in Virginia, Maryland, and North Carolina. The sons of well-to-do planters migrated to Alabama and Mississippi, carrying with them whatever capital they could collect, and even a great many older heads were enticed away to the new country. Land in the far South could be obtained for a "song" and a profit of fifteen per cent. could be speedily realized on the money invested. On the other hand, land in Virginia had lost one-half its value, and where planting was unprofitable, of course slaves became a burden on their masters. Real estate could not easily be disposed of, but negroes could, and they were sold in large numbers to the cotton growers of the Gulf states.[1]

Between 1820 and 1840, the population of Mississippi increased by 300,000 souls, and the property valuation was many times greater at the latter than the former date. The long strip of country bordering the Mississippi had widened and lengthened at the cost of the Indians, who had been obliged to give up their hunting-grounds, and migrate to the less desirable lands beyond the great river. This drain upon the economic life of the old South was so heavy that even such well-established men as Jefferson and Madison came near being forced to sell their estates. The slave markets of Richmond, Norfolk, and Wilmington manifested a feverish activity. Good men disliked to part with their slaves; but the constant dread of bank-

[1] Richmond *Enquirer, passim;* Collins, *The Domestic Slave Trade.*

ruptcy necessitated their disposing of property that could no longer be made profitable. The flower of the old states was transplanted to the new ; the way was preparing for this section to enter upon the leadership of the South and, for a while, of the country. Not only were Virginia and the Carolinas called upon to make large contributions to the upbuilding of Mississippi and Alabama, but also Kentucky, Tennessee, and Georgia. Davis says, in his fragment of an autobiography, that, in his boyhood days, the population of lower Mississippi was composed of about equal parts of emigrants from the seaboard states and the recently settled western communities. Such a mixture of the new and old elements, of the energetic and vital forces of the South, could not but produce important results.

The extraordinary prosperity of the new region reacted upon the political views of the mother states. South Carolina declared slavery a blessing at an early date. Jefferson favored the institution in 1820, Madison lost hope in the cause of gradual emancipation by 1830, and Chief-Justice Marshall defended it, as he would any other form of property, long before his death in 1835. Calhoun launched his scheme of slavery expansion in 1837, and before 1840 the South was "solid" for the indefinite fixing of the institution upon the country.

The building of these commonwealths on their firm economic basis of cotton-growing had wrought the change. Slavery was a necessity, it was thought, in these states ; it was therefore not only not wrong, *per se*, but right and a blessing. This idea was championed not only by Southerners but by almost every newcomer from all parts of the country : Robert

J. Walker, one of the ablest champions of the new Mississippi, was a Pennsylvanian; John A. Quitman, slavery's militant protagonist from 1840 to 1858, was a New Yorker. And it was indeed an excellent civilization in many respects, which these younger sons of the South built on the black and apparently impregnable foundation of negro servitude. The Davis home itself was a fine product of it; and these thoughtful students of things political and literary, the aristocratic owners of "Hurricane" and "Brierfield," were then, and would be now, an honor to their day and generation. The whole South was made up of men of the same type in 1850, with slight variations in the different localities.

Another phase of this Mississippi life must be sketched, if we would understand the almost boundless opportunities and the discouraging limitations of Jefferson Davis when he emerged from the great sea of obscurity in 1844. With land rapidly going up in value, negroes rising faster still, and the world looking more and more to this region for its necessary supply of cotton, it is not unnatural that the spirit of speculation should seize the people, and sweep off their feet the best of their leaders.

In the early years of the century, the Territory of Mississippi had incorporated the Bank of Mississippi. After the territory's admission into the Union in 1818, its capital was augmented, and the name of the institution was changed to the Bank of the State of Mississippi. At the same time the corporation was given a monopoly of the banking privileges in the state, with power to establish branches in the various towns. The rapid growth of population and wealth brought a strong demand for the withdrawal of these franchises or the foundation of rival institutions. Consequently in February, 1830, the Planters' Bank of Mississippi was created. Its capital stock was $3,000,000, of which the state itself subscribed two-thirds. Thus the public became responsible for the losses of creditors and depositors in proportion to the state's share of the capital. In order to pay for this stock, bonds were issued and sold during the next two years to the amount of $2,000,000, the rate of interest being five per cent. annually. It was expected that the dividends from the bank would pay the interest on the bonds, for whose security quite naturally the faith of the commonwealth was pledged; that is, the state became indebted to the extent of two million dollars in order that a new bank might be opened. The institution did a successful business without loss to any one until the general panic of 1837. This taste of the sweets of high finance only whetted the appetites of certain classes of the population. But before the mania for fictitious riches had fairly seized the people at large, a new constitution was adopted in which, according to the Jeffersonian dogma, it was made unlawful for the legislature to pledge the faith of the state for future payment of present obligations, except after giving public notification and on approval of two successive assemblies.

The craze for banking and other speculative schemes was not to be stayed by mere clauses of a constitution, drawn up too in 1832 before men knew the joys of paper wealth. Had not the United States government set them the example and stimulated them by promising large deposits on favorable terms? And

were not all the states of the North and West getting
rich by similar methods? Abraham Lincoln, as a
member of the Illinois legislature, was showing his
people how to run his state into debt, as he thought,
without danger.

In addition to the Bank of the State of Mississippi
and the Planters' Bank, with its three millions of
capital and its branches in the various trade centres,
still a third institution was incorporated in 1837 under
the name of the Union Bank of Mississippi. The
capital stock was placed at $15,500,000, to be sold by
the directors to the people, the income of the colossal
establishment being promised *pro rata*, to the sub-
scribers. Citizens of other states were forbidden by
law to hold stock. To secure these shares, the state
issued five millions in five per cent. bonds to the bank
directors, who were to dispose of them in the markets
of the world, appointing at the same time several of
the directors as a guarantee that her interests would
be safeguarded. These bonds were redeemable at
short intervals. The remaining ten millions of bonds
authorized by law were left to be sold or held, at
the discretion of the bank. The five millions were
purchased by Nicholas Biddle, Jackson's "monster"
bank president, who resold many of them in England. When this good news reached Mississippi,
bonfires were kindled and torchlight processions instituted in the leading towns as though some auspicious
national event were to be celebrated. The great bank
opened its doors at the capital in 1839 ; and branches
were established soon after throughout the state.

All this was done in a community of 350,000 people
and during the panicky years of 1837 to 1840. In-

deed, it was a part of the program to relieve men of their financial difficulties. Stock was sold on credit, liens on real estate, slaves or cotton being accepted in lieu of more substantial collateral. Thus property of uncertain value was made to yield certain dividends without its sale and in addition to regular crops. Money which the state collected for its bonds or which the bank received on deposit or for stock was loaned to insolvents on the promise of payment of interest and one eighth of the principal each year for eight years. Everybody was trying to "get rich" with the aid of the government; and to do so two successive legislatures and two governors endorsed this extravagant scheme so that the terms of the constitution might be complied with. In three years the debt of the state had been increased to nearly seventeen millions at an annual interest of almost a million—a per capita indebtedness of more than forty-five dollars. The total income of Mississippi to-day with a population three times as great is scarcely more than was then voted annually for the maintenance of the banking schemes of 1839. Two hundred and fifty thousand dollars of this interest was payable in London, *i. e.*, in gold. Did ever an Anglo-Saxon community take such risks or so certainly invite bankruptcy?

In 1841 Governor McNutt declared in his annual message that both the Planters' and Union Banks were insolvent; that the latter bank had $4,000 in good money and that its immediate liabilities were more than $3,000,000. He recommended the repudiation of all those bonds which had been sold to Biddle, on the ground that the transaction was not in exact accordance with the law of the state and because the charter of the United States Bank of Pennsylvania forbade the purchase of bonds other than those of the United States government and of Pennsylvania. The legislature, be it said to its credit, was almost unanimously of the opinion that the bonds should not be repudiated. The Democratic state convention—and the Democrats had been responsible for the Union Bank scheme—met a few days after this sensational message was published, but not a word was said about the bonds or the interest due on them. The Whig party, on the other hand, took decided and high ground, declaring that the debt was lawful and must be redeemed. Before the campaign had far advanced, it was clearly evident that Democratic success would mean repudiation. That party was victorious in the election which followed and the Union Bank bonds were declared void and worthless; even those of the Planters' Bank were canceled in the same way some years later. Great excitement prevailed during the "repudiation" campaigns, and most men of wealth, generally in the older counties, voted for the validity of the recent extravagant acts of the legislature. Some even offered privately to aid in the payment of the debts of the state; but nothing came of their efforts and Mississippi's credit was permanently impaired.

Both Jefferson Davis and his brother Joseph opposed, as was natural for wealthy men to do, all these wild banking schemes; though neither of them seems to have hazarded his popularity by heading a party revolt.

As the test year of 1844 approached, another and even more important matter was absorbing the minds of Southerners, particularly of the Mississippians: the proposed annexation of Texas. That state won her independence from Mexico in the year 1836, under the leadership of a favorite of President Jackson ; the new constitution [1] was drawn up and signed, with two exceptions, by Americans who had not been very long naturalized.   It made provision for property in slaves, notwithstanding that, under Mexican rule, slavery had been formally abolished.   Mexico, however, in the early forties, had not recognized the independence of her erstwhile quarrelsome province.   It was but natural, under these circumstances, that leading Texans should favor annexation to the United States. Formal application had been made in 1836, and in 1837 Calhoun espoused the cause.   He declared again and again that the United States had improperly and unwisely assented to the " restoration" of that vast region to Spain in 1819 in part consideration for Florida, although he himself had been a member of the administration thus assailed.

The election of Harrison and Tyler was a blow to the Texas propaganda ; but the succession of the Vice-President turned the scales.   A " Texas " man, Abel P. Upshur, of Virginia, was called to the State Department in place of Webster.   Thomas Ritchie, editor of the Richmond *Enquirer*, took up the matter and Virginia was added to South Carolina in the campaign for the " Lone Star" state.   Upshur was accidentally killed by the explosion of a gun on the warship *Princeton* in February, 1844.   Tyler had long been at odds with Calhoun, but in the following March, the astute Virginia politician, Henry A. Wise, found a way to get the South Carolinian into the cabinet for the express purpose of annexing Texas, peaceably if

[1] Cf. Garrison, *Texas* in American Commonwealth Series.

possible, by warlike methods if necessary. By this
time Mississippi and Alabama had become as ardent
annexationists as South Carolina had ever been. In
1836 Mississippi had sent a company of volunteers,
under the command of John A. Quitman, to the aid of
Sam Houston in the bitter war against Santa Anna.
Though these would-be liberators did not take part in
the contest, they returned to Natchez, to work in the
state like the proverbial leaven in the lump until
public sentiment was in complete ferment.

Calhoun proceeded to his great task and completed it
in a short time, submitting a treaty of annexation to
the Senate for ratification in April, 1844. The Whig
Senate rejected his work, and he and the President
began to lay plans for the accomplishment of their
ends, despite the opposition. Meanwhile the politicians who controlled the party machinery, the "bosses"
of that day, were brought face to face with the popular
issue in the approaching presidential convention.

The Richmond *Enquirer* and its clique of wire-
pullers desired annexation, but they also longed for a
Democratic victory. Tyler and Calhoun, without whose
assistance success was impossible, were unpopular in
the North. Van Buren was therefore Ritchie's candidate for the Democratic nomination ; but he opposed
annexation and was consequently unacceptable to the
South. To force the New Yorker into line and to unite
the Northern with the Southern Democrats, a letter
from the sage of the "Hermitage," Andrew Jackson,
bearing date 1843, was now published as if written in
1844. The great ex-President urged annexation.
Still Van Buren could not be coerced and Calhoun became the logical candidate. Ritchie feared defeat

with such a leader, and the convention, in the hands of the annexationists, arranged their program. They held out the expansion of the Northwest to the followers of the able and popular Lewis Cass of Michigan, an old Jacksonian war horse. "Reannexation of Texas and the reoccupation of Oregon" were made the slogans of the convention. It being thought impossible to elect any really distinguished man of pronounced views from either North or South, James K. Polk, a popular Tennesseean of fair experience, was, to the surprise of the country, made the standard-bearer of Democracy. This left Tyler and Calhoun to themselves, which was nothing new to the latter who had never been a good party man. How had Polk gained the support of the South and made himself acceptable to the delegates of the Northwest?

This was the work of United States Senator Robert J. Walker, the wizard of Mississippi, a leader in the party of repudiation in 1841, a bankrupt himself half his life, but an able, far-seeing politician who sometimes approached the dignity of a statesman. Walker controlled his own state. He made an alliance with Thomas Ritchie and the *Enquirer;* Simon Cameron of Pennsylvania also joined him ; Bancroft and the Massachusetts politicians yielded ; and with these influences behind him, he was able to bring the Northwest to favor Texas and to accept Polk as the candidate of the party.[1] It was this "whiffle" of a man, this stooping, diminutive, wheezy-voiced leader, of "vaulting ambition," who first brought the dynamic forces of Missis-

---

[1] Claiborne, *Reminiscences of Mississippi*, Vol. I, pp. 415–423; the Vicksburg *Sentinel* of Feb. 1, 1845, speaks of Walker as the "lion" of Mississippi politics.

sippi to bear on national affairs. He, it was, who did most in the South to discard Calhoun, leave Tyler stranded high above the water's edge,—and yet "annexed" Texas. He, too, was responsible indirectly for the first appearance of Jefferson Davis in national politics.

Unlike the bank issue this new policy of his party appealed strongly to Davis. He was ready to commit himself publicly and there is no reason to suppose he was not supported by his more powerful brother.

In 1843, the Whigs had a fair chance of electing the legislature of Mississippi and reversing the shameful policy of the Democrats on the subject of repudiation. The famous Sargent S. Prentiss was the champion of the party and the bitter assailant of the Democratic program. Somehow the Whigs of Warren County permitted two of their representatives to enter the race for the state House of Representatives. Their common opponent who, under these extraordinary circumstances, should have had a fair chance of election, was a weak candidate and withdrew in due season. Jefferson Davis took his place and undoubtedly began a vigorous campaign, although he does not admit as much in his own account. He, in common with his Whig neighbors, had opposed his party on the repudiation of the Union Bank bonds, holding that they were state obligations whose value ought to be determined by the courts. As the judiciary was then constituted, this was tantamount to saying that they should be paid. With such a Democrat in the canvass, Whigs might as well desert their own divided party and vote for him.

Davis's rival opponents, however, "made up" their

differences, leaving only one candidate in the field
against him. This meant certain defeat in his first
race for political honors, but he did not give up
the struggle. On election day Prentiss was to speak
against the Democrats. Davis met him in the court-
yard at Vicksburg, dangerous as it was to do so, and
one of the great discussions of Southern politics took
place, not to the entire discomfiture of the ambitious
young aspirant. The debate continued through the
better part of the day with a result for Davis not
unlike that of John Randolph against Patrick Henry
at Charlotte court-house in 1798. He was henceforth a man of mark in Mississippi, being looked
to by the Democratic managers as a strong leader in
a forlorn section of the state. Thus equipped, surrounded by a growing, ambitious community, he devoted himself to the better life of his country. A
friend of slavery and a follower in a vague way of
Thomas Jefferson, he stood ready to enter upon the
crusade which leading Mississippians were inaugurating on behalf of the expansion of the South.

This work, as it was planned by Calhoun and put
into a practical party program by Robert J. Walker,
was intended to widen the area of slavery at the expense of Mexico and Spain. The first object was to
annex Texas before any plan of emancipation could be
put into effect there; the second was to get possession
of Cuba and other islands of the Gulf of Mexico. To
this end Calhoun worked in Washington in the year
1844 as he had never worked before ; and Tyler formed
the first joint-resolution scheme to override an opposing Senate. Mississippians, proving themselves more
practical leaders of the people, as already explained,

laid the large plans which brought the Democracy to
their view and then secured such enthusiastic support
from the uncertain Northwest that the election turned
in favor of Polk as against the "peerless leader" from
Kentucky,—the vacillating opponent of annexation.
This was an imperialist plan; it gave birth to the
contagious ambitions of the succeeding decade.

What did Davis have to do with the far-reaching
movement? He joined the ardent Mississippi political
crusaders, who had control of the Democratic machine
and who proposed to lift the local party out of its
dangerous dalliance with repudiation and turn its face
toward Washington. Walker was the master of this
group of aggressive Democrats. He was aided by
John A. Quitman, the famous Henry S. Foote, the
later Senator A. G. Brown, and Jacob Thompson, all
young men of power and none too scrupulous as to
methods.

Davis was a member of this active body; he was,
however, a Calhoun man who sought to gain his end by
pledging the delegates to his favorite as a second
choice, knowing certainly, through Walker's wire-
pullers, Ritchie, and others, that Van Buren could
not be nominated. Indeed, it was already decided
that the two-thirds rule should be adopted in order
to defeat the ex-President. Davis failed to accomplish
his purpose, but he was later made a Polk and Dallas
elector, thus coming into full coöperation with the
Walker machine. He now for the first time visited
all the counties of the state, speaking for the principles and measures of his party. He proved a strong
and popular orator. The success of this canvass
practically closed the repudiation issue, turned the

local party toward greater things, gave him a reputation which must ere long bring him high political honors and made Walker Secretary of the Treasury. It was a strange stroke of fortune that the man who did most to ruin Davis in the day of his tragic greatness, should have brought him into the larger affairs of his state and thus prepared the way for the coming bitter rivalry.

While engaged in the canvass of 1844, his mother died at the home of his sister, who lived on the old Woodville estate. At the same time he was addressing Miss Varina Howell of Vicksburg—the granddaughter of Governor Howell of New Jersey, and a very brilliant young woman, who soon became his wife and who ever afterward aided him in the discharge of his public duties. Her family was prominent in the Whig party and, like Lady Washington, could not at first realize how a gentleman and a Democrat could be united in the same person. Davis overcame these obstacles and in the end probably proved as much of an aristocrat as even a Howell could desire. The bridal tour took them to New Orleans, and to the famous St. Charles Hotel, where they met the fashionable society of the Creole city. They returned after a few weeks to "Brierfield," their favorite home until the war cast them adrift and gave occasion for the looting of the fine old place.

The next summer, as a sort of reward for his useless campaign of 1843, and his expensive canvass as an elector in 1844, Davis was brought forward as a logical candidate for the national House of Representatives. To the surprise of the party leaders, he openly announced his opposition to the Democratic attitude on repudiation, the one live local issue.[1] But there was possibly some method in this madness. He hoped to add weight to the ticket in northwestern Mississippi. Strongly to censure this feature of Democratic rule was not likely to lose him as many votes as it would gain. The "organization" probably did not approve of this sort of contempt for their authority; but they feared to make an issue of it. When the nominating convention met, there was little chance of defeating so popular a candidate, especially since Davis commanded a powerful social "backing" in some of the Whig counties. He was chosen without a contest. The canvass he made was undoubtedly a vigorous one; in view of the future of the young leader, it is unfortunate that no reports of his speeches have been preserved. He was elected and took his seat in the House of Representatives in the following December.

In the autumn of 1845, Calhoun who, in the meanwhile, had been advising his friends not to accept office in the Polk administration, made a tour of the South and West as far north as Cincinnati. He was received with enthusiasm such as few Presidents have aroused. In Mobile, in Montgomery, and in Memphis he spoke to vast crowds.

When he reached Vicksburg, Jefferson Davis was fittingly appointed to present the speaker in a short address. The Mississippian was much concerned about Calhoun's strange advocacy at Memphis of a new plan of internal improvement; he could not bring himself to refer to this subject, though it was the topic of conversation in every gathering. Nevertheless, the introduction passed off smoothly and Calhoun made another

[1] *Memoir*, pp. 204–205.

of his logical Southern and states' rights speeches, without reference to the improvement of the "inland seas," says Mrs. Davis, who was present and a most interested auditor.[1]

The day after—late in November—Davis and his wife set out for Washington, going by way of the Mississippi and Ohio Rivers as far as the boats could take them. The remainder of the journey was made by stage-coach. They reached the capital in time for the opening of Congress and took lodgings at the National Hotel, where Polk had stopped when he came on for the inauguration. Calhoun, reëlected to the Senate by his faithful South Carolina, tarried a while at his home, making clear to himself the policy which he would pursue relative to the threatening crisis.

[1] *Memoir*, Vol. I, pp. 211–213.

CHAPTER IV

A DANGEROUS ISSUE

THE new theatre in which Davis was to play so tragic a rôle was just now the centre of a dangerous agitation. The Democratic party had shrewdly gauged public opinion when it emblazoned "Texas and Oregon" upon its banners; the country gave it a free hand. The President was commissioned to "re-annex" Texas and to "reoccupy" Oregon; both the Senate and the House were in the hands of the Democrats. But the bold language of a popular campaign is not appropriate in international relations. To incorporate Texas, even after the events of early 1845, was to "assume" the responsibility for a war with Mexico, of which no one could foresee the outcome; to seize the whole of Oregon as rightfully belonging to the United States when the American government had admitted a partnership with England since 1818 was a still more dangerous policy. The leaders of the Democratic party had placed themselves in a very serious attitude. The people had been taught that their rights were coextensive with their cupidity; they had been influenced to believe that neither Mexico nor England would fight, or, if they should, that Americans could march unimpeded either to the Mexican capital or to the frigid zone. Elected, then, with such high hopes, these same teachers of the public were now confronted with the consequences of their radical but popular plans.

Besides these perfectly obvious difficulties, others were certain to arise. If Congress annexed a region to the Southwest in which slavery had already been planted—a region several times larger in area than all New England—what would be the effect on the Northern Democracy? The Northwest might possibly be content with her equivalent, Oregon; but not so the populous East and North. Might not the party lose its hold on such states as New York and Pennsylvania, by whose loyalty it had won all its victories since Jefferson's election in 1800? The East and North were unwilling that five or six new slave states should be brought into the Union, for the reason that the Senate would then be permanently in the hands of men who represented slave-holding interests. Such a condition would consolidate hostility to slavery by making its continuance equivalent to Northern political bondage; that is, the North's preponderant population and wealth could never suffice to secure her control of the national government. Could the South thus risk the alienation of its old friends?

The President in his inaugural message, in March, 1845, had embarrassed gray-heads in the party by almost defiantly proclaiming, as he had done during the campaign, that the American claim to all of Oregon was unquestionable. He repeated this declaration when Congress assembled; and matters were speedily made worse by the resolutions of Senator Allen of Ohio, calling for a formal notification of England that our partnership as existing since 1818 was dissolved, which practically meant war, because "reoccupation" was supposed to follow this proposed "notification."

Davis entered Congress amid these trying and delicate circumstances. He at once made friends with the group of leaders from the South, some of whom were soon to desert him, though they later regained his confidence and then, finally, did most to ruin him when all were embarked on the dangerous and stormy sea of Southern independence. William L. Yancey, Robert Barnwell Rhett and Jefferson Davis were the younger leaders of this extraordinary school of Southern politicians. Calhoun was their prophet, and he now planned a larger imperialism, which should win all the ends aimed at in the Democratic national convention in Baltimore while not endangering the existence of the Union. For this he had yielded at Memphis his beloved strict construction theories, and advocated Clay's vast scheme of internal improvements, adding even the suggestion that the national government should aid in the building of railways connecting the north central with the south central states and finding an outlet to the Atlantic at Charleston.

What the great South Carolinian proposed appeared at once reasonable to Davis, Rhett, and Yancey, except they were not certain that even he could win all Oregon for the Northwest without war, and for this alternative they would in no wise accept responsibility.

Had Calhoun been retained as Secretary of State, it is more than probable that he could have secured both Texas and Oregon without involving the country in war. He would have given in to Mexico on minor points and delayed a solution of the English question until he was ready to assume a bold policy. Then having become a second time a believer in broad national powers, he could have realized some of his plans enunciated or suggested at Memphis by yielding large expenditures of public moneys in the North or perhaps granting a fair protective tariff.[1] The presidency could no longer have been denied him and the ambition of a long and remarkable career would have been satisfied.

Yancey and Rhett were not men of Calhoun's calibre. They insisted that Texas should at once fall into the lap of the Union, for the benefit of their own section. Rhett, in his famous paper, the Charleston *Mercury*, began to decry the Oregon policy, and labored to prove that the claim of the United States to that region was a humbug;[2] he did what he could to call down upon the heads of the Democratic leaders the charge of Punic faith, already finding a place in the more acute journals of the North and West. Yancey was an ally of his. Both made insulting and useless speeches, Rhett declaring that the North was voting for "notification," in order to win the Northwest from the South; and Yancey insisting that war with England would result in the loss of Oregon and the gaining of Canada, a poor exchange from the viewpoint of radical Southerners.

Davis made his first set speech in Congress on this resolution. He manifests here, in his early efforts as a legislator, some of the larger views of national life and development which have been so persistently ignored by those who have chronicled his career.

[1] As Everett was urging him to do: *Report Amer. Hist. Ass'n*, 1899, Vol. II, p. 1081.
[2] See Washington *Union*, Nov. 17, 1845.

First he did what few other members of the House
had the industry and patience to do,—examined all
the available authorities on the subject, going back to
Cook's and Dixon's voyages, and closing with a very
respectful and sensible use of Gallatin's recent public
letter on Oregon and the present crisis.[1] The wild and
unreasoning appeal to arms, the jingoist's boast of
recent months, he deprecates as positively harmful.
He then manifests his West Point spirit in the plea for
a little better preparation for hostilities before too
much bragging is indulged; "the cry, 'the whole of
Oregon or none, now or never,'" leads directly to our
ruin.   As to the declarations of the Baltimore platform
he says: "Some advocates of this immediate notice
have urged their policy by reference to the Democratic
Baltimore Convention and contended that the question
was thereby closed to the members of the Democratic
party.   That resolution does not recommend immediate notice, but recommends the 'reannexation of
Texas and the reoccupation of Oregon at the earliest
practicable period.'   The addition of territory to our
Union is a part of the Democratic faith, and properly
was placed in the declaration of our policy at that
time."[2]   He goes on, however, to justify Southern
haste in regard to Texas, as contrasted with his willingness for delay in Oregon, because the former
Mexican province is further advanced and more inti-
mately identified with American interests, all of which
was true, though unquestionably he saw a reason for
the eagerness of his section, that he did not care

---

[1] Published in the *National Intelligencer*, about this time, but not
republished in Gallatin's works.

[2] Twenty-ninth Cong., 1st Sess., Feb. 6, 1846.

to state in the House of Representatives. The final gentle hint to the Executive to act wisely manifests a disposition to cajole those who are not his positive opponents, into the adoption of what he regards as the best policy.

There was much of the sophomoric element in this first speech; something of insincerity, too, but he was supporting Calhoun's larger plans, and was not anti-national, desiring to conciliate the North rather than defy it, as Rhett and Yancey were already doing. Besides, Davis had a personal acquaintance with many of the Western leaders,—the Dodges of Iowa and Wisconsin, and George W. Jones. And he himself was animated with some of the buoyant and boundless patriotism of the Northwest.

Two abuses, already grown common in Washington, received the attention of the young Mississippi member before the close of this short term of the House. Internal improvements for local purposes or, as Stewart, a representative from Pennsylvania, put it, to "cement the union," received scant courtesy. On March 16, 1846, Davis narrowly examined the items of the current River and Harbor Bill, finding that the representatives from Illinois and Michigan had combined to procure appropriations for certain localities with small regard to the national benefit. St. Louis and Lexington had both succeeded in getting their hands into the Treasury under the terms of the bill. Davis held that these methods of "log-rolling" the nation's money into private or local pockets was unworthy of honorable men. When asked if he did not lend his own support to appropriations for Mississippi's benefit, he retorted sharply that he would ask for nothing which could not be justified in the minds of men living most remote from the locality ; he would not ask even for this, if he were compelled to vote for some of the appropriations carried by the general bill on this subject.   When he had shown the need of removing certain obstructions in the Mississippi River, some member, bent on his favorite local expenditure, interrupted him to ask, " Will you vote for the Lake appropriations ? "   He responded : " Sir, I make no terms.   I accept no compromises.   If when I ask for an appropriation, the object shall be shown to be proper and the expenditure constitutional, I defy the gentleman, for his conscience' sake, to vote against it.   If it shall appear to him otherwise, then I expect his opposition, and only ask that it shall be directly, fairly and openly exerted.   The case shall be presented on its single merit ; on that I wish it to stand or fall. I feel, sir, that I am incapable of sectional distinction upon such objects.   I abhor and reject all interested combinations." [1]

Davis then attacked the protective system as unconstitutional, because special in design and operation. It was, he maintained with much force, the source of most of the abuses in the River and Harbor Bill appropriations from year to year.   Let the government aid all classes by releasing them from duties or other taxes not absolutely necessary for the general defense.   The least government possible at the least possible cost was the ancient Jefferson dogma which he resuscitated at a time when politicians were striving to make the republic a mutual benefit society.

At the close of his remarks, we have another proof

[1] Twenty-ninth Cong., 1st Sess., March 16, 1846.

of his hopeful optimism. He says that the size of the Union is not a matter of concern to him; that loyalty, unlike gravity, increases the further one goes from Washington; and he cites his experience in the far West and the lower South as proof of his assertion. "The extent of our Union has never been to me the cause of apprehension," said he; "its cohesion can only be disturbed by violation of the compact which cements it." [1]

The efforts of Calhoun in the Senate, aided by Davis and others in the House, resulted in a reduction of the demands on England, so that what remained of the Allen resolutions was quite inoffensive. Great Britain was not challenged. With the Oregon side of the crisis passed, what would become of the Texas embroglio? The President, not Congress, settled this question by causing the American army, under Colonel Zachary Taylor, to threaten the Mexican position on the Rio Grande. Hostilities followed as a matter of course, and from the White House the word came to Congress early in April that war already existed and called for troops. Calhoun arose in his place in the Senate and demanded to know the authority of the Executive in usurping the rightful powers of Congress; Davis made a similar protest at the same time in the House. The South Carolinian continued to arraign the President's policy, while Davis, parting company with his greatly admired friend, yielded his support to the war and deprecated all criticism of Taylor and his men for their unnecessary advance. Rhett became an almost bitter opponent of Calhoun, on the ground that war was necessary if annexation was to be com-

[1] Twenty-ninth Cong., 1st Sess., March 16, 1846.

pleted, and annexation was already an ultimatum of the Southern extremists. They would go to war with the North, it was openly repeated, if this new region were not to be incorporated into the Union. Rhett, Yancey, and Davis had their way in respect to Texas—the result need not be anticipated.

Having favored the war, the Mississippian was selected to command the first regiment enlisted in that state, called the Mississippi "Rifles." He resigned his seat in the House in June and set out for Jackson, going thence to the scene of active hostilities. Congress had dallied while the dangerous crisis came on, and the Executive seized the reins and drove directly into war. The country was left to judge between Calhoun and Polk.

CHAPTER V

ONE YEAR OF WAR

THOUGH the circumstances of the reconciliation are not known, Zachary Taylor and his son-in-law appear to have become friends before the outbreak of the war with Mexico. The young Mississippian had no love for General Scott. How natural was it then for the commander of the Mississippi Rifles to have had an understanding with the President that he and his men were to remain with Taylor until the close of the war, or the expiration of their term of enlistment.

Davis set out for New Orleans, the rendezvous of his regiment, early in June, 1846. After a short stay at "Brierfield," where he procured a trustworthy servant and horses, he continued his journey, embarking in New Orleans on the *Alabama* for Brazos, St. Iago, near Port Isabel in southeastern Texas. He and his troop reached there August 2d, and were immediately encamped for some weeks of hard drill such as only a West Pointer knows how to give. They occupied a neck of sandy land near the sea and were compelled to endure the hot, sultry, August weather with but brackish water to drink. It was not a pleasant outlook for volunteers whose business it was "to fight," not always to be preparing for the conflict. Sickness afflicted many and others were disillusioned; it was a difficult matter to maintain discipline and keep these spirited soldiers in harness.

However, Davis was popular with the men, many of whom had enlisted from his immediate neighborhood, and he kept the regiment together and in good cheer. On August 12th, they marched to the mouth of the Rio Grande, nine miles south. Here they again encamped, awaiting means of transportation up the river to Camargo, where they would become a part of Taylor's " army of invasion." The drilling was renewed, much to the regret of the men ; but at last they joined Taylor, and were pronounced the best trained and most orderly volunteer troops in the army.[1]

It was a remarkable organization. The privates were men of wealth and high social standing. They had their negro servants and extra provisions. Their guns were of a new model and proved to be wonderfully effective in battle. Before leaving his seat in Congress, Davis had insisted that his regiment should be armed with rifles. Later, when Secretary of War, he introduced into the regular army the improved guns he now used in the Mexican War ; and they were to be employed later in the Civil War. It was a good regiment, comprising altogether, with companies full, a little over nine hundred men. It was indeed a welcome addition to the weakening American force since the enemy was increasing in numbers daily.

After reaching Palo Alto, Taylor had occupied, without serious resistance, the town of Matamoras ; he now extended his lines up the river to Camargo, the new

[1] *Memoir*, Vol. I, pp. 288-289.

base of supplies for the army of invasion, not re-
linquishing his hold on Port Isabel. It was here that
he selected the force which he proposed to lead in the
direction of Saltillo, more than a hundred miles distant on the road to the City of Mexico. Taylor commanded now, late in August, 1846, 12,000 men, of
whom 9,000 were volunteers, enlisted for short terms.
Few officers of the regular army esteem very highly
the citizens who offer for short terms. Taylor was no
exception to the rule. The Mississippi Rifles had enlisted for a year; they reached Camargo about September 1st and were put in charge of Brigade Commander Quitman, who panted for the conflict. It was
perhaps due, therefore, to Davis's military training
and experience in the West that this brigade was
chosen for the active duties of the advance movement,
for Taylor selected only 6,000 men for this purpose,
leaving the other 6,000 for guard and garrison service
at the various points already seized.

The army moved southwestward on September 5th;
two weeks later they approached the town of Monterey,
which was one hundred miles from Camargo, and held
by 10,000 troops under command of the Mexican
general Ampudia, who was in high favor with the
restored Santa Anna. The latter had infused a new
spirit into the armies of Mexico, and it was with every
prospect of success that he viewed the coming battle.
Monterey was strongly fortified and the American
general had no heavy artillery. Ampudia's army was
made up of 7,000 regulars and 3,000 recruits; Taylor's
advance force consisted of 3,000 regulars and 3,000 recruits. The Mexicans defended their homes while
he had penetrated far into the country of a foe. But

the attack was vigorously made on September 21st.
The first and third regiments of the regulars led the
fight. Having entered the town, the assailants received a galling fire from public squares, barricades,
and private house-tops. Men and officers were wavering when Taylor hastened a much stronger force into
the city under Butler and Quitman.

Davis now had the opportunity to show his mettle.
The main point of resistance was Fort Teneria.
Quitman, Davis, and McClung, Lieutenant-Colonel in
the Mississippi Rifles, made an irresistible charge,
carrying everything before them, and seized the fort,
which they held for two hours under the hottest fire.
A second fort three hundred yards farther on was
attacked, but was not captured that day. Night came
on and the invaders encamped on their advanced
ground. During the same day General Worth, another
of the excellent officers who commanded under Taylor,
seized the line of Ampudia's retreat and at nightfall
held the road to Saltillo. On September 22d, the
Americans made no vigorous forward movement; but
the next day Worth occupied the public square of the
town and by evening the Americans had improved their
position so much that the morrow must have brought
a fearful slaughter but for Ampudia's offer to treat.
Taylor accepted the proposal and appointed three
commissioners to agree upon terms.

It is proof enough of the high regard in which Taylor
now held Davis to know that the young Mississippian
was named as one of the commissioners, in preference
to ranking officers. Ex-Governor Henderson, commanding the Texas forces; General Worth, of the
United States Army, and Jefferson Davis, of the

Mississippi Rifles, were appointed to conduct the negotiations. It was agreed that Monterey, its fortifications, cannon, other munitions of war, and all public property should be delivered to the Americans. In consideration of the offer to surrender without further loss of life, it was stipulated that the Mexicans should march out of the city with the honors of war and retire beyond a line in the rear of Saltillo, forty miles distant. Both parties accepted an armistice of eight weeks, time enough for each to hear from the home authorities.

This was liberal treatment; but Ampudia had won it by hard fighting and a timely surrender. Besides, the enemy's strength was not entirely broken. The losses had been very heavy on each side, and it was not Taylor's policy to exasperate the Mexicans and bring down upon himself the inveterate hatred of the surrounding population. It was hoped at the American headquarters that the Mexican government would regard this vigorous beginning as a clear manifestation of the purpose of the United States and would now offer to make terms of peace. Davis wrote his wife on October 5th, that there were good reasons to believe that Mexico would soon yield and withdraw the forces just defeated at Monterey. This was a mistake. Santa Anna issued a proclamation, saying that he would yet dictate terms to the enemy on the banks of the Sabine.

If we may judge from certain indications and from the statements in the letters of Mississippians at the front, Davis had made a reputation which transcended that of any other officer except Taylor himself. One wrote: "If the time of our regiment expires and our colonel even then thinks that we could be useful, there is not a man in his regiment who would not sacrifice his life to obey him, so much has his gallant conduct raised him in their estimation. The degree of power his coolness, courage, and discretion have acquired for him in the army generally would hardly be believed at home." [1]

But the politicians in Washington were not pleased with the liberal terms made with the enemy at Monterey. The armistice was declared to be abrogated, while Taylor was ordered to assume the offensive. How the administration meant to reward him—he was as yet the only victorious commander in the field—can best be judged by the dispatches which now began to reach him. On October 10th, he received the information that one of his subordinates, General Patterson, then at Camargo, was to march with a large contingent of the troops toward Tampico ; and early in November he got word that he was to make no further advance movements, but to fortify himself at Monterey. At the same time Patterson's army was definitely stated to be 4,000. On November 14th, a letter from General Scott informed Taylor that 10,000 men were to be taken from the army, and that he himself, instead of Patterson, would command them. The objective was now declared to be Vera Cruz. Finally on November 24th, Scott wrote that he was coming south, not to supersede Taylor but to march away with his men, leaving him to await the pleasure of Congress in regard to raising a second army.

Was ever a deserving officer so badly treated? The administration was in sore straits for a commander of

[1] *Memoir*, Vol. I, p. 308.

high rank who would not become, on the successful termination of the war, a formidable candidate for the presidency. It was limited in its choice to General Scott and his next ranking subordinate, both of whom were known to be Whigs.[1] Following the Machiavellian principle that a general should not be allowed to grow too great, Polk and Walker thought first to slight Scott, and advance Taylor; but when the latter had won his second battle and his name began to be mentioned for campaign purposes, they turned again to Scott, who was still willing to go in person to Mexico and reap laurels, the seeds for which had already been sown by his subordinate. Scott proposed that an army should be collected at Vera Cruz, whence it could be led along the road made famous by Pizarro four centuries earlier, direct to the capital of Mexico. Undoubtedly this was a proper plan; Taylor had said as much in a letter to his friend Senator Crittenden. But to entrust the whole movement to Scott, after the magnificent campaign just completed, was little less than insulting to the hero of Monterey.

Happily, Taylor was far from the scene of intrigue and, having already received the order to break the armistice, he was free to make such disposition of his forces, now 15,000 if Patterson's division be included, as he deemed best. He advanced beyond Saltillo, holding the country on the seacoast in the direction of Tampico, whither Patterson was already directed to conduct his command. Butler had been left at Camargo,

[1] Thurlow Weed's letter to Taylor seems to show that his attitude in politics was now understood to be favorable to the Whigs. *Autobiography of Thurlow Weed*, I, 58, quoted in Schouler, Vol. V, p. 22.

with the greater portion of the army, including recent
accessions, under his immediate supervision. The
country between the Rio Grande and Tampico, extending westward to Saltillo, was, by the end of December, under the control of Taylor, the commander-
in-chief being at Victoria, the capital of the province
of Tamaulipas, near the seacoast, almost three hundred
miles south of Camargo.

General Scott now executed his purpose of depriving
Taylor of his troops and without a conference with the
latter, ordered Butler to put in motion, for Tampico,
all the men he commanded, adding to these practically
the whole Army of the Rio Grande. These movements were being effected during January, 1847. But
the instructions of Scott, relative to the new disposition of the men hitherto operating under Taylor, fell
into the hands of Santa Anna, who at once prepared
to cut off the remnant of the force and compel the surrender of all the troops remaining on the advance line
of Saltillo and Victoria. It was a great opportunity
for the Mexican commander and he embraced it
promptly.

In February, Taylor was allowed to select for himself a regiment of volunteers, Bragg's and Washington's batteries, and a squadron of dragoons, for which
service the Mississippi Rifles were chosen. To this
detachment was added General Wool's little Army of
the Northern Department of Mexico, hitherto an independent organization, amounting to some 4,000
volunteers. During the early days of February, 1847,
Taylor, with his small force,[1] marched rapidly toward Saltillo to effect a junction with Wool. No

[1] Davis's report, *Memoir*, Vol. I, p. 315,

serious attempt was made by Santa Anna to prevent
this movement, which was successfully accomplished.
Taylor now commanded 5,400 men of whom less than
one-third had ever been under fire. On February 22d,
Santa Anna approached the American position—a
high plateau eight miles south of Saltillo. His army
of 20,000 men attacked Taylor's left. A regiment of
volunteers was in full flight when Davis was ordered
forward with the Mississippi Riflemen, much reduced
in numbers on account of losses at Monterey, and two
extra companies detailed for this special duty. He
gives an account of his day's work as follows : [1]

"This position, important from its natural strength,
derived a greater value from the relation it bore
to our order of battle and line of communication
with the rear. The enemy, in number many times
greater than ourselves, supported by strong reserves, flanked by cavalry, and elated by recent
success, was advancing upon it. The moment seemed
critical, and the occasion to require whatever sacrifice it might cost to check the enemy. My regiment, having continued to advance, was near at hand.
I met and formed it rapidly into order of battle. The
line then advanced in double-quick time, until it was
in the estimated range of our rifles, when it was halted
and ordered to fire advancing. . . . We steadily
advanced, and as the distance diminished the ratio of
loss rapidly increased against the enemy ; he yielded
and was driven back on his reserves. A plain now
lying behind us, the enemy's cavalry had passed
around our right flank, which rested on the main
ravine, and gone to our rear. The support I had ex-

[1] *Memoir*, Vol. I, p. 321.

pected to join us was nowhere to be seen. I therefore ordered the regiment to retire, and went in person to find the cavalry which had been concealed by the inequality of the ground. I found them, at the first point where the ravine was practicable for horsemen, in the act of crossing—no doubt for the purpose of charging our rear. The nearest of our men ran quickly to my call, attacked this body, and dispersed it with some loss."

The regiment was reformed on the ground which it had occupied at the beginning of the fight that day and from which it had retreated. "Here," says Davis, continuing his account, "a heavy fire was opened upon us by a battery which the enemy had established near the centre of his line. The battery was withdrawn for the moment and a large cavalry force advanced to the attack on our left. The Mississippi regiment was filed to the right, and fronted in line across the plain ; the Indiana regiment which had been operating with us was formed on the bank of the ravine in advance of our right flank, by which a re-entering angle was presented to the enemy. While this preparation was being made, Sergeant-Major Miller of our regiment was sent to Captain Sherman for one or more pieces of artillery from his battery. The enemy came forward rapidly and in beautiful order—the files and ranks so closed as to look like a mass of men and horse. Perfect silence and the greatest steadiness prevailed in both lines of our troops as they stood at shoulder [?] arms awaiting an attack. At eighty or a hundred yards in front of us the enemy came almost to a halt. A few files of our men fired without orders and both lines then instantly poured in a volley so destructive that the mass yielded to the blow, and the survivors fled. Their retreat was followed by a very effective fire by Captain Sherman who had now arrived with his field-piece until they were out of range."

This was Davis's celebrated stand, which was reported all over the country. It had saved the day for Taylor. The Colonel of the Mississippi Riflemen did other valiant work in this battle—all the time suffering from a painful wound in the foot—but nowhere else was the issue so close and the conduct of his men so heroic. In his detailed report of the battle of Buena Vista of March 6th, Taylor said :

"The Mississippi Riflemen, under command of Colonel Davis, were highly conspicuous for gallantry and steadiness, and sustained throughout the engagement the reputation of veteran troops. Brought into action against an immensely superior force, they maintained themselves for a long time unsupported, and with heavy loss, and held an important part of the field until reënforced. Colonel Davis, though severely wounded, remained in the saddle until the close of the action. His distinguished coolness and gallantry, and the heavy loss of his regiment on this day, entitle him to the particular notice of the government."

This was the last battle General Taylor was to fight, Santa Anna retiring to San Luis de Potosi with hardly half as many men as he had commanded on the previous day. The general had shown admirable qualities ever since the government had practically repudiated him. He had borne Scott's insulting conduct without throwing up his commission ; had so stationed his forces as to meet the enemy on greatly advantageous ground; and during the fierce fighting of the 23d, had remained unperturbed in the midst of his troops, disposing them to the best advantage, while he encouraged the faint-hearted and restrained the headlong. He had triumphed over an enemy four times as strong as himself—proof enough of his good leadership. It was his third victory on the enemy's ground, against forces greatly superior to his own.

The government had again grown uneasy about the little Army of the Rio Grande. Scott's disposition of the forces had become known and it was feared that Taylor had been surrounded and his men put to the sword, a sacrifice to the ambition of the commanding general. The news of Buena Vista was even more grateful than had been that of Palo Alto. The people breathed easily once more and the names of Taylor and Davis were toasted from one end of the country to the other.

While the ostensible candidate for the next Whig nomination was moving in all pomp and splendor toward Vera Cruz, the deserted and neglected subordinate had won a brilliant victory against the greatest odds. There was now nothing more for Taylor to do but to guard the Rio Grande and hold the ground he had taken. He was left by the government idly to watch the Vera Cruz expedition. But his three successful encounters, and, above all, that of Buena Vista, had won him the presidency at the hands of the people of his country, who loved fair play and were determined to reward him for his faithful services.

The term for which the Mississippi Riflemen had enlisted was about to expire. There was no longer any real need of them, and Davis, after formal arrangements with his chief, marched the remnant of his command to the harbor near Port Isabel, where they took ship for New Orleans. They reached the Southern metropolis on June 9th, nearly one year after their departure. The city outdid itself in honoring the returning heroes. They were marched along Canal Street, amidst deafening applause, and finally to La Fayette Square, where S. S. Prentiss delivered an oration of unsurpassed eulogy—not at all like the speech he had made at Warren County court-house, against Davis four years before. The commander replied in amiable terms to the eloquence of his old political opponent. From the speech-making, the regiment marched to the Place d' Armes, where they were feasted at the public expense.

The next day, the Riflemen took ship and disbanded as they went up the stream, groups of men being left at each wharf. Mrs. Davis came on board the vessel at Natchez, where she had spent the past year at the home of her father. There were also twelve young ladies, with a quantity of flowers, who crowned the officers—let us hope some privates too—with wreaths. From this place to Vicksburg, it was a continuous ovation which the planters gave their neighbor, the returning master of "Brierfield." After a day in Vicksburg, Davis and his wife went back to their estate, where the wounded foot continued to give trouble, compelling the hero to depend upon crutches for a year or two.

A significant and somewhat impertinent act of Davis's now closed his Mexican career. Polk forwarded him, through a friend, a commission as brigadier-general of volunteers. Its recipient returned it with the remark that the President of the United States had not the authority to make such an appointment,[1] that power inhering in the states alone.

[1] *Memoir*, Vol. I, p. 360 ; Schouler, Vol. V, p. 77.

CHAPTER VI

GOVERNOR ALEXANDER G. BROWN designated Davis to represent Mississippi in the United States Senate within two months after his return from Mexico. The appointment was for the interval to elapse before the next session of the assembly, the vacancy being due to the death of Senator Jesse Spaight. The legislature soon met and unanimously elected him for the remainder of the unexpired term. There was scarce a ripple of disapproval of these acts, either in the public press or on the platform. The state had become overwhelmingly Democratic ; but all parties joined in honoring the brilliant young Colonel of the Mississippi Rifles, the unstinted praise of Sargent Prentiss in New Orleans having done much to reconcile stanch Whigs and anti-administration men.

When Davis appeared in the Senate, two problems of serious import confronted him and his party. The first was the evolution of a definite Southern plan with reference to the large annexations of territory which, by common consent, had come to be regarded as the natural result of the war. The second was the winning of a sufficient number of Northern votes to make the new program effective. The President had already committed his party to the policy of a large extension of territory ; he had even attempted, as Davis must have known, to carry through a scheme for the entire

dismemberment of Mexico.[1] Calhoun, whose influence was in no way waning, had already declared, in
his famous speech at Charleston, in the preceding
March, that the new region was to be thrown open to
the settlement of slave-owners. And ardent followers
of the South Carolina statesman had begun to raise
afresh the long quiescent question of the Missouri
Compromise. It was boldly asserted by influential
leaders in the South that the settlement of 1820–21 was
unconstitutional and that the Northwest ought now to
be opened to slavery.

Davis's friends, Rhett, Walker, Yancey, and Jacob
Thompson, were impatiently urging the President forward in his policy of annexing the whole of Mexico.
They even threatened secession in the event of their
being denied what they held to be Southern rights in
the new territory.

Robert Barnwell Rhett, descended from an ancient
South Carolina family, editor of the already famous
Charleston *Mercury*, and member of the national
House of Representatives since 1835, was coming to his
own. He had always been an agitator. His first field
was the Colleton district in the southeastern part of his
state. The occasion had been the tariff of 1824, and
in 1828 he was able to carry much of South Carolina
with him. In the same year Calhoun experienced his
first change of heart on the subject of the national
tariff, and by 1829 the younger had won the older man
entirely to his view of the tariff and states' rights—a
view which had obtained almost universal acceptance
in Virginia during the last decade of Jefferson's life.

[1] Professor E. G. Bourne's article in *Amer. Hist. Rev.*, April,
1900.

Calhoun and Rhett worked side by side in the days of nullification, and the aristocratic eastern or tidewater section was the basis of their power. On the failure of nullification, Rhett made the slavery issue paramount in his state; when the Texas agitation began, he thought in advance of Calhoun, championing that leader's measures in the House from 1835 to 1845. But when Calhoun began to fear the outcome of the Texan trouble and raised his voice against the war with Mexico, Rhett refused to listen to conservative counsel, even from his own recognized chieftain. "War and conquest" was the slogan of the editor of the *Mercury*. Now that the end was near and a rich harvest was almost within his grasp, would Rhett yield for Calhoun's sake? Or would the older man surrender to the younger and himself become a radical?

Experienced heads in the Democratic party saw that this extreme Southern program could not succeed. Ritchie and other conservative Virginians combined with Northern Democrats to urge upon the President a moderation of his views, which was absolutely essential if they expected to continue in control of the country. The cabinet yielded to this sane outside pressure. Davis took the same position and hoped to combine all elements in the interest of Calhoun; but the bitter contempt of the latter for the administration, based on a natural resentment at being so completely ignored by those whose importance had been the outgrowth of his own planning, rendered co-operation impossible. Davis was therefore forced to break with the South Carolina leaders, who were themselves not united, and ally himself with Cass and others who espoused the measures of the cabinet. Failing, then, to enlist his Southern colleagues on the basis of a common, moderate program, he decided to take such a position as would appeal to the greater number North and South, though in doing this he sacrificed much of what he thought ought to become a part of the Democratic policy.

Without solving the problem of Southern unity, Davis became the coworker of Cass, the powerful Democratic senator from Michigan who was also Chairman of the Senate Military Committee, and other leaders of the Northwest, in the hope that this section might yet be attracted to the policy of the administration and in the end obtain enough Northern votes in support of his views to make the party reasonably safe in its position. Personally, however, he remained on the most friendly terms with Calhoun, and at heart expected to bring that statesman into sufficiently harmonious relations with the leading elements of the Democratic party to render feasible his nomination for the presidency in 1848. For this result, Everett of Massachusetts and a strong party in Virginia, including R. M. T. Hunter, were also laboring.[1]

But to force Mexico to yield as much of her territory as was required, it was deemed essential that large reenforcements for the armies stationed there should be raised and equipped. The President called for ten regiments and stated his object to be the overawing of the enemy and the occupation of its southern provinces. The war had now continued for nearly two years and peace with "security for the future" was still distant.

[1] Annual Report, Amer. Hist. Ass'n, 1899 : Jameson, *Correspondence of Calhoun*, pp. 1066–1081.

Polk found a ready champion in Cass, and Davis at once became a strong advocate of the administration. Long debates ensued on the Ten Regiments Bill, as it was called, from December 30, 1847, through the following months. The Mississippian was an important member of the Committee on Military Affairs and urged that the delay of a single week in its passage would be harmful to the country. Other leading senators thought the case not so pressing and instituted various tactics to achieve postponement. During the month of January, 1848, nothing of consequence was done in the Senate except to debate this measure of doubtful necessity, and incidentally arraign the motives and the policy of the President. On March 17th, it was passed by a vote of 29 to 19, with such powerful Southerners as Calhoun, John Bell of Tennessee, and Berrien of Georgia disapproving. Only Virginia, South Carolina, Florida, Alabama, and Mississippi voted solidly. In the House, where the anti-administration party was in control, the bill received scant courtesy, finally being pigeon-holed in the rooms of the Committee on Military Affairs, Howell Cobb and Robert Toombs of Georgia leading the opposition.

The discussion of this measure and the resolutions and amendments that were proposed during the debate, are of importance to the student of Davis's life only because they show, first, his public policy and his powers as a legislator ; second, the attitude of the states which later entered the Southern Confederacy. The bill was a part of an imperialist scheme which, as the war wore on, was seriously designed to bring all Mexico into the Union.[1] Its advocates were bold

[1] See Bourne, *Amer. Hist. Rev.*, April, 1900.

Southern expansionists who saw in this the realization of Calhoun's pro-slavery policy; and imperialists of the West and Northwest, such as Benton and Cass, who thought that the hand of "manifest destiny" ever pointed to the shores of the Pacific as the true western boundary of the country.

That Davis wished to see Mexico dismembered and annexed to the United States can hardly be doubted, if circumstantial evidence has any value, though he had not at first taken this view. His speech of January 3, 1848, against Calhoun's resolutions, declaring that annexation was not the purpose of the government; his repeated assertion that not a week's delay should be permitted in the passage of the Ten Regiments Bill; his persistent advocacy and defense of the administration, which he knew had badly treated his father-in-law—all speak eloquently for Calhoun's charge that nothing short of annexation was intended.

Another side of Davis's character was manifested in the debate on the Crittenden amendment to the Ten Regiments Bill, proposing to substitute volunteers for regulars. He opposed the suggestion, at once, maintaining that the chief business of the new force would be in garrisoning the towns and strongholds of Mexico, for which volunteers were unfitted : "The high-spirited citizen-soldier goes to war for battle, not the dull routine of army posts; he is active, alert, restless, not accustomed to drudgery, and therefore unfitted for anything less than the dangerous duty of the battle line." On the other hand, the man who enters the regular army comes from a lower class of the community. He is unaccustomed to personal refinements, willing to be commanded, driven and kicked if necessary—a West Point opinion of the private soldier then as well as now, and a view of social life in general which prevailed all too widely in the South in 1848. So apt was Davis's description of the Southern attitude toward the two classes, that Calhoun hastened to approve this part of his opponent's remarks. That neither senator was rebuked for these speeches is significant of the times, as well as of the character of the annexation propaganda.[1]

Calhoun still further embarrassed his ardent states' rights followers by charging the President with usurping authority not properly belonging to the Executive, when he had practically declared war upon Mexico. In answering these allegations, Davis and Rhett outdid the Federalists of 1798 in ascribing powers to the President. To declare war, Rhett said, was not the function of Congress, while Davis was willing to leave every military question to the President and his advisers.

But Davis and Cass found it difficult successfully to defend the policy of the administration against Webster, Calhoun, Berrien, John Bell, and Crittenden. The whole Whig galaxy now joined the recalcitrant Democrats in combatting every proposal of the younger politicians. Davis knew no better way to silence these great speakers than to charge them with the responsibility for the war. He said: " We had information from a special agent, sent to Mexico in 1844, that he had commenced preliminaries, and had the prospect of settlement by negotiation of all difficulties then pending. On the fourth day after the negotiations had been opened, two celebrated letters,

[1] Thirtieth Cong., 1st Sess., Jan. 5, 1848.

published that year, reached Mexico. One was dated
at Raleigh [Clay's] and the other at Lindenwald [Van
Buren's]. On the arrival of these letters, forwarded,
it is said, by the Mexican minister at Washington,
the negotiation was immediately suspended." If the
Mexicans have "their hopes revived again with the
prospect of a refusal here to supply men and money to
prosecute the war," Davis continued, "they will again
reject negotiations in the expectation that a new administration may come into power in the United States.
. . . We have erred on the side of leniency in our
dealings with Mexico ; I think we are about to retro-
cede territory to Mexico. I hold that in a just war
we conquered a larger portion of Mexico, and that to
it we have a title which has been regarded as valid
ever since man existed in a social condition—the title
of conquest : it seems to me that the question is now,
how much shall we keep, how much shall we give up,
and that Mexico cedes nothing." [1]

Arguing thus, he proceeds, with the true imperialist's instinct, to suggest the annexation of Yucatan,
lest England or another nation shall acquire it. And
when some one cautiously intimated that the British
government might resist the continued advance toward
the Isthmus he replied by saying that he would then
make war on Great Britain. The West Indies, and
finally an inter-oceanic canal, were not without the
scope of Davis's policy. And, as if preparing for his
own future undoing, he vehemently declared : "I have
no confidence in the humanity of Great Britain, the
great slave-trader of the world. If she should interfere
on any pretext in the affairs of Cuba in order to get a

[1] Thirtieth Cong., 1st Sess., March 17, 1848.

footing there, I would regard it as a proper occasion to interfere. . . . The very necessity of defending the United States requires that we should take whatsoever should be necessary always to secure the great point of exit and entrance to a large portion of the American coast [the Gulf of Mexico]."

Before the close of the session of 1847–48, Davis unfolds the vast scheme which had seized the minds of young Southern statesmen. In the Oregon debate, he laments the narrow view of those who see in the expansion of the country only the advancement of slavery. Such a position he combats in a vigorous fashion, prophesying that, after the sectionalists of the day have forced a dismemberment of our " glorious Union," the old flag will again be "unfurled over the continent-wide republic." [1] And at the next session he advances to the position of Calhoun, as outlined in 1845, which he had viewed askance when entering Congress. He is now ready to champion the cause of a Pacific railway, beginning of course at some point on the Mississippi below St. Louis, preferably at Vicksburg ; but he, like the South Carolina statesman, never admits the reasonableness of Benton's project for a road whose eastern terminus should be at the junction of the Missouri and Mississippi Rivers.

Peering still further into the future of American political planning, he outlines a scheme for a Panama railway under government control, to be operated in the interests of international commerce and for the defense of the Pacific coast states. Thus with ever-enlarging view, we find this ambitous young senator progressing toward the goal which "great Americans"

[1] Thirtieth Cong., 1st Sess., July 12, 1848.

have ever kept in mind. In order to carry out these designs, he makes advances to such Northern and Western members of the Senate as Stephen A. Douglas, John S. Dickinson, and the aged Cass. Could he have included the able and sturdy Benton among his friends, and offered what the great Missourian so much loved, a meed of harmless flattery, his aims might have come much nearer their realization.

But the fearful slave-issue stood threatening in the way. The quickening conscience and sectional jealousy of the North already gave assurance of the failure of these larger schemes and the precipitation of a crisis more acute than that of 1820. Davis hoped, however, that the prejudice of the people of Ohio, Indiana, and Illinois against the free negro, whose immigration they so much dreaded, would whip into the Democratic line enough senators and representatives to save the day for the South. All three of these flourishing young commonwealths were at this time forbidding the negro to settle within their bounds. Might they not finally reject the overtures of the reformers of the Northeast and the Western Reserve and accept the embraces of the imperial South?

To forward these plans Davis became one of the first advocates of a "Home Department," with duties not unlike those of the English Home Office—another scheme of Robert J. Walker. A geological survey, coast surveys, and numerous naval improvements also received the attention of the future Confederate President during these happier days. Alexander D. Bache, a classmate at West Point, and Matthew F. Maury, America's great ocean surveyor, were his friends. Many writers of note, and men interested in astronomy and pure mathematics were entertained at his hospitable board, where his accomplished wife presided, his views thus being enlarged by contact with men prominent in every walk of life.

CHAPTER VII

SLAVERY, AND THE COMPROMISE of 1850

WHILE Davis had been an ardent nationalist since the day of his entrance with Walker upon the Polk campaign, he had always acted on the supposition that slavery was a fixed institution of the South and possibly of the country at large. Without advancing such arguments in definite terms, he had expected the annexation of Texas and the Mexican acquisitions materially to improve the political condition of the Southern states. When he favored the expansion of the Northwest, he openly said that the new territory should not for reasons of policy be closed to the slave-owning immigrant. And the Southern advocates of Oregon expected the beneficiaries of the increasing area of the nation in that direction to say nothing against the claims of their section to regions beyond the boundaries of the ancient Louisiana purchase.

But if Cass, Hannegan, and Douglas had given assurances of the acquiescence of their states in the policy of the South, they had reckoned without their host in so far as it involved the question of slavery expansion. When the bill for the creation of Oregon Territory came before Congress in 1848, the Northwest was almost unanimously opposed to the proposition to leave the matter unmentioned. It was remembered that Oregon lay beyond the boundaries of the Louisiana region, and that, under the Constitution, the master might carry his slaves into any possession of the nation, unless expressly prohibited by law of Congress. The Compromise of 1820 did not suffice. Davis saw the advantage of leaving the knotty problem untouched : this inactivity would not cause slavery to take root in the far Northwest, but would secure for the spread of Southern institutions the more congenial territory south of the line of 36° 30', where new states might be built up to counteract the growing power of the North. But when it was proposed to apply the Northwest Ordinance to Oregon, Davis introduced [1] a proviso "that nothing contained in this act shall be so construed as to authorize the prohibition of domestic slavery in said territory whilst it remains in the condition of a territory of the United States."

Calhoun defended the Davis proviso, contending that the Ordinance of 1787 applied only to individuals ; that it could not be fairly considered a precedent because Thomas Jefferson, its author, had in 1820, in a letter written to Holmes, of South Carolina, declared against it ; and that Congress had no power in the premises, states alone having authority to regulate slavery. In other words, the Compromise of 1820 had been extra-constitutional. Davis spoke to his own proviso and laid down his doctrine on this one great question of his life. He had sought, with Calhoun, to bring about a state of things which would leave the South secure, and isolate that section of the North hopelessly opposed to slavery. This had failed. The country was now confronted with the pressing issue : Shall slavery enter the new territory of the nation ? Since the question must be met, Davis inclined to yield his greater Americanism for the particular inter-

[1] Thirtieth Cong., 1st Sess., June 23, 1848.

est of Mississippi and her sister states of the Lower South.

The speech followed somewhat closely the trend of thought in Calhoun's recent addresses and letters. Eleven states, said Davis, have declared, through their legislatures, that slavery shall not be protected in the new states and hinted that it must be destroyed in the old ones. This looks to the isolation of the slave-states and the final abolition of property in slaves. He then presented the doctrine that Congress could not legislate against property guaranteed by the laws of any state, but that it must protect such property, no matter at what cost, else the Union was not doing the tasks it was created to perform. The idea which he had in mind, and which he clearly stated, was that the Constitution did not grant primary authority, only secondary and delegated rights. It had, so to speak, given Southern masters and their successors, by formation of the Union, a perpetual franchise over the labor of negroes. This franchise, like any other contract, could not be abrogated without the consent of both parties to it. On the question, then, of lawful right, Davis was immovable. It mattered not to him how much the world argued against the wisdom of slavery; how inhuman the masters were declared to be. He stood here on the constitutional compromise; he demanded his "bond," regretting the short-sighted policy of the Southerners in 1787 and 1820, in yielding their interests and their privileges for what seemed to be a humanitarian and fraternal object. That the letter of the law and the Constitution favored him will not be disputed by many competent students to-day. What would be the alternative of this hard and fast position, Davis does not now fully declare, though there is every reason to believe that his mind was made up on this question.

So much for the rights of the slave-holders as Davis viewed the issue.   What of their policy?   On this point he said that there was no intention to carry slavery into Oregon, no purpose of imposing the institution on unwilling embryo states; it was only desired to leave the fundamental law in such a form that Southern property might be safe there.   Slavery, he thought, could not flourish in northern latitudes. All that he really aimed at was to put a stop to adverse legislation on the matter and forestall the Wilmot Proviso, which was still a sort of spectre likely to make its reappearance in Congress at any moment. He would have secured a vantage-ground north of the line 36° 30', in order later to compromise successfully on its extension to the Pacific, though he was no friend of compromises on this or any other subject.

He closes his speech in a remarkable defense of slavery—the more remarkable because of the year in which it was made, 1848 : "If slavery be a sin, it is not yours.   It does not rest on your action for its origin, on your consent for its existence.   It is a common law right to property in the service of man ; its origin was Divine decree—the curse upon the graceless son of Noah."   He then traces what he thinks has been the history of the institution through Spain to America, through the native tribes, and through Dutch and English traders, concluding :

" But the sons of Shem [Indians] were not doomed to bondage ; they were restless, discontented and liberated because they were unprofitable.   Their places were supplied by the sons of Ham, brought across the broad Atlantic for this purpose; they came to their destiny and were useful and contented. Over the greater part of the continent Japheth now sits in the tents of Shem, and in extensive regions Ham is his servant. Let those who possess the best opportunity to judge, those who have grown up in the presence of the slave institutions, as they exist in the United States, say, if their [the slaves'] happiness and usefulness do not prove their present condition to be the accomplishment of an all-wise decree. It may have for its end the preparation of that race for civil liberty and social enjoyment. . . . Sirs, this problem is one which must bring its own solution; leave natural causes to their full effect, and when the time shall arrive at which emancipation is proper, those most interested will be the most anxious to effect it. . . . Leave the country to the south and west open, and speculation may see in the distant future slavery pressed by a cheaper labor to the tropical regions where, less exertion being required for support, their previous preparation will enable them to live in independent communities. They must first be separated from the white man, be relieved from the condition of degradation which will always attach to them whilst in contact with a superior race, and they must be elevated by association and instruction: or, instead of a blessing, liberty would be their greatest curse."

As to the motives of the two great parties to the struggle over slavery, Davis said:[1] "The question is before us; it is a struggle for political power, and we must meet it at the threshold. Concession has been

[1] Thirtieth Cong., 1st Sess., July 12, 1848.

ever the precursor of further aggression, and the spirit of compromise has diminished as your relative power increased.   The sacrifices which the South has at other times made to the fraternity and tranquillity of the Union are now cited as precedents against her rights. To compromise is to waive the application, not to surrender the principles upon which a right rests, and surely gives no claim to further concession.   .   .   . If the folly and fanaticism and pride and hate and corruption of the day are to destroy the peace and prosperity of the Union, let the sections part like the patriarchs of old and let peace and good-will subsist among their descendants.   Let no wounds be inflicted which time may not heal.   Let the flag of our Union be folded up entire, the thirteen stripes recording the original size of our family, untorn by the unholy struggle of civil war."

Before Davis spoke on the Oregon question, both houses had been wrangling for two months over the status of the prospective states of California and New Mexico.   The House had inclined to prohibit slavery there ; the Senate to permit it.   Finally, the latter body referred the whole knotty problem to a special committee, headed by John M. Clayton of Delaware, which reported a bill making territories of California, New Mexico, and Oregon.   Oregon was to be free from slavery, while California and New Mexico were left to decide the question in their own courts, with a right of appeal to the United States Supreme Court.   This was thought to be a manœuvre favorable to the pro-slavery party, since the latter was deemed safe for the Southern interest.   The House refused to assent to the proposition, having meanwhile passed a bill making Oregon a free territory. This was amended in the Senate so as to extend the line 36° 30′ to the Pacific, securing slavery to all national ground south of this boundary. The measure was returned to the House with this radical change, where it was promptly stricken out, and on the last day of the session, the bill became a law with slavery excluded from Oregon and without any declaration as to the future of California and New Mexico, or the line of 36° 30′. The South had failed in this parliamentary duel and Davis returned to Mississippi a disappointed man.

He was there confronted with another question. Whom should he support for the presidency? His father-in-law, General Zachary Taylor, had been nominated by the Whigs in their Philadelphia convention while Congress was yet in session. The Democrats, still under the influence of the now somewhat conservative Southerners of the Polk imperialist school, had named General Cass as their standard-bearer. He had ably championed the administration of Polk, had polled a large vote in the Baltimore convention and was generally regarded as the logical candidate of the party. But under the pressure of Northern sentiment, he had been forced to declare himself on the question of slavery expansion.[1] His statement was but half satisfactory to the South and it failed also to conciliate the North.[2] The coalition of South and West therefore was visibly weakening just when success was in sight.

[1] See Nicholson letter, as discussed in McLaughlin's *Life of Cass*, p. 231.
[2] Letters to Calhoun in Report of Amer. Hist. Assn., 1899, Vol. II, pp. 1120, 1132.

For a while before the meeting of the Philadelphia convention, Davis had manifested a disposition to support Taylor, who, it must be remembered, was a large Louisiana planter and slave-holder. Rhett had inquired of him, for Calhoun, whether the Whig candidate were "safe" on the great questions affecting the interests of South Carolina. Up to the nomination, it was uncertain whether Davis would support the popular military hero, with whom he had been on the most intimate terms since his brave conduct at the storming of Monterey. South Carolina was in doubt for a long time whether to vote for Taylor while repudiating his party, or to support the candidate of the Northwest. At the last moment the vote was given to the regular Democratic nominee, Calhoun and Rhett acquiescing. Davis likewise remained true to the organization ; but, for obvious reasons, he did not enter the campaign against Taylor. Indeed, he once came out boldly in the brave old soldier's defense, when some over-zealous Democrat attacked Taylor's character. Davis was thus true to his nationalist traditions, while at the same time he was not risking the existence of slavery. He was a party man of the strictest sect as this canvass shows.

At the next session of Congress, the slavery issue again occupied the attention of both houses. The New York senators and representatives reported that their instructions from Albany required them to exert themselves to the utmost to prevent the extension of slavery to the new possessions. John P. Hale, a senator from New Hampshire, introduced petitions on behalf of free negroes going to Liberia, and still others, calling for the dissolution of the Union. This irritated

Davis, the more since the constitutional convention of Kentucky, then in session, was debating a plan for emancipating that state's slaves and sending them to the new African republic. It was Douglas who replied to Hale, lamenting the offensiveness of his language and suggesting to the Senate his own later famous policy of leaving each territory to settle for itself and for Congress the status of labor within its boundaries. That is, the existence or prohibition of slavery in new territories was to be submitted to the determination of the territorial lawmakers, an idea which Cass had probably invented and which Bagby of Alabama had defended as the only proper method of evading the troublesome issue. Davis thanked Douglas for his speech without committing himself to the policy thus presented by the influential senator from Illinois. He closed his remarks with the warning that the Union would certainly be broken up if Northern gentlemen continued their practice of intermeddling with the affairs of the South : "It is an idle waste and a base abandonment of the duties of members upon this floor thus to squander time which should be devoted to some useful purpose. All this talk about slavery begins and ends and has its middle with the negro race. I can hear nothing else, sir ; of nothing which is progressive in human reform, nothing which does not concentrate itself in this question concerning the African race." [1]

Aside from the relaxation offered him by his management of the inauguration of the new President—Davis was chairman of the Senate committee appointed for the purpose—this short session gave rise only to anxiety and forebodings concerning the future of his

[1] Thirtieth Cong., 2d Sess., Jan. 10, 1849.

beloved Southern civilization.   He returned once more
to Mississippi to report nothing but signs of ill-omen
in the Northern skies.

Soon after the election of 1848, various Northern
legislatures renewed their agitation of the slavery
question by again endorsing the Wilmot Proviso, so
offensive to the South.   Before the close of 1849, four-
teen states had adopted in principle, at least, the hated
idea.   The legislature of Virginia was first to make a
formal reply.   Her resolutions declared in so many
words that the application of the Wilmot Proviso or the
principle it involved would be " resisted at all hazards
and to the last extremity."   These bold words, whether
they were originally sincere or not, were taken up in
every Southern state and approved by mass meetings
and formal legislative assemblies.   Calhoun gave out
the word in Mississippi that a movement looking
toward a Southern convention ought to be made ; and
Whigs and Democrats at Jackson joined in a call for
this purpose.   Delegates were chosen for the famous
Nashville Convention of June, 1850.   Other states
followed suit—South Carolina going so far as to call
out her militia and vote $300,000 for their equipment.
Charleston and Columbia, S. C., and Jackson, Miss.,
were the centres of the agitation.   Georgia, Alabama,
and Texas were also aroused ; but Virginia, despite her
bold resolutions, followed " afar off."   Still dissatisfac-
tion and feverish excitement prevailed everywhere.   The
formation of a Southern Confederacy, with Calhoun as
its first President, was the talk of after-dinner speakers
and of political conventions.   The Charleston *Mercury*,
the Richmond *Enquirer*, the Montgomery *Advertiser*
were fanning the discontent of the people and urging

politicians to act worthily and to respond to the high-spirited sentiment of their constituents. Davis was in the midst of the agitation and lent his influence to all these schemes looking to the "redress of the grievances" of the South. In fact, he had grown so popular and was so nearly in complete harmony with Southern extremists that Yancey proposed him to Rhett and the South Carolina junto as a suitable "Southern Rights" candidate for the presidency. Nothing came of the suggestion, but Calhoun designated him during this excitement in regard to the Nashville Convention as the future leader of the South.[1]

When Congress next assembled, the whole country was uneasy : the South awaiting the first step toward the exclusion of slavery from the new territory ; the North resolutely declaring that it should never be planted on soil already " dedicated to freedom." The various Southern states were "instructing " their delegates to Nashville, while the newspapers stirred the fires of discontent. Charleston was anticipating a great future for the new empire, whose boundaries were to extend to the Pacific and the Isthmus of Panama ; and New Orleans, located in its very heart, was not less expectant.

But while the excitement grew, California organized as a state, drew up and adopted a constitution forbidding slavery, and sent two senators and one representative to Washington to ask for admission into the Union. Counter attempts were made in New Mexico to form a government favorable to the "institution" of the South ; but a population of less than one thou-

---

[1] Statement of A. P. Calhoun to John W. DuBose of Alabama, repeated to the author, May, 1905 ; see also Rhodes, Vol. I, p. 390.

sand Americans was not sufficient to leaven a lump of
forty thousand Mexicans accustomed to the free labor
system, so far as there was any labor in this easy-going
region.   To procure two senators and one representative favorable to the Southern cause from this barren
and inexperienced section, would have been a farce indeed, as Henry Clay declared when the subject came
to his ears.   The next resort was to claim, on behalf
of Texas, a large strip of New Mexico, and then in due
time make of this mammoth commonwealth a half-
dozen slave states as counter-weights to the expanding
Northwest.   Every sort of scheme, every imaginable
device was suggested by the fertile-minded leaders of
the lower South.

In full sympathy with his section and his state, Davis
entered the Thirty-first Congress, where the angry seg-
ments of the dissolving country met to settle their differences.   In view of the serious aspect of things,
Henry Clay returned once again to the scene of his
former conflicts and disappointments.   Chastened by
the defeat of his darling ambition to be President, he
now entered the Senate, the acknowledged champion
and beloved leader of his party,—the party which
never won a victory except in the wake of the éclat of
some military hero, and which was now about to render its last great service to the country and die in the
act.   Massachusetts still retained in the national Senate, Webster, who, next to Clay, was to contribute
most to the pacification of the warring North and South,
and who, like his party, was to bankrupt his popularity for the sake of peace.   Calhoun, disillusioned at
last of his magnificent scheme of 1844–45, and too old
and broken in health again to aspire to the presidency,

was in his wonted place and awaiting what he regarded
as the onslaughts of the enemies of *his country.*   Benton, the victor over the combined ability of the trio in
1834 ; Thomas Corwin, Stephen A. Douglas, of the
rising Northwest ; and a half-dozen followers of Calhoun from the South,—Mason and Hunter of Virginia,
Butler, Yulee and Soulé, completed the list of leaders.
Of this distinguished assemblage, Jefferson Davis was a
willing and a welcome member, though the program
for which he now so inflexibly stood was anything but
acceptable to the body.

Recovered somewhat from his life-long malady, facial
neuralgia and neurosis, his wound of Buena Vista entirely healed, with an elastic and resolute step he now
entered the lists for his class, the great monopolists
of the time.   Full six feet tall, rather lean of face,
with large gray-blue eyes, overhung with heavy brows
and set off to advantage with a high and masterly forehead, he appeared as handsome as resolute, challenging
the attention of every newcomer and the confidence of
those whom he represented.

The serious situation of the country was shown soon
after Congress opened by the presentation of the
Vermont and the North Carolina resolutions.   Vermont, through her legislature, declared that slavery
was a crime ; that it could not be permitted longer to
exist in any territory or under any jurisdiction of the
United States ; and that her senators and representatives were thereby instructed to use their utmost endeavors to carry their wishes into execution.   A more
significant series of "instructions" were those from
North Carolina, a most conservative Southern state.
On February 6th, Senator Mangum, an ardent "Clay

Whig," read a petition, prepared and signed by men assembled in mass meeting at Wilmington, who were not accustomed to take part in popular uprisings— men of property and most respectable standing of both political parties, yet not great planters.   They insisted that, if Congress yielded to the demands of the North in the new territories, their state would be justified in withdrawing from the Union.   Mangum, in presenting the petition, said emphatically : "All parties in the South are merged on this question and will stand together, shoulder to shoulder, to defend those rights which we mean to defend, which we can defend, and which we will defend at all hazards—at all hazards, sir." [1]   He went on to report that the mass meeting had issued a call for a state convention in Raleigh ; had appointed a committee to confer with a general Congressional district convention in March following ; and finally had selected thirteen most trusty men to act in the meanwhile as a committee of safety.

Wilmington was then as now the largest town in the state ; its citizens had been the first to move in the Revolution of 1776.   A demonstration like this had not occurred there since January 1, 1775.   Such action at such a place was but typical and common in the early months of 1850 throughout the South, as that of Vermont was equally representative of Northern feeling.   Both statesmen and politicians in Washington felt on this occasion a pressure from their constituents which was as disconcerting as it was alarming.   The Wilmot Proviso had been and was now the touchstone of elections everywhere and the representative of a Northern community who did not approve this popular

[1] Thirty-first Cong., 1st Sess., Feb. 6, 1850.

demand, was sure of defeat at the polls; similarly, the Southerner who did not regard it as the consummation of all villainies could not hope to remain in office.

To render matters worse for the country, Clay, on his arrival in Washington, attempted to dictate the President's policy. Now Zachary Taylor was the last man to surrender his just prerogatives. He had a plan of his own for the settlement of the difficulty before him; he was, besides, the elected head of the nation, and as a military man had been accustomed to obedience from subordinates. Taylor had sent an agent to California, who had presided at the birth of the new state. It was then a result of his own work that Senators Gwin and Frémont now appeared at the doors of Congress, asking admission. As to New Mexico and the Texas boundary dispute, the President was less disposed than Clay to yield to the South.[1] He preferred to let these matters await the development of events, which, after the first months of 1850, was the view also held by Senator Seward, who had become a confidential adviser of the Executive.

Davis had been intimate with Taylor before the election; he had received a letter from his former general and reconciled father-in-law just previous to the nomination, saying that the South must resist boldly and decisively the encroachments of the North.[2] And after the election, even after the inauguration, Taylor had shown a disposition to consult the Mississippi leader. But this expression of confidence soon changed to the passage of mere social civilities. William H. Seward,

[1] James F. Rhodes, *History of the United States*, Vol. I, pp. 119, 121.
[2] Speech of Davis, at Raymond, Miss., Oct. 1, 1848. The *Mississippi Weekly Independent*, Oct. 14, 1848.

the rising senator from New York, rapidly won his way to the closet, and there convinced the President that Davis and his followers actually meant to secede unless they succeeded in obtaining what they regarded as security for the future ; *i. e.*, slavery extension westward to the Pacific.   Davis could not now do otherwise than hold aloof.   He was sorely disappointed, and the bitterness of his feelings found vent in his speeches on the floor of the Senate.

With these explanatory paragraphs, we are better prepared to understand the rôle of Davis in the interminable debates of the winter, spring, and summer of 1850.   On January 29th, Henry Clay proposed his long anticipated plan of compromise.   It offered to the North the admission of California as a free state and the settlement of the Texan boundary dispute so as to approve the New Mexican claims, while it declared against the continuance of slavery in the District of Columbia.   The advantages offered to the South were the erection of a territorial government in New Mexico without a prohibition of slavery ; the payment of the Texan public debt contracted prior to annexation ; the enactment of a fugitive slave law ; and a guarantee that Congress would exercise no power over the interstate slave-trade.

These propositions, reasonable enough as we now read them, were to Davis a complete surrender of the most vital contention.   Representatives from slave-holding states raise their voices for the first time in disregard of long admitted rights ; the senator from Kentucky offers to bribe Texas to give up her rightful possessions ; he denies to the South the right of equality in the territories ; he asks it to yield to the clamors of

Abolition. Arguing thus, Davis goes on to outline his own positive views, which laid down, as the first condition of peace, that the line of 36° 30′ should be extended to the Pacific, his last demand of a year ago ; that any citizen of any state should have the right to go with his property into any landed possessions of the Union—the negro always being property ; that the prohibition of slavery in the District of Columbia was a direct blow at the South ; and that the very suggestion of the national government's restricting the interstate slave-trade was insulting to this section.

He was in accord with Calhoun and that old leader's aggressive followers on every point ; and the difference between the Clay proposal and his ultimatum was chasm-wide. How could it be bridged ? Davis decided not to allow California to enter the Union without a clear agreement that the line 36° 30′ should be extended to the Pacific with a positive guarantee of the permanence of slavery south of it. This was his compromise : To yield the admission of California half-slave and half-free and accept therefor the fee simple to all the new acquisitions south of that line, leaving the return of fugitive slaves to their owners to the laws of the border states. Indeed, the gift of this vast region would not be satisfactory ; he said later, "I wanted all the country drained by the Rio Grande," that is, when the treaty of peace was negotiated.

The exciting debate went on through the winter and spring and summer. Davis availed himself of every opportunity to accomplish the defeat of the Clay Compromise. There was reason to expect success. The President was not friendly toward the plan ; the Northern extremists also desired a settlement to meet their own views, so that with wise, yet bold management, the South might win.   But the almost sudden demise of President Taylor on July 9, 1850, changed the outlook.   The new President, Fillmore, was under the influence of Clay.   Friends of the Compromise took seats in the reorganized cabinet and the much-delayed pacification came.   The Whig party had rallied for one short season ; they kept together long enough to prevent probable secession on the part of the South and were able to secure a truce of ten years between our radically divergent civilizations.   They exorcised the Abolitionist to a temporary silence, the resolute monopolist of the cotton states being the immediate gainer.   The program which Clay presented at the beginning of the session had become the law of the land, despite the impassioned protests of Davis and his group.   Leading Southern senators presented in form, duly signed, a solemn remonstrance against the Compromise and secured its insertion in the *Congressional Globe*, to the open disgust of the radicals of the North.

CHAPTER VIII

THE interesting question now was, what would Davis do? He had been beaten. The South was offered a compromise which he had declared to be insulting. Would he acquiesce or would he yield to his ardent friends, Rhett, Yancey, and Quitman, and help them form a new confederacy composed of as many states as might secede from the Union? In order to understand his attitude at this time, it is necessary to review some of the events of the previous year.

Henry S. Foote, his colleague in the Senate, had taken the side of compromise in the recent struggle and each had appealed to the people of the state to support him. The future course of Davis in public affairs depended largely on the issue of this contest. When the two senators had last been in Mississippi, they were friends; both had taken extreme positions on the question of slavery expansion; both had helped organize the state against accepting any compromise; and both had favored the movement which looked to united resistance on the part of the South. This movement had then seemed to appeal to all parties in Mississippi and, up to the death of Calhoun in March, 1850, it appeared likely that the coming convention would decree Southern independence. In the Mississippi address of May, 1849, the voice of Whig and Democrat alike found expression; and at the election of delegates to the Southern convention, the Whigs were represented in the person of Chief-Justice Sharkey and others of great respectability. Davis had been more prominent in this work than Foote, but not more positively in favor of resistance.

In midsummer of 1849, Calhoun's famous Southern address was read in almost every home in Mississippi. There was little dissent from its conclusions, which were in favor of secession in the event of the adoption of the Wilmot Proviso, at the coming session of Congress. Davis spoke to a large concourse at Jackson in July. The burden of his thought was resistance ; and finally on October 12, 1849, on the eve of his departure for Washington, he addressed a letter to the people of the state, outlining in detail the position he later took on the Clay Compromise. He closed significantly enough : "The generation which avoids its responsibility on this subject sows the wind and leaves the whirlwind as a harvest to its children ; let us get together and build manufactories, enter upon industrial pursuits and prepare for our own self-sustenance." [1] While there was some objection to this aggressive policy, it was not strong, and the leading Whig paper at Jackson said : "The Wilmot Proviso will be such a breach of the Constitution as to justify and make it the duty of the slave states to take care of their own safety." [2]

In leading this agitation, Davis was in full possession of the confidence of his people. The *Weekly Independent*, an important Whig organ, said of him : "Perhaps no man stands higher in our state than Jefferson Davis.

[1] *Mississippian*, October 20, 1849.
[2] The *Weekly Independent*, October 13, 1849.

Possessing the respect and esteem of all parties, while true to his own political faith, he yet possesses the proper dignity of a senator and knows that he represents Mississippi. It is well for her name and honor that she has *one* such senator." [1] The same paper spoke of the mass-meeting and the issues involved on June 16, 1849, as follows : "If there is no prior settlement of the controversy, the action of President Taylor in vetoing a bill (passed by the Wilmot men) might bring about the election of an Abolition President, and by his election a hundred questions might be started into active life, which now only have vitality in the fanatic heart and madman's brain."

Foote was an able but coarse man, unscrupulous in the use of offensive language in debate both in Congress and on campaign tours. He had migrated early in life from Fauquier County, Virginia, to Alabama, thence to Mississippi in the "flush times" following the organization of the new commonwealth. He won immediate distinction; became a member of the Walker wing of the Democracy and was chosen to the United States Senate in 1847. He gained such favor with the leaders of that body as to receive the appointment of chairman of the Committee on Foreign Relations, one of the most responsible posts in the national legislature.

Foote, Davis, and other stanch Southern expansionists lodged together, while in Washington, in a "mess" managed by a Mrs. Owner. On Christmas Day, 1847, for some unexplained reason, Davis and Foote had become involved in a personal difficulty which led to blows. They were separated by friends and a truce

[1] October 14, 1848.

was arranged, every witness being solemnly enjoined never to mention the circumstance. Howell Cobb, Abraham W. Venable, and others were present and assented to the compact. The fisticuff of itself was not a great matter, but the fact that both parties were leading members of the Senate was likely enough to lend importance to it; and while they managed to cover up their personal differences and keep their secret until 1874, and those who had been present never spoke of the affair until requested by the principals, it was morally certain that the two could not labor together in the bitter struggle of 1850–1851, especially since Davis assumed in a decidedly dictatorial manner to speak for Mississippi.

In that state, as well as in Alabama, the effect of Clay's return to the Senate became evident in the early months of 1850. Old Whigs began to regret their part in the recent agitation and inventive journalists sought a way out of the difficulties so fast thickening around them. In several papers and in public speeches, the idea of leaving the slavery question in the new territory to the settlers themselves was mooted—the germ, as will be recognized, of Douglas's famous "squatter sovereignty" doctrine of 1854. Before March, 1850, a decided change in public opinion in Mississippi became manifest. Foote, though he had been a far more extravagant defender of slavery than Davis, welcomed the apparent rift and espoused the cause of those who opposed radical action on the part of the South. His next step was to champion Clay's Compromise. The break with Davis was now complete. He denied the reiterated assertion of his colleague that Mississippi stood firm in her determination not to yield to any compromise. An appeal to the voters of the state was natural and speedily agreed upon.

Meanwhile, the time approached for the assembling of the South in convention at Nashville. The conciliatory policy of the stronger Democratic party during the preceding autumn in electing former rivals and opponents of the Mexican War as delegates, begins to bear fruit. When the movement culminated in the meeting, it was found that those who had originated it, and felt the pressing need of action against the "encroachment of the North" were in the minority. The method of resistance rather than resistance itself came to the fore in the discussion. South Carolinians desired immediate secession in the event of the passage of Clay's program ; but Georgia held back. Alabama inclined to the party of coöperation, demanding united and simultaneous withdrawal of all the Southern states from the Union, which was an impossibility. Chief-Justice Sharkey had been made chairman of the convention and he now opposed radical action of every kind. The result was much secession talk, but no positive resolves ; the Nashville Convention became ridiculous and the leading separatists, Rhett and Yancey, returned to their homes discredited, though none the less determined in their attitude. The former, who was about this time chosen to Calhoun's seat in the United States Senate, after a few months in Washington, resigned in disgust and retired to his plantation near Charleston to be called forth in dramatic fashion in 1860.

The Mississippi Democrats were not content with the Nashville fiasco. They nominated Quitman for governor in 1851 on the platform of resistance to the laws of the Union. This was such a challenge to the reviving Whig party that they looked about for a leader to oppose him. Foote, the former Democrat, answered the need. He was put forward as a "Unionist" candidate. Clay and Webster endorsed him and Judge Sharkey took up the cudgels in his behalf. Quitman's extravagance in the cause of state sovereignty and the sacred rights of slavery rendered almost certain his defeat. Foote returned to Mississippi in the spring of 1851 in most blatant fashion. He met his rival on the stump and nearly vanquished him. A few more encounters convinced the Democrats that they were engaged in a losing fight.

Davis's challenge to Foote in the Senate, as well as his general popularity, suggested him as a suitable champion. But he had already returned to the quiet of "Brierfield" and seemed indisposed to meet his boastful opponent. Already two opportunities for a joint discussion had been permitted to pass unimproved.[1] Had Davis decided to acquiesce in the Compromise, or was it dread of the rough and unseemly conduct of Foote on the platform that caused him to remain silent? Events forced him to a decision more rapidly than he was wont. The last legislature had called a state convention to consider the future relations of Mississippi to the Union. While Foote and Quitman were vomiting forth their personal and political vituperation from Holly Springs to Gulfport, the counties were engaged in the canvass for the convention. The questions hotly discussed everywhere were, secession or "submission," and if the former, whether by single

[1] At Columbus, October 12, 1850; see *Mississippian*, October 11, 1850.

state action or coöperation.   The result of the contest,
with many personal challenges and actual encounters,
was the election of a "Union" convention which at
once settled the great question.

This decisive victory for the conservatives, as we may
call them, caused the Democratic state committee to
waver in their loyalty to Quitman, whose personal unpopularity was evidently counting against the cause.
To prevent an irretrievable retreat at the coming regular
election, it decided to ask him to withdraw, while Davis
was chosen at this late day to take the leadership.

He entered the race in September, with his party
beaten by eight thousand majority.   Foote called
loudly for a joint discussion, but Davis declined, giving ill-health as his excuse.[1]   As a matter of fact, the
tide was turning against extreme measures and Davis
himself was now constrained to take the defensive ; he
had admitted that the time had not come for secession,
which was equivalent to saying that the Compromise
should be supported.   There was then no good reason
for the Democratic campaign.   Foote had kept his ear
closer to the ground than his opponent, though the latter saw clearly enough that public opinion was against
his cause.   But Davis had been popular since he first
appeared on the public stage.   In the autumn of 1849,
there had been no man in Mississippi who could com-
pare with him, all parties uniting to do him honor.
He entered therefore upon a vigorous canvass, visiting
every county in the state.[2]

[1] *Memoir*, Vol. I, p. 468.
[2] Letter in State Department MSS. Washington.   These letters
were recently brought to light by Mr. Waldo G. Leland, of the
Carnegie Institution, Washington.

Foote was elected governor by a majority of one thousand, and the exciting struggle was at an end. The defeated candidate had already indicated that he would accept the new conditions and was now a stranded politician. His successful rival did not fail to boast of the victory over "General" Davis. It was indeed the first defeat he had ever met, and it must have been a bitter one, for not only the South, but the nation at large had closely watched the Mississippi campaign. Like Thomas Jefferson, his political patron saint, he repaired to his plantation to cultivate the soil and meditate upon the means of avoiding the repetition of such a disaster.

CHAPTER IX

IN THE CABINET

THE nomination of Franklin Pierce in 1852 by the Democratic national convention was the result of a carefully laid plan of Massachusetts and Southern Democrats. After four days of earnest effort on the part of the old politicians to secure the great honor for Cass or Buchanan or Douglas or Marcy, leaders whose prominence and party services could not be disputed, the name of the New Hampshire militia general, who had seen some service in Mexico under General Scott, was brought to public attention by the loud hurrahs of the Virginia delegates. On the fifth day of the session, a stampede for Pierce secured him the nomination. To appease the Northern Democrats, who had approved the course of events in 1850, and to weaken the Southern Whigs, a champion of Clay's last great compromise, William R. King of Alabama, was given the second place on the ticket. The convention closed with a love feast and the succeeding campaign was conducted on the specific assurance that he who even mentioned the now officially "dead" slavery issue should be forever ostracised. The November elections proved conclusively that the sober sense of the nation was with the Democrats. General Scott, the fourth military hero of recent presidential campaigns, unlike his predecessors, was overwhelmingly beaten—the worst defeat since 1820.

In this remarkable canvass, Davis took a conspicuous part, making speeches in Louisiana, Mississippi,
and Tennessee. Such activity was a repudiation of his
doctrine of resistance so strenuously advocated in 1851.
His explanation of the seeming inconsistency of his
course was his readiness to accept the popular verdict as final and to put himself in harmony with the
majority of his people—the doctrine which his career
continued to exemplify with far-reaching consequences
in 1861.

The result of the election was to give the Democracy
carte blanche, with promises of a long lease of power in
the years to come. As in 1844, the "dark horse"
candidate, after coming to the President's chair, inaugurated the most important policies. Davis was
suggested to Pierce for a cabinet position,[1] we are told,
by Caleb Cushing of Massachusetts. This fact, however, is not firmly established. The proposition was
made the Mississippian at the close of the year and
declined. Later the President-elect wrote him to come
to Washington, if possible, for the inauguration.
This request was heeded and as a result of the personal
interviews which followed, Jefferson Davis became
Secretary of War. There was no Southern protest
against this appointment. It was regarded as a recognition of the states' rights wing of the successful party,
as it also gracefully testified to the strong friendship
existing between the two men. It really meant the
introduction into the administration program of Calhoun's comprehensive ideas of 1845. Naturally the
North was not satisfied with Davis, because of his sign-
ing, with Mason, Hunter, and others, the protest of

[1] Rhodes, *History of the United States*, Vol. I, p. 393.

1850.[1] Still there was no outcry, for had not everybody voted the Democratic ticket? And the new Secretary was the foremost Southern Democrat. The other members of this notable cabinet were William L. Marcy, whom Davis did not like and whose appointment was held up some days, possibly on this account; James Guthrie, of Kentucky; James C. Dobbin, of North Carolina; Robert McClelland, of Michigan; James Campbell, of Pennsylvania; and the able Caleb Cushing, of Boston. Marcy, Davis, and Cushing were the forceful members, the primacy in influence over Pierce resting with the Secretary of War. In fact, Davis could not have been a member of any political body without largely dictating its course of action. He was at this time enjoying the best of health; intellectually he was in his prime and morally there was hardly a more commanding character in the country.

"I had in my imagination," writes Carl Schurz, "formed a high idea of what a grand personage the War Minister of this great republic must be. I was not disappointed. There was in his bearing a dignity which seemed entirely natural and unaffected—that kind of dignity which does not invite familiar approach but will not render one uneasy by lofty assumption."[2] As to fitness for his position there was nowhere, not even among his most inveterate opponents, the slightest doubt. His West Point training, his long apprenticeship in the regular army, and his distinguished career in Mexico, were sufficient guarantees. There had not been another such Secretary of War since Calhoun served under Monroe, and even the South

[1] *Ante*, p. 121.
[2] Letter of Carl Schurz to the author, Dec. 23, 1904.

Carolinian, deficient as he was in the knowledge of the details of the proper organization of an army, must not be placed above him.

Davis was not slow to show forth his fitness; he revised the regulations of the service, introduced new tactics, and caused the infantry to be provided with rifles constructed on the latest models, such as, for example, his regiment had used with telling effect in the campaigns of Monterey and Buena Vista. The " Minie" ball, so familiar to every soldier of a later day, was an innovation of his, as was likewise the medical corps. He experimented with the camel, in the hope of bringing our distant western posts closer together; and he dreamed of changing the methods of promotion so that merit, and not age, should determine rank in the service. But in this he failed. Seniority still retains its accustomed place in the American army, and as for Davis's predilection, we shall see what sad havoc it wrought for him and his cause a decade later.

Still other schemes revolved in the brain of this imperious man from the lower South. His old schoolfellow, Robert E. Lee, was superintendent of the national military academy, while Davis was Secretary of War. They decided to introduce extensive improvements, which should make West Point the equal of any other military school in the world. New quarters for the officers, detailed to teach at their *alma mater*, were recommended by Lee, and Davis successfully urged Congress to make the necessary appropriations. The best men, said they, must be sent to West Point to train the young cadets, who must also have improved hospital service. Davis found the actual strength of the regular army 11,000 officers and men ; he raised it to 15,000 effectives, with 17,000 on the rolls. He planned larger and stronger fortresses at important and exposed points without favoritism[1] to his own section ; and he secured what was but a just increase of pay to rank, file, and field, salaries having remained stationary during the last twenty-five years, while, as he thought, the cost of living, due to the increase of gold and silver, had advanced at least forty per cent.

These were all matters of detail, yet their prompt and decisive execution infused a new spirit into the army, and officers and men remembered with gratitude the era created by "their own man" in the War Department until the bloody years of 1861 to 1865 embittered their minds.   The army became another and different organization, and Congress, responsive to these legitimate demands, made liberal appropriations in order that the able Secretary might have his own way.   They even entrusted new duties to his Department : the improvements in the District of Columbia were left to his supervision, and the annex to the Capitol—the completion of the magnificent building as we now see it—was planned and executed under the direction of Jefferson Davis.   " Cabin John Bridge " was also his work and his name used to adorn one of the great stones of that then broadest arch in the world ; but Congress, in one of its fits of meanness, such as invented the excuse of confiscating Robert E. Lee's estates, ordered it to be erased.   The bridge itself stands as of yore and bears its daily burden of busy humanity and hurrying commerce.

[1] See reports of Secretary of War to 33d Congress, 1st and 2d Sessions ; *Memoir*, Vol. I, Chapters XXXIV and XXXV.

But the master hand was seen in the policy of the administration rather than in the important matters just described. Like Polk, Pierce was an imperialist. He desired the expansion of the boundaries of the Union, and, realizing that Canada could hardly be won, he turned his attention to the South, where Davis had long been pointing out the road to national aggrandizement. Cuba, the Mesilla Valley, a region embracing 45,000 square miles south of New Mexico, and Central America were the objects of his ambition, and any fair, possibly some foul, means would have been resorted to in order to acquire them.

The relations between the President and the Secretary of War were of a most intimate character. They had been friends for some time and acquaintances since the winter of 1836–37.[1] Both were Democrats of the school of 1844 ; both had helped on the expansionist program in that year ; and whatever Davis really desired, Pierce was apt to grant.

The Baltimore convention of 1844 had fallen into the hands of the more radical Southern politicians, whose leading policy had been the expansion of the South. They had satisfied the Northwest with fine promises and won the election, then carrying the flag of the Union victoriously to the capital of Mexico.   They had annexed as much Mexican territory as was thought desirable, and not even the New Englanders dared repudiate their work.   Only the popularity of a military hero had won from them the elections of 1848, and notwithstanding the bitterness of the contest of 1850 over the status of slavery, practically the whole country accepted the Democratic, not the Whig, program.   Thus

[1] Mrs. Davis's *Memoir*, Vol. I, p. 369.

those who opposed expansion had been relegated to back seats in the national legislature, when they had not been turned out altogether.   Indeed, the time had never been when the people would repudiate leaders who had pleaded for a "Greater America"; why should they change their attitude now?

Thus Davis reasoned as he reëntered political life on the invitation of his friend from New Hampshire. That the Constitution set no metes and bounds to our lusty young republic he fully believed.[1] He had not been satisfied with the modest acquisitions of 1848; why should he not now reach out to Panama and the islands of the Gulf of Mexico?

The one objection which could be made was that the annexation of new lands in those regions would raise once more the slavery question; for Cuba and Mexico, if acquired, would, in all probability, offer themselves as slave states.   Certainly the former would do this, and the latter might safely be entrusted to the care of such vigorous propagandists as William Walker and John A. Quitman.   If the Northern people did object to this one-sided growth of the country, would not time reconcile them as it had done in regard to Texas and New Mexico?   Such was the lesson of recent politics.   And as to slavery itself and its final effect on the South, Davis had no scruples and few fears.   As will be seen in the next chapter of his life, he was rapidly coming to believe that it was a blessing both to the negro and his master, and that consequently the country must one day seek to expand rather than restrict the "institution."

With these well-fixed views in mind, Davis at once

[1] Davis's speeches on Oregon and other debates of 1847–48.

began to shape the course of the administration for their realization. He secured the appointment of Soulé, senator from Louisiana, and a co-protestant with Davis against the Compromise of 1850, to the Spanish mission. If there was one thing that Soulé desired above all others it was the annexation of Cuba. Marcy, the Secretary of State, opposed the appointment of such an avowed expansionist, especially to the court of the kingdom which he so ardently wished to despoil. But Davis and President Pierce prevailed, and Marcy made out the commission. John Y. Mason, of Virginia, was also an advocate of Cuban annexation. He had served in the cabinet of Polk and was not likely to oppose the purchase or seizure of any portion of Mexico which that unfortunate country might not be able to govern satisfactorily. Mason was suggested to Marcy by Davis as the minister to the court of Napoleon III.[1] James Buchanan, the new Minister to England, was a Northern expansionist. He had preëminent claims on the party. There is no proof that Davis named him for the post at the court of St. James; but he certainly did not oppose the sturdy Pennsylvania partisan who had done such valiant service in the cabinet of President Polk. Even Marcy himself thought that two new stars ready to be set in the American crown of states—wrested from the grasp of decrepit Spain—would be a drawing card for the Secretary of State at the next Democratic convention, and he lent all his great ability to the accomplishment of the plans of his able rival from Mississippi, notwith-

[1] See letter of Mason to Davis, thanking him for his appointment, written from Virginia in March of 1853, in State Department archives.

standing their personal dislikes. Other leaders of the party outside of the cabinet favored the new schemes, all forgetting, it would seem, that the decision of the people in their recent elections was based upon the tacit and avowed assurance that negro slavery was henceforth never again to be discussed in Congress or in the country at large. Within a period of six months the chief aim of the administration was one which would involve the renewal of all the antagonisms of 1850.

Soulé had scarcely arranged his household in Madrid when the *Black Warrior*, an American trader plying between New York, Havana and Mobile, was seized off the coast of Cuba and unlawfully ordered to give up her cargo—$100,000 worth of cotton—on the plea that she had violated the tariff laws of Spain. A fine of $6,000 was also laid upon the captain of the ship. That the crew had been guilty of irregularities was not disputed ; but the demands of the Cuban officials were outrageous. Rather than submit to search and the heavy fine, the ship itself was surrendered by its officers. This occurred in February. In April Soulé presented a categorical demand that before the expiration of forty-eight hours the Spanish government must agree to pay an indemnity of $300,000 and dismiss every one who had been officially concerned in the affair. A refusal meant that the United States must either go to war about this insignificant incident or repudiate the action of her minister. Spain declined to reply to Soulé, who was left practically suspended from office from April till late summer, when he was ordered to meet Mason and Buchanan in Paris, with a view to elaborating an American policy for the West Indies.

Before taking his departure, he gave the Spanish court the comforting assurance that the United States would purchase and pay liberally for the coveted "Pearl of the Antilles."

After full discussion, the three ministers issued from Ostend, October 18, 1854, their famous manifesto which can scarcely be regarded as a master-stroke in diplomacy. This remarkable paper, which was probably the product of Soulé's pen, declared in effect that "Cuba lay close to our doors, therefore it should be ours; that, however, the American government would buy the island at a good price if it were disposed of promptly, otherwise it would be seized without remuneration." One thing must be said in Soulé's behalf: he broke down all the ordinary restraints of formal diplomacy and told Europe just what his nation wished to do. There was no mistaking the purpose of this bold American representative.

When Marcy received the report of this conference, he was not at all pleased. Such placarding of one's plans was highly questionable in the mind of so shrewd a man as the Secretary of State, and only a short time elapsed before the imperious Louisianian was recalled. Meanwhile the Spanish government had settled the claims of the owners of the *Black Warrior*, without resorting to diplomatic methods. The incident was closed and Cuba remained in the undisputed possession of its ancient proprietor.

Even before this difficulty arose, John A. Quitman prepared to bring powerful aid to the policy of the government by leading an expedition to Cuba for the purpose of attack. To advance this cause, Senator Slidell, of Louisiana, introduced into the United States

Senate a resolution, temporarily suspending the neutrality laws of the country. This effort failed ; but much interest was felt in the Quitman enterprise. Men and money were supplied and all eyes were turning to Cuba. When Soulé was recalled, very much against the will of Davis, an order went out from the President's office, warning the people against the filibustering expedition. The doughty Quitman was arrested, brought before the United States court in New Orleans, and required to give security for his future good conduct and the observance of the neutrality laws of the nation. The Secretary of War yielded with as good a grace as possible to Soulé's return, knowing that this did not mean a repudiation of his general views. The North cordially enjoyed the disgrace of the late minister, and the South rewarded the lawlessness of Quitman with a seat in Congress. But the policy which lay so close to Davis's heart must be temporarily abandoned.

The attention of the administration had meanwhile been directed to the extension of our southern boundary. The Mesilla Valley, as has been said, was another object of our growing appetite. The treaty of Hidalgo Guadaloupe had not proved, in all respects, satisfactory : one of its clauses bound the United States for the protection of Mexico against Indian depredations ; but the red men had been no respecters of persons. They plundered Mexican and remote American settlements with the utmost impartiality. Consequently a number of claims had been presented to the Washington authorities. It soon came to be regarded as an unfortunate thing that the United States must protect the Mexicans against invasion by American savages.

Why not leave that to Mexico ?   A second consideration was the fact that the topography of New Mexico
was very unfavorable to the building of a transconti-
nental railway to California.   By crossing the boundary
into northern Mexico an excellent route could be found.
Why should not the United States own all the land over
and through which the road was to be constructed ?
And lastly, the acquisition of a large region in this
latitude would probably redound to the benefit of the
South—the home of the expansionists.   James Gadsden, an energetic South Carolina politician, was therefore dispatched to Mexico to obtain such changes of the
treaty of 1848 and such concessions of new territory as
should satisfy the wants of the administration.   In
order to make these propositions more palatable to the
Mexican authorities, the commissioner was empowered
to offer a large sum of ready cash—$10,000,000.   He
was highly successful in his negotiation.   The desired
alterations were made in the treaty of 1848, and a
valuable strip of country was annexed, while the
Mexicans were induced to assume the responsibility for
their own defense.   The new treaty was agreed upon
and sent to Washington in the early days of January,
1854.   It was ratified without difficulty by a friendly
Senate.

The next project in which Davis, rather than the administration as such was interested, was the establishment of a protectorate over Central America and certain parts of Nicaragua.   Nearly all intercourse with
California and the Pacific possessions of the country was
conducted over the Nicaragua route ; i. e., travelers,
emigrants, and freight were taken on board ships at
Greytown on the Gulf of Mexico, carried to the mouth

of the San Juan River, whence the way led across Lake Nicaragua and a narrow strip of land to the Pacific and from there by water to the Golden Gate of San Francisco. England had exercised some sort of jurisdiction over a portion of Nicaragua known as the Mosquito Coast. Americans felt that this meant an attempt to gain possession of the routes to the Pacific and thus hamper control of their new western possessions—especially in the event of war.

In the many revolutions which occurred in this region of petty strife, there was naturally a chance for an enterprising foreigner to establish himself, and finally bring about close relations with his own government. Such a person appeared in 1855 in the vigorous and able chieftain, William Walker, a Southerner of the Quitman type. Walker was invited by the weaker party in a conflict then waging in Nicaragua to bring what aid he could and, in case of common success, to receive his share of the rewards. He hastened to accept the offer, adding a company of Americans to the forces of his allies, and won for them a victory which was fruitful for him in that he was made dictator of a portion of Nicaragua for a year. Davis was interested in Walker and favorable to his schemes for he saw in them the opportunity to take the initial steps for a future canal or railway ; but could not of course intervene to prevent the filibuster's early defeat and banishment.

Southern extremists, such as the Rhetts of South Carolina, Quitman now in the House, Slidell and Benjamin in the Senate, took up Walker's cause. The Charleston *Mercury* proclaimed him a hero and benefactor of mankind. Had he succeeded, he planned to make Nicaragua a slave state and if possible bring it into organic relations with the United States ; but the dictator of a single year found that the quicksands of Spanish-American statesmanship were shifting again. He was forced to leave his little republic, as it was called, and find consolation in laying broader and more far-reaching plans for future success. Walker and his filibustering expeditions remained a disturbing factor in American politics during the succeeding half decade, when finally he lost his life in 1860, still trying to carve a slave-state out of the chaotic map of Central America. Under the rising tide of Northern opposition Davis was unable to accomplish anything either through Walker or otherwise and he gave up reluctantly plans which have with modifications become a part of our national policy.

On July 18, 1853, before the new administration had got well into the harness, Davis made a speech in Philadelphia in which he announced, on behalf of his "honored chief," that no schemes for local internal improvements would be approved, the President being opposed to the principle involved. On the other hand, a plan to assist in the building of a railway to the Pacific, beginning at Memphis and following the lower route to California, would receive his hearty sanction. He made haste to say, however, that such an undertaking, involving probably a hundred millions of dollars, could not be prosecuted under the famous " general welfare " clause of the Constitution, but only under the powers granted for the public defense, within the states and especially in the territories ; that is, the railway was to be built as a military necessity. The national government had no authority to clear the channel of the Mississippi, or to construct a road for the public good, yet possessed the power to do both these things under the grant requiring it to provide for the public defense.

Calhoun, as we have already seen, had taken the same position at Memphis when he said that national funds could be used in the improvement of the Mississippi and its tributaries on the ground that they were to be regarded as "inland seas," the nation unquestionably being free to spend money in building lighthouses and removing obstructions in the channels of harbors, no matter where they were located. Davis changed the reasoning at a single point: for military purposes internal improvements could be undertaken in states and territories as well as "inland seas." When Calhoun made his Memphis speech, he had in view the consolidation of the South and West as against the North and East. At Philadelphia, Davis was planning for the same thing: a great railway from Memphis to California would empty the commerce of the growing West into the holds of lower Mississippi boats. Vicksburg and New Orleans would be much benefited. A railroad from Memphis to Charleston, via Montgomery and Atlanta, was already in part constructed; another was planned via Jackson to Mobile. The political effect of such a development would have been incalculable: Tennessee would have been linked to the lower South; Kentucky would have leaned the same way; the growth of the Southwest instead of the Northwest would have been fostered as a result of national initiative; and the commerce of Illinois and Indiana would also have been drawn southward rather than over the mountains or through the

Erie Canal to New York. Davis was planning for the South as Calhoun had done, but with far greater chance of achievement. Had he been successful it is interesting to speculate as to the result of the Civil War, if indeed that great struggle had ever been entered upon.

When Congress assembled in December, 1853, the President strongly commended the project just outlined, making it the feature of his first annual message and the leading item in his policy for the coming four years. After proving—at least to the satisfaction of the Democratic party—that internal improvements were by no means permissible except to the states, Mr. Pierce went on to say :

"For the progress made in the construction of roads within the territories, I refer you to the report of the Secretary of War. . . . The power 'to declare war, to raise and support armies, to provide and maintain a navy, and to call forth the militia to execute the laws, suppress insurrections, and repel invasions,' was conferred upon Congress as a means to provide for the common defense and to protect a territory and a population now wide-spread and vastly multiplied. As incidental to and indispensable for the exercise of this power, it must sometimes be necessary to construct military roads and protect harbors of refuge. To appropriations by Congress for such objects, no sound objection can be made. . . . The magnitude of the enterprise [the Southern Pacific Railway] contemplated has aroused and will doubtless continue to excite a very general interest throughout the country. In its political, its commercial, and its military bearings, it has varied, great, and increasing claims to consideration. The heavy expense, the great delay, and, at times fatality attending travel by either of the Isthmus routes, have demonstrated the advantage which would result from inter-territorial communication by such safe and rapid means as a railroad would supply." [1]

Henry Clay himself could not have surpassed this reasoning of his Democratic opponents, now come to power. This remarkable message fell upon willing ears, since the Democrats were in control of both houses by large majorities. Behind the administration was a settled and prosperous people, tired of agitation and trusting fully in the leaders to whom they had recently given over the government. It cannot reasonably be doubted that this principal recommendation of Pierce's program would have received endorsement; appropriations would have been made and public attention would have turned to this vast work of internal improvement, but for the reopening of the slavery dispute. The results could not have failed to be beneficial. In a political sense, they must have tended greatly to increase the power of the South. It is not unlikely that Pierce would have been reëlected, and that his party would have obtained such a hold on the country as could not have been broken in two decades. Such was certainly the hope of Davis, for in this state of things he could not have failed to reap suitable rewards for his bold and able administration.

The best of plans "gang aft a-gley." Stephen A. Douglas was chairman of the Senate committee on territories, and the vast tract then known as Nebraska,

[1] Richardson, *Messages and Papers of the Presidents*, Vol. V, pp. 220-222.

embracing an area equivalent to a dozen states, was already so well settled that preparations were making for its organization as a territory. Under the Missouri Compromise, as generally understood, no question could be raised as to the exclusion of negro slavery from this region. A bill for the organization of Nebraska, making no reference to the subject, had failed in the Senate in the winter of 1852-3 on the ground that the Indians were not treated fairly. A measure proposing the same plan was introduced in the Senate soon after it met in December, 1853, and was referred to the regular committee. Douglas threw it aside and, on January 4, 1854, reported one of his own invention. This bill was a veiled repeal of the Missouri Compromise, shrewdly calculated to inspire pro-slavery leaders with zeal for the aspirations of its author.

But Southerners had grown wary of laws bearing on their favorite institution. Douglas declared that the compromise measure of 1850 had formally transferred the decision of slavery disputes in new possessions or in territories not regularly organized, to the parties most vitally concerned—to the settlers themselves. The South had not so regarded the laws of 1850 ; her leaders now hastened to examine this new Northwestern interpretation. They had long been acquainted with Cass's doctrine of "squatter sovereignty" as a possible remedy for Wilmot Provisos ; but they had not been ardently in favor of it. Douglas had borrowed the idea from his rival and he now designed to attach it as a sort of codicil to the treaty of peace between the sections, agreed upon with so much difficulty four years before. It was a manoeuvre for the Democratic nomination in 1856. Should the South accept this strong hint, Douglas would distance his competitors, Pierce, Marcy, and even Cass, and find himself safe in the President's chair after the close of the present term. The proposed law provided, too, that all disputes in the territories as to the ownership of slaves should not only be heard in the local courts but be subject to appeal to the United States Supreme Court —a suggestion that this bench should determine the status of slavery.

On January 16th, Dixon of Kentucky, "the successor" of Henry Clay, advocated an amendment of the bill in such a way as to repeal, in distinct terms, the slavery section of the Missouri Compromise. Douglas was surprised and possibly alarmed. He could not retreat. Dixon represented the South, now beginning to be aroused to the possibilities of the new policy. From Richmond, Charleston, Montgomery, and other ardent pro-slavery centres, came urgent recommendations that the Southern senators should demand the passage of Douglas's bill. The bold Illinois leader felt impelled to meet their requirements, or yield forever his chances for the presidency. He decided for the South and in the direction his ambition pointed. But the decision necessitated several days' consideration, for he did not know at first that he had crossed the Rubicon. He visited Dixon at his residence and, after long conversation, completed the plans for the further advancement of the dangerous undertaking.

Thus far, Douglas had operated without consulting the President or any representative of the administration. In fact, he must have felt that he was preparing the petard that was to hoist the popular occupant of the White House from his much coveted seat. Now that the hostile sections of the country were forcing his hand, the Illinoisian felt constrained to approach Mr. Pierce in the hope that he might not lose both his present and future fights by a division of the party. It was indeed a very ungrateful request to make of a President who was to suffer most from the schemes thus inaugurated. Douglas did not hesitate. On Sunday morning, January 22d, with some Southern adherents, he called at the home of Jefferson Davis, who conducted them to the White House and procured for them an interview, contrary though it was to the custom of the President, always conscientious in his religious scruples.[1] This was the most important act of Davis's cabinet career. It meant the ruin of his larger and more humane plans, as it presaged a future bitter struggle over the slavery question. That he approved of the repeal of the Compromise of 1820 cannot be doubted ; though, when its consequences were known, he stoutly denied having favored the scheme. And Douglas he denounced repeatedly as a demagogue and a treacherous man.[2] The President gave his approval of the Dixon amendment, and became, with Douglas, the Northern champion of slavery expansion, for that is what the bill meant. After many angry sessions and much party caucussing, the measure passed both houses and was finally approved by Mr. Pierce.

The "sleeping dogs" of Abolition were unchained. Douglas was burned in effigy throughout the North ; he became a hero in the South. That his own section opposed repeal was regarded in Richmond, for example,

[1] Rhodes, Vol. I, pp. 425–437.
[2] Letter to Pierce, June 15, 1860, *Amer. Hist. Rev.*, Vol. **X**, p. 365.

as a sure sign that justice could never be obtained on this vital subject. "A bold attempt is even now on foot to deprive the South of every semblance of equality in the Union," said the Charleston *Mercury*.[1]   "If forced to go out of the Union," remarked the Richmond *Dispatch*, "[the South] can go with colors flying, *with arms in her hands*, and with all the honors of war."[2] From this time forth Southerners manifested a fixed purpose to secede, should the territorial question be decided permanently against them. But what emigrants they could spare were hastened to Kansas, the lower end of the Nebraska region. The North sent half a dozen times as many more, and the battle-scene which Douglas had begun in the Senate was shifted to the West, where neighborhood war prevailed for six years to come. Thus Davis had aided in opening the very question which all had pledged themselves never again publicly to discuss. Within less than a year Pierce had violated the pious promises of his inaugural speech, and wittingly or unwittingly laid the foundation of his own destruction and the ruin of his party. All Davis's imperialistic plans, so carefully wrought out, were now destined to come to naught.

[1] Charleston *Mercury*, February 27, 1854.
[2] Richmond *Dispatch*, March 1, 1854. The *Dispatch* was considered unpartisan and decidedly conservative at this time.

CHAPTER X

THE IRREPRESSIBLE CONFLICT

DAVIS closed his administration of the War Department by publishing an account of the various surveys he had caused to be made, of the possible routes for a railway connecting the Mississippi River with the Pacific Ocean. It embraced ten large octavo volumes, containing a vast amount of information about the country which the road was to penetrate. Scientists and artists were employed in the engineering parties, and the reports which they made of the plant and animal-life of the great West are a monument to the energetic Secretary. Davis was not a small-minded man ; he loved ambitious undertakings and he delighted to employ scientific men and to associate with them. Ten thousand copies were placed at the disposal of the Senate and five hundred in the hands of Mr. Davis himself. Senators found partial sets of this large work on their desks when they met in December, 1857. The ponderous tomes were not read with avidity by these staid and practical politicians, but they were consulted during the coming years and became the basis of much discussion and controversy. They were campaign documents, as well as scientific surveys, intended to convince a stubborn Senate that it was best and most economical to build a railway to the Pacific via the Gila Valley and the Southern passes of the Rocky Mountains.

Davis had been hopeful of being elected to the

Senate by the Mississippi legislature in 1854 when
A. G. Brown had been chosen, but his partisans
managed things so badly that his name was not even
presented.   Fearing that a second blunder of this kind
might be made in the election of 1856, he wrote his
friend, C. S. Tarpley of Vicksburg, on December 19,
1855, distinctly stating his position.   He desired above
all things that his career as an ardent "Southern
rights" man should not be repudiated.   He wished
his course in the crisis of 1850 to be endorsed ; and
finally to have it understood that he was not privy to
the reported scheme of "running" him for the vice-
presidency in 1856, which was designed, he thought,
to secure his defeat for the Senate.   The Secretary of
War was uneasy about the outcome and there is no
doubt that his candidacy was kept well before the
public mind throughout the year 1856.   His opponent,
or rather, rival, was Jacob Thompson, an equally
ardent Southern rights man and an able politician of
the Walker school of 1844.   Some capital was made
of the fact that Davis, with most of the other leaders,
was a resident of southwestern Mississippi.   When the
Democratic caucus met to nominate their candidate,
the preference of the party was very much in doubt.
Tarpley, who was present, was active in Davis's behalf.
It was recognized to be a very close contest, and one of
the members of the legislature, as he journeyed on
horseback to the meeting-place, inquired of every
voter he met, the choice of the neighborhood through
which he passed,[1] with the result that sentiment was
seen to be almost evenly divided.   This gentleman was
made chairman of the Democratic caucus.   The first

[1] Reuben Davis, *Recollections of a Mississippian*, pp. 353, 354.

ballots resulted in a tie.   The vote of the presiding officer was cast for Davis, the report was made in his favor, and the legislature, without a struggle, chose the man who had thus been designated, though it was by no means such a victory as he and his friends could have desired.

The transfer from the cabinet to the coveted seat in the Senate had not been easy for this reason : Mississippi, as late as 1856, was not unanimously in favor of the radical program associated with the name of her most distinguished son.   While Thompson undoubtedly represented similar lines of political action, he was supported by many who opposed much of what Davis laid down as the ultimatum of the South.   Thompson was said to " know no North, no South " ;[1] he represented at the time the more timid, the politicians especially, of his party.

The Washington *Union* and other Democratic journals hailed the result of the election with delight and when, in the early spring of 1857, Davis returned to his estate, he received a great ovation.   At Vicksburg, on May 18th, a barbecue was given in his honor ; another followed at the state capital a short while afterward. In the autumn he made a sort of tour of Mississippi before setting out for Washington, to resume his old place in the Senate.   He had spent but little time among his people since the presidential campaign of 1852, and he seems now to have tried to bring them into fuller harmony with his favorite views.

His most significant speech was made at Mississippi City on October 14, 1857.   There he said that the administration of Pierce had done well to send Soulé to Mad-

[1] Washington *Union*, January 26, 1856.

rid for the express purpose of obtaining Cuba, and that, had the *Black Warrior* episode been managed properly, in his belief, the United States would have acquired the island. "General" Walker, he thought, was doing American civilization a service by filibustering in Nicaragua, and should he succeed, Davis hoped the government would act with a firm and aggressive hand. "Squatter sovereignty" had seemed to offer the South much in 1854, but its promises had not been realized, and now he favored taking the ground which ought to have been maintained from the beginning,— that the national government must protect negro slaves in the territories as it did every other species of property. He did not admire apologists ; he declared openly and boldly that "African slavery, as it exists in the United States, is a moral, a social, and a political blessing." These utterances were well received and it cannot be denied that a majority of the slaveholders of Mississippi endorsed his views in preference to those of the more moderate Thompson.

The country had been greatly agitated during the preceding spring and summer by the dictum of the Supreme Court in the famous Dred Scott case. Dred Scott, a slave whose master had taken him into a free state and there held him in bondage, had sought to secure his liberation on the ground that such residence entitled him to it. The suit had been instituted in the local courts of Missouri, was appealed to the national tribunals and obtained a final hearing in December, 1856. The great points for the whole country were :

1   Could a negro, even if free, sue in the courts as a citizen ?

2. Was the Missouri Compromise, which forever prohibited slavery in territory lying north of the line 36° 30′, constitutional ?

The court answered these questions after some effective pressure from the South as follows : [1]

(1) A negro cannot become a citizen, and therefore has no status in the courts.

(2) Congress had no authority to make the Missouri Compromise ; that is, property in slaves was not different from other property and must be protected alike in every part of the Union.

This was the contention of the Southern extremists. It was exactly what Calhoun and Davis had maintained ever since 1847. The court, revered by the country since Marshall made it the vehicle of nationality, had now declared in favor of Yancey on the only important subject in dispute. The Democrats of the South and the Douglas wing of the northern Democracy were gleeful ; the Republicans must henceforth contend against the bulwarks of the Constitution. Davis himself was very much elated. He challenged his opponents to attack the Supreme Court and for a while seems to have supposed that they were silenced. Not so ; the party of the future did not hesitate to assail the court and its judges, Republican leaders seeing in Chief-Justice Taney only an ally of the slave-holders.

While Davis's great surveys in the Rocky Mountains were going forward ; while the pro- and anti-slavery parties were laying waste the fertile fields and budding cities of Kansas ; while the Supreme Court was preparing its ambitious and dignified scheme, the merchants and bankers and speculators had plunged

[1] Rhodes, Vol. II, pp. 253–254.

the country into an economic and financial panic. The President was forced to propose some sort of remedy for the troubles which came home to every man, regardless of his views on slavery. Wall Street was insistent; it could not, like "Bleeding Kansas," be thrust aside for a while. Merchants had closed their doors by the thousands; bankers refused to redeem their pledges; railway trains stood still. What would angry, partisan and ignorant congressmen do with this even more pressing problem?

And finally, as if to embarrass even Providence, ambitious and unscrupulous Southerners were again sending forth their filibustering expeditions against the governments of their neighbors, bordering on the Gulf of Mexico or the Pacific Ocean. "General" Walker, whom Davis mentioned so favorably in his Mississippi City speech just before he took up his journey northward, was collecting forces along the Mississippi River, in Texas and New Mexico preparatory to the attempted conquest of Nicaragua.[1] And the Spanish authorities in Cuba were on their guard day and night lest Quitman take them by surprise in another foray and annex the beautiful isle to the United States.

The new President, Buchanan, was not an able man; and the House was now hopelessly divided. It devolved on the imperious Senate to solve these difficult problems. Davis, Douglas, and Seward were its foremost members, the sovereigns of the nation—if there was such a thing as sovereignty or a nation in this Western world in December, 1857. The President sent to Congress a long and sensible message, as soon as it organized for the transaction of business. While

[1] *Amer. Hist. Rev.*, Vol. X, pp. 792–811.

the new members were getting acquainted with their surroundings and Buchanan was pressing for some reform in the banking laws of the country, as a means of escape from the financial ills of the time, news of recent events in Kansas was received. The election of December 21st was being denounced by the press and in Abolitionist platforms. Robert J. Walker, the recently appointed free-state governor, though fast becoming *persona non grata* to the Southern leaders, was plying his well-known arts on the President and cabinet in behalf of the anti-slavery men, who were manifestly in the majority in the territory.

Always bold and sometimes happy in his expedients, Douglas astonished the Senate and the country by coming out positively for Walker and his party in Kansas. He denounced those who would defraud his "squatters" of their right to determine forever the status of slavery in the new state.[1] The principle for which he had contended so long and against such overwhelming odds was now about to be violated. He thus took the Southern men, especially Davis, by surprise. The President, wavering between the influence of Walker and the North on one side, and that of Southern extremists on the other, was outclassed. He must either accept Douglas and appear before the country in the leading strings of a new group of Northern politicians, or else he must surrender outright to Howell Cobb and Jacob Thompson, of the cabinet, and allow Jefferson Davis to voice the administration in the Senate. Buchanan chose the second alternative and on February 2, 1858,[2] sent a

[1] *Cong. Globe*, 35th Cong., 1st Sess., Dec. 9th.
[2] *Messages and Papers of the Presidents*, Vol. V, p. 471.

message to Congress, espousing the side of the Kansas pro-slavery convention, and urging the acceptance of the so-called Lecompton constitution. Douglas now became the object of especial hatred on the part of the administration. But the senator from Illinois had regained many of his former Northern supporters, as well as strengthened himself for the coming contest in his own state, where Abraham Lincoln was to gain distinction in so notable a way. Douglas outwardly accepted the dictum of the Supreme Court in the Dred Scott case and took the strongest ground possible for any Northern Democrat. Walker had unquestionably caused his influence to be felt, and if he could have brought Buchanan to his own and Douglas's position, his long cherished ambition might still have been gratified. At any rate, he could have made Douglas President.

Davis said but little on the subject of Kansas until after the message of February 2d. Then he commends Mr. Buchanan as a statesman and a patriot[1] and proclaims it as his creed that, when the interests which a senator represents no longer find protection under the laws of the Union; when they are, indeed, constantly warred upon, he holds it to be his duty to retire, as would an ambassador from a foreign country on the eve of war.[2] This speech, while particularly directed against Fessenden of Maine, was intended for the Republican party, now grown as aggressive as the Southern Democracy. Mason of Virginia, Benjamin of Louisiana, and other leading Southern senators, joined Davis in his hearty commendation of the President, thus bringing the slavery question once again to the

---

[1] *Cong. Globe*, 35th Cong., 1st Sess., Feb. 8, 1858.
[2] *Ibid.*

first place in Congress and in the country at large, despite the many and grave financial difficulties then pressing upon the people.

The fate of the vast railroad schemes, for which Davis had sacrificed some of his states' rights views while a member of the cabinet, had not yet been determined. Indeed, it was just at this time that he and his friend Gwin of California, formerly of his own state, were evolving a plan for bringing the matter before Congress. The senator from Mississippi having done so much to further the cause, it seems to have been decided that the Californian should there present a resolution committing "so much of the President's message as related to the subject" to a select committee of nine. Gwin became its chairman; Davis, Hunter, and Iverson were the forceful Southern members and Douglas was appointed in recognition of the Northwest. A report was duly made and a bill regularly introduced, when Davis, representing the minority of the committee, moved an amendment, providing that the President should let the contracts. It was accepted; but no debate was had on the subject until late in the session. Several intense states' rights men, under the lead of Slidell and Benjamin, resolutely opposed the building of any road, on the ground that it was unconstitutional. Gwin could not get a vote on his favorite measure. Davis himself was taken seriously ill early in the session, and during the larger part of the winter and spring, he was not able to leave his home. At the next session, the bill was reintroduced and it occupied much of the time of the Senate. When it finally passed, all that remained of it was a resolution, authorizing the Executive to receive

estimates on the cost of roads by the three possible
routes described in the magnificent surveys of the ex-
Secretary of War !

Of these, Davis had made up his mind long since
that the Southern was the cheapest and most practicable, and it certainly would have been the most advantageous to the lower South.   Under the leadership
of Senator Green of Missouri, a plan was presented for
building the railway from some point near Kansas
City by the easiest passages over the Rocky Mountains
to San Francisco.   Still another group of politicians
insisted on a road from Omaha to Puget Sound.   The
advocates of the various lines had local, not national,
interests in mind, and Davis was hardly an exception
to the rule.   Indeed, it was repeatedly contended that
the main purpose of the surveys, conducted under his
direction, had been to prove that the extreme Southern
route was the only practicable one.   These charges,
while containing a semblance of truth, did him much
injustice.   He was really anxious to turn the attention
of the country from the discussion of the slavery question to that of a great national undertaking.   His
tender conscience, however, would not permit him to
believe Congress could build a railway through a state
for any other than military purposes, and, least of all,
to administer it when it was completed.   States might
do all these things, but not the nation.   What, then,
was his justification?

Now, as in 1853, when he first broached the subject,
it was this : A road connecting the East with the
Pacific coast was absolutely essential from a military
point of view, as well as for commercial purposes.
But it could be undertaken only while the region

through which it was to go remained in the territorial stage ; for after it was cut up and converted into states by the progressive enterprise of private parties, the United States would no longer have permanent rights over the soil.   The necessity for the railway and the possibility of constructing it by the central government being clearly shown, he was not yet satisfied ; for, after the work was done, the government could not possibly operate the road.   How could this obstacle be overcome ?   Davis thought that a private company should be incorporated in one of the states ; that it should be given the right of way through the territories, with a loan of $10,000,000 on easy terms, and the privilege of selling alternate sections of the public lands along the line.   With these concessions, it was believed that private parties would build the road in due time.

Such a railway, he argued, would be the means of uniting the hostile portions of the country; it would bind the sundered West to the heart of the " Confederacy " ; give us control of the Pacific and render certain the destiny of our " continent-wide republic." [1]   That so happy a result would have followed is of course doubtful enough ; that Davis hoped for such an outcome is creditable to him.   It shows that he was not a secessionist *per se*.

Had he been able to secure the appropriation for the Southern Pacific Railroad, his next move looked toward the incorporation of Mexico into the United States.   He also renewed his plans and endeavors for the purchase of Cuba, as was foreshadowed in the speech at Mississippi City in October, 1857.   But since the acquisi-

---

[1] *Cong. Globe*, 35th Cong., 2d Sess., Jan. 19th and 20th.   See also Appendix for same date.

tion of that island was left for Slidell to advance as best
he could and because of the precarious condition of his
own health, Davis played a secondary rôle in the debates on the matter.   The second annual message of
President Buchanan renewed the recommendations of
its predecessor on this subject and urged Congress to
vote ample supplies of money for the purpose of taking
over Cuba, whenever a favorable opportunity offered.
It was even urged that the "Pearl of the Antilles"
should become a part of the United States in order
that the African slave-trade encouraged there might
be suppressed.[1]   Practically all leading Southerners
endorsed this proposition, and it was hoped in the
South that at least two new slave states would thus be
brought into the Union to balance the growing power
of the North in the Senate.   Douglas favored this
course, notwithstanding his quarrel with the President;
and the Democrats generally were willing to embark a
second time upon a policy of expansion, in the hope
that they might again win the acclaim of imperialists,
everywhere so easy to arouse.   It was unpopular to
oppose the widening of the boundaries of the country,
even though the pro-slavery party must certainly get
the "better half" of the bargain.

When Buchanan yielded his own convictions on the
Kansas embroglio to the demands of his Southern supporters, he steeled himself to enforce his own view in
regard to another complication, just then coming to his
knowledge.   "General" William Walker had gone a
second time to Nicaragua.   Soon after he had landed
and begun his operations, he was seized by Naval
Commander Paulding and carried under arrest to the

[1] *Messages and Documents of the Presidents,* Vol. V, pp. 509-511.

United States. As guilty as ever Aaron Burr had
been, the President determined to make the filibuster
feel the heavy hand of the law. Davis and Toombs
thought Walker had been illegally imprisoned, and
they desired his speedy release, the latter charging
that the arrest had been made only because the adven-
turer, if left to himself, would establish slavery in
Central America.[1] His cause was not vigorously
pressed by his friends in Congress, because it was
thought best to let the President have his way in this
instance, lest he break from the Southern program
in Kansas. The offender was placed under bond to
keep the peace, but it was only a short while before he
was again directing attacks on Nicaragua and Central
America. He was finally captured and, as already
noted, shot on the scene of his usurpations.

The break of Douglas with the South and with the
administration created new political constellations.
Robert J. Walker was now both hated and feared in the
slave states. With the "Little Giant" for a coadjutor,
he might, a second time, prove himself a maker of
presidents, or possibly reach that high station himself.
Davis denounced Walker as untrue to his section and
called upon the party to repudiate him. This made
the Governor of Kansas only the more popular in the
North ; and Douglas's demand for a fair trial of the
popular sovereignty idea in the territories also regained for him the rank and file of the Democratic
party there. Though once regarded as a "Northern
man with Southern principles," Douglas now became
a real leader of the Democracy in his own section, and

See Johnston and Browne, *Life of Alexander H. Stephens*, p.
328.

one who might command the larger portion of the old
Southern Whig vote in the coming election.   As for
Walker, he was a man without a party after his removal from office as Governor of Kansas in December,
1857.   The Southern people could not forget his brilliant leadership of 1844, nor forgive his change of
front, as they thought, in the recent crisis.   The
North, on its side, was glad to have his testimony in
favor of its contention in the territories, but could
not excuse his long and efficient pro-slavery service
under Polk.   Though an exceedingly able man, he
never quite won the confidence of any party.   He remained in Washington until the outbreak of the war,
when he was employed by President Lincoln to go to
Europe for the purpose of destroying the credit of the
Confederacy by defaming the leading characters in its
government, which he did with eminent success in the
strategic year, 1863.   He died in Washington in 1869,
unlamented and almost forgotten.

Douglas, now at the head of a reunited Democracy at the North, was preparing to offer battle to the
Republicans, whom not a few conservative people
feared.   If he could regain some of his former popularity in the South, his chances of success in 1860 were
many and promising.   Davis and his co-workers began anew their plans of 1850 for consolidating their
section, so that no Northern man could well hope to
carry a single state there.   They thus sought to do
for the South what the Republicans, in 1856, had well-
nigh accomplished for the North.   In that year all
branches of the old Democratic party, not excepting
the Yancey men, had agreed to let the slavery question
settle itself in the territories.   Their convention,

which met in Cincinnati, had been remarkably harmonious, though Buchanan's small electoral vote showed how much ground had been lost since 1852.

Yancey and Rhett had grown old in urging a purely sectional creed upon the South.   Only once since 1847, had they yielded to the policy of expediency—in the Cincinnati convention.   The hope of the party had then been that by overwhelming, or even decided, success, the South would again come into the control of the government and possibly turn the issue or confuse it with other important questions as in 1844–1846.   But with all possible manœuvres, the slavery conflict, on the plains of Kansas and Nebraska, was steadily reaching a solution adverse to the South. Douglas's dangerous stroke of 1854, at first so promising, turned rapidly into worse than a Pyrrhus victory. The growing popularity of the great Illinois senator in the North only too certainly pointed to the fact that slavery could not compete in the open field with free labor ; that Douglas had only appealed the case from Congress, which had always been reasonably friendly, to the majority of the newcomers in Kansas, who would undoubtedly be inimical to the cause of slavery in the West.   The South was clearly beaten ; Douglas was at once named as the responsible man.

In this state of things, the leaders of the extreme party of 1850 came back to power.   The logic of events had justified Yancey and his following.   The agitation was now renewed in several forms :

(1)   Vigilance committees and committees of correspondence were voluntarily formed, and leading slaveholders, who had hitherto manifested indifference toward the many controversies of the party, were made

to understand that their property was being endangered by the steady gains of the Republicans.

(2) The North was felt to be gaining more and more economically through its manufactures and trade. This advantage must be destroyed. The South must export its valuable crops direct to Europe and buy in a foreign market, rather than remain longer under the galling yoke of the Yankee. From 1854, Southern commercial conventions were held annually in such cities as Charleston, Montgomery, and Memphis. Very alarming pictures of Southern bondage were presented and every assemblage closed with the most solemn vows never again to buy from the hated North ; —yet local merchants continued to keep large open accounts in New York.

(3) The next and most difficult problem was that of consolidating the Southern states, of bringing them to act together as a unit. Failure to do this had broken the back of the movement of 1850, causing the isolation of South Carolina and the defeat of Jefferson Davis in 1851.

In addition to the natural jealousy manifested by Southern politicians and to an extent, too, by the South generally toward everything Northern, there was the everlasting negro problem. Hitherto Southerners had been content to hear slavery denounced as an unavoidable evil, an oppressive burden. The best of them, as late as 1840, agreed on these points. At the same time, since 1820, there had been a corporal's guard who denied the existence of an evil. By 1837 Calhoun gave his powerful influence to the view that slavery was a good, a blessing both to master and bondman. He held that in Southern climates, it was an economic necessity. This idea grew apace. Young Virginian leaders in the ranks of both parties asserted in 1840 that the Calhoun doctrine was the correct one. As nearly as can be ascertained at the present day, the first positive propaganda in support of this new contention, began at William and Mary College under the able direction of Professor Thomas R. Dew. The College of South Carolina early embraced the same theory, and later most Southern schools ranked themselves behind the doctrine. Before 1850 the great democratic religious denominations of the country, the Baptist and Methodist, divided on the moral issue involved in slavery. The Presbyterians likewise separated. The sectarian and theological schools became as thoroughly imbued with pro-slavery principles as the secular institutions. Dr. B. M. Palmer, a foremost Presbyterian divine, championed in the pulpit the cause of the slave-propagandists, declaring that the institution was a blessing *per se* and that he who planned for its overthrow was an anarchist. President William A. Smith of Randolph-Macon College in Virginia, published, in 1856, a labored book on the subject, in which he cited the Bible as positively authorizing it. The pulpits of all the churches were largely occupied by men who thought negro servitude the basis of the natural and divine order of things. As early as 1845, the election of bishops in the great Methodist and Episcopal churches hinged on the question of slavery. It was a sort of test which men unconsciously applied to everything.[1]

Socially the institution had even a stronger hold, for

[1] Calhoun Correspondence, Report Amer. Hist. Ass'n, 1899, Vol. II, pp. 1046–1048.

every one in the South who exercised any influence was a master or mistress of slaves. Young gentlemen carried their negro valets and black groomsmen to the University of Virginia, the College of South Carolina, and elsewhere. In Richmond, Charleston and New Orleans, the whole social fabric rested on negro servitude. The handsome if not luxurious country houses from one end of the South to the other, were filled with picked and trained servants who stood ready at all times to do the slightest bidding of their masters. It is needless to give here any description of this well-known *ancien régime.* Now that slavery had won a rating in the moral code; obtained recognition in all the great branches of the Christian church; and had been declared an economic and social necessity, it should occasion no surprise that leading men defended the institution before the whole civilized world as of divine origin and sanction. It was only the leader, the thoughtful and responsible representative of the people of the South, who should have foreseen the consequences of these new and very remarkable teachings.

But Davis said in most of his public speeches after 1856 that he was "tired" of apologies for "our institution." We must take a higher and more defensible position. Reaching backward in his own history, he again finds the Bible arguments which he had used in his speeches on the Oregon bill in 1849–50. He now admits that the young South differs from the great leaders of 1776–1830 ; that slavery had not been understood by these older men ; and that they had inadvertently yielded to the arguments of their opponents on this subject and allowed the passage of the Northwest Ordinance—the "beginning of our woes,"—and later the Missouri Compromise, which, unconstitutionally, to be sure, limited the freedom of one section of the Confederacy while the other was given an advantage. The speech of October, 1857, in which slavery was defended as a divinely established institution, not to be apologized for, was then no mere bid for popularity. He was now, from 1858 to 1860, openly and somewhat defiantly enlisted in the cause of slavery extension, for nothing occupying so high a place in the political and social system of his section could be permitted to be restricted and limited to a particular locality. There can hardly remain a doubt that in 1858, when the issue forced its way once more to the first place in the Senate, he looked forward to gaining new victories over the North by means of the Supreme Court decision and through the control of the presidency and possibly also of the Democratic party. It was in his mind a dangerous period for the South but it does not seem to have portended secession. The election of 1856 was, he said, but a truce between the great sections—a time for both sides to gather strength for another struggle which might give either the mastery.[1]

As might have been foreseen, the pressure of the Southern extremists for victory in Kansas, and the equally strenuous fight of the radical anti-slavery party of the North for the control of that region, forced aside all other questions before Congress. Finance, filibustering expeditions, the purchase of Cuba, vast railway schemes,—all yielded to the one vital "irrepressible conflict." Seward, the long-time opponent

[1] Speech in Jackson, Miss., October 14, 1857.

of Davis in all his pro-slavery plans, had gained an
influence with the people almost equal to that of
Douglas.   Henceforward a certain and ever-increasing
tide of popular favor rallied behind the resourceful
leader from New York.   The Mississippian, on the
other hand, had secured prestige with the President, so
that officially at least he occupied the vantage ground.
He could initiate measures looking to the campaign of
1860.

But, as already noted, Davis was taken seriously ill
early in the winter ; he was seldom seen in his place
during the session.   On rare occasions he appeared and
spoke with the very form of disease sitting upon him.
With head bandaged and leaning on his cane, yet with
a zeal and earnestness unmistakable, he presented his
views at critical stages of the Kansas debates.   After
all, little progress was made on either side save the removal of Walker from his place as governor, and the
organization of the Democratic official party against
Douglas and his friends.   The vital question remained
unanswered ; while business enterprise and the natural
buoyancy of the American spirit, rather than any law,
restored the embarrassed finances of the country.[1]

At the close of the session, Davis decided to spend
the summer on the Maine coast, in the hope of repair-
ing his broken health.   He left Washington, accompanied by his sprightly family and most popular wife
in the early days of July.   It was to be his last pleasure
trip into the North, and he seems to have felt the near
approach of the fatal conflict.   He journeyed by sea
from Baltimore down the Chesapeake ; past ominous

[1] Public letter of May 14, 1858, in all the leading Southern
papers.

Fort Monroe; out into the ocean at Cape Charles, hard
by the scenes to be made historic by the *Monitor* and
the *Merrimac;* thence to Boston, the home of William
Lloyd Garrison; and on to Portland, where many
Southerners of prominence were accustomed to spend
the summer.   Montgomery Blair, an intimate friend of
the Davises, had his cottage there; and the Shipleys
and Carrolls of Maryland also belonged to this group
of interesting sojourners.[1]

On the way from Boston to Portland, Davis made an
address to his fellow passengers.   It was July 4th.
He warned them against the dangers into which all
felt that the Union was being thrust by the agitators
of *both* sections.   Again, in Portland, he was called
upon to speak on several occasions.   Happy as were
his party and personal relations, made more so by
the rapid recuperation of his health, he insisted each
time on the immanence of the coming storm.   Finally,
during the early days of October, he set out for Washington.   Everywhere he went, he was received with
the highest marks of courtesy and popular esteem.
While Northern and Eastern men did not agree with
the Mississippi leader politically, they valued him
highly, and remembered with gratitude, even pride,
his able and fearless public service both in war and in
peace.   In Boston he became the guest of the city and
was invited to address an audience in Faneuil Hall,
that charmed spot of New England patriotism and
local pride, which had been closed to Webster after
his Seventh of March speech.   Davis was introduced
by his devoted friend, Caleb Cushing, while Robert C.
Winthrop and Edward Everett honored the event by

[1] *Memoir*, Vol. I, pp. 584–586.

their presence on the platform and entertained the distinguished visitor in their homes.[1] It was a Democratic assemblage, however, and it was openly acknowledged that no adherent of this party had been elected in Massachusetts "in many a day." It was a remnant of the conservative wing of years agone, made up of men who trembled at the thought of war and who hoped against hope that the Republicans would be defeated in the coming presidential campaign.

Davis won laurels on that October day. He spoke with evident feeling and genuine love for the Union. The history of ancient Boston was rehearsed; the stanch resistance to the adoption of the national Constitution in 1788 touched upon; and the later pride in the Union emphasized. But the ever-present slavery problem bore down upon the minds of all; the one theme then uppermost in every locality could not be repressed, especially by Jefferson Davis. He confessed himself a member of the so-called slave-expansionist group of the lower South; inveighed against agitation and intermeddling in the affairs of sovereign states; arraigned the motives of Douglas, without mentioning his name; and argued warmly in support of the decision of the Supreme Court in the Dred Scott case. In all that was said there was an earnest and anxious tone as of one who foresees an impending calamity. He threatened no one, nor indulged in any braggadocio; but he let it be clearly understood that all his hopes for the safety of the Union depended on the Democratic party, which was already dividing into Douglas and Yancey factions. There is no doubt that Cushing,

[1] *Memoir*, Vol. I, p. 594.

Winthrop, and B. F. Butler, influential men in New England, thoroughly agreed with these views. It was they who held out longest, less than two years later at Charleston, for Democratic harmony ; they who voted again and again for the choice of Davis himself as the candidate of their party for the presidency.[1]

From Boston he journeyed to Washington where he left his family, and went once more, early in November, to Mississippi to gauge the sentiment of his state. It was to a sullen and discontented constituency that he now returned ; and he did not quiet the troubled waters. No one could have done so at this time, least of all Senator Davis, whose visit North was looked upon with dislike and jealousy in all the Gulf states. The sojourn in Maine was not regarded as necessary for the recovery of his health, but as a bid for New England support in the coming Democratic convention. "Davis is at sea," was a phrase often applied during the years 1858 and 1859. This impetuous, angry, defiant community would not tolerate anything like lukewarmness in their leaders, still less a yielding to Northern demands. The Boston address had not been to their taste. It was well that its author came back to "render his account," if he desired to continue his career in the Senate of the United States.[2]

[1] See Butler letter in Johnson Papers, Library of Congress. "I voted fifty-seven times for the nomination of Jefferson Davis," said this rather doubtful character in American history.

[2] See speech of November 11, 1858, in Jackson, Miss., *National Intelligencer*, November 27, 1858.

CHAPTER XI

THE BREAK-UP OF THE DEMOCRATIC PARTY

THE Republican party sprang into being, not only as a protest against the repeal of the Missouri Compromise, but for the purpose of setting metes and bounds to slavery. It appealed at once to the North as offering the only possible way of wresting from the Democracy the control of the Union. The strong sectional prejudices of the people of these states, naturally aroused by the fear of a long lease of power to their opponents, were cultivated as strenuously as were those of the South by the extreme slavery propagandists. The programs of the party in 1854, 1856 and 1860, were aimed at a consolidation of all anti-slavery interests. There was hardly a hope that any Southern state would ever join their ranks, and up to the present time the South has remained "solid" against all their leading policies. The North had grown strong enough to seize by mere force of numbers the control of the Union if they could unite. It required only a few years to bring about this necessary harmony of action with such a goal in view.

The new party was not scrupulous in its use of weapons. The protective tariff of the Whigs was brought into the platforms to win the Pennsylvania vote against a powerful local Democratic machine. The Declaration of Independence was, as ought to have been expected, made to do valiant service on be-

half of emancipation. Like all revolutionary parties,
it condemned and attacked conservative institutions :
the Constitution, the Supreme Court, the United States
Senate. By every available means, the young and
vigorous organization forged its way on to success.
No one doubted that in the course of a few years Republican leaders would occupy the great places in the
national government.

Davis's erstwhile friends and co-workers, Rhett,
Yancey, and A. P. Calhoun, early in 1857 prepared
to renew their campaign against the North. Their aim
was to organize the South as thoroughly as the other
section appeared to be. Thus united, they meant to
enter the Democratic conventions whenever they might
assemble and demand the adoption of their program,
which called for absolute guarantees for slavery in the
territories. If in this they were successful, they
would support the only remaining party with a
unionist outlook ; should this party fail in a presidential election, they would fall back on their compact organization and urge secession as the last remedy at
hand.

The Southern commercial conventions were used as
a means of agitating afresh the slavery question. At
Knoxville in 1857 it was seriously proposed to reopen
the foreign slave-trade, under the ban of national legislation since 1808. L. W. Spratt of South Carolina was
appointed chairman of a committee to investigate the
subject and report at the next meeting. He did so at
the Montgomery convention, which met in 1858, urging Southern members of Congress to do their utmost
to obtain a repeal of the law. Yancey championed
the new proposition and rallied his followers to the

cause. The motive for raising the embargo on the importation of native Africans was to increase the population of the South and thereby secure a larger representation in Congress; to lower the price of negroes so that the small farmers and poor whites might become slave-owners, thus rendering Southern society more homogeneous; and of course to enable slave-holders the better to fasten their grip on new territories.

The border Southern states, whose citizens sold annually as many as ten thousand negroes to the lower South, to say nothing of the larger migration to the "cotton country," opposed the proposition. Roger A. Pryor, editor of *The South,* an important newspaper published in Richmond, replied to Yancey in lively fashion, and was able to secure a postponement of the decision until the next meeting. A year later at Vicksburg the Southern interests represented in these assemblies put themselves on record, by a large vote, as favoring this method of indefinitely increasing the negro population.

As a result of the agitation, foreign slavers and smugglers from the Northern as well as the Southern seaport towns, seized every opportunity to land cargoes of their African freight on the Southern coast. In Charleston, Savannah, Mobile and along the river banks, thousands of natives were unloaded and disposed of to eager purchasers at low prices.[1]   In no case could the local grand juries be induced to bring in bills of indictment against men engaged in this miserable business. It can hardly be doubted that between 1856 and 1860 as many as fifty thousand negroes,

[1] Collins, *Domestic Slave Trade,* pp. 19, 20.

direct from their jungles, were sold in the United States.

Davis favored this new propaganda, though he did not become its champion. As for Mississippi he thought it already had enough slaves to satisfy the demand; but he said in 1859 that Louisiana and Texas might stand in need of a fresh supply. When the legislatures of Southern states, Louisiana, for example, enacted laws providing for the importation of "black apprentices," designed to circumvent the national laws of 1819, on the subject of the slave trade, he found no words of condemnation, but suggested the repeal of too harsh general measures. As an earnest of his good-will, he steadily exerted his influence in Congress to make easier the course of the African slaver in the lower Atlantic. He must therefore be classed as an advocate of this item of Yancey's extreme program; and it was but natural, since he openly proclaimed negro slavery a blessing and a divinely established institution.

In the crisis of 1850, Davis had urged his Mississippi followers to build manufactories, to learn the arts and trades; in short, to render themselves independent of the outside world.[1] In 1854 the Richmond *Enquirer* advocated larger state appropriations to the new Virginia Military Institute at Lexington on the ground that trained men would one day be needed. South Carolina had long liberally supported her famous cadet school, the "Citadel" in Charleston. The Universities of Alabama, Mississippi, and other states added military departments and employed competent drill masters.

[1] Public letter of November 18, 1849, in leading Mississippi papers.

Louisiana established a military academy and engaged
William T. Sherman as its superintendent. A num-
ber of smaller schools, such as "Bingham's" of North
Carolina, enjoyed a good patronage.

Meanwhile, pressure was brought to bear on the
patrons of Northern colleges. From time immemorial
there had been large Southern contingents at Yale,
Princeton, and Harvard. After the Silliman episode
at Yale in 1854, most Southern newspapers published
editorials condemning parents who permitted their sons
to attend these "Abolition" schools. "If our own
schools are not good enough, let them be improved by
a more hearty support; if this is not enough, then
patronize the universities of Europe rather than aid or
abet in any way the bitter enemies of the Southland."
Such was the tenor of opinion in the more conservative journals. Not only colleges but books and works
of art of Northern origin were decried. Every occasion was used to encourage Southerners to renew their
connections and affiliations with England and France.

This was not the spirit of friendliness and mutual
forbearance demanded by the voluntary union of 1787 ;
but one which ought to have convinced thoughtful men
that separation was inevitable. For this hostility was
wide-spread ; it permeated all grades of society to a
greater or less degree, while the ruling class—the large
slave-owners—was extremely bitter. Papers like the
Richmond *Dispatch*, whose avowed purpose was to give
the news and eschew politics, yielded to the all-per-
vading feeling and before 1856 were almost daily denouncing some Northern man or institution.

The outcome of Walker's course in Kansas [1] was in-

[1] *Ante,* Chap. X.

tensely disappointing to the South; the apparent though not real change of position by Douglas, the consequent breach between him and the Democratic administration, embittered Southern men against him who had promised them everything in 1854. When the North saw the new attitude of the senior senator from Illinois; *i. e.*, when they understood that local sovereignty in the territories invariably meant anti-slavery supremacy, he became as popular as he had been hated in 1854. Douglas was the only Northern Democrat who could hope to "carry" a Northern state. He was not as "dead" after the Lincoln debates as has been assumed, since there were strong reasons for believing that the next Democratic convention would nominate him without a serious bolt. In that event, Lincoln could not have defeated him in 1860.

But intrigue plays a rôle in democracies as well as in despotisms. The regular Democratic organization was in the hands of John Slidell, Senator Bigler of Pennsylvania, August Belmont of New York, and Caleb Cushing of Massachusetts. Slidell was one of the worst corruptionists at the time active in American politics; he was aided by a clique of Massachusetts minority leaders and the Pennsylvania machine. The lower South lent its support because it was promised the privilege of dictating the next platform, which also meant that Douglas was marked for defeat, since he could never yield his favorite territorial policy without losing everything to the Republicans in the North. Buchanan was able to arrange matters so as to control the national committee, although the great majority of Northern and some Southern Democrats favored the nomination of Douglas. During the year 1859, the

main business of the party managers of whom Davis
was certainly a conspicuous leader, was to secure his
defeat.

The first visible step in this direction was to call the
national Democratic convention to meet in Charleston,
the centre of hatred for the "Little Giant." The
South Carolina metropolis and the beloved city of the
slave aristocracy was at that time one of the most important towns in the United States. It was the intel-
lect of the lower South, where the best of her ideals
could be seen in every-day life. William Gilmore
Simms, Henry Timrod, and Paul Hamilton Hayne all
lived there and contributed much to the culture of that
remarkable society. The *Mercury*, for which these
brilliant authors wrote, issued daily from Charleston.
Owned by the Rhett family ; edited by the finest talent in the South ; devoted to the cause of slavery-ex-
pansion ; representing, too, the Calhoun tradition, this
newspaper was an engine of opposition to and ridicule
of Douglas. Its power in the South could hardly be
over-estimated. What the *Mercury* said was echoed in
every local organ of extreme Southernism from Richmond to New Orleans in the short space of a single
week. If Charleston were consulted, no half-way measures would be taken and no half-way men nominated
at the coming convention. The senior Rhett, the retired senator would be made the standard-bearer of
the party ; and if the country should fail to elect him
on an extreme platform, she would lead the South out
of the Union and proclaim herself the capital of a
new Confederacy based on cotton, slavery, and free-
trade.

The aristocracy of South Carolina, which prided itself on birth, capacity and wealth, centred in this city by the sea. There was unquestionably good blood in the veins of these scions of the Huguenots. The ability and resolute will of the Calhoun generation of politicians and statesmen cannot be disputed ; and there were some millionaires whose riches were not their only title to distinction. Such profusion, ease, luxury, and *esprit* as characterized this metropolis of the old South was hardly to be paralleled in the country in 1860.

To such a city, under the shadow of the *Mercury* and in the midst of hostile sentiment, the friends of Douglas, on whose success depended the peace of the country, were forced to go by the Democratic executive committee in April, 1860, and Davis must be held responsible to a large extent for this action.

That point decided, all parties renewed their efforts to secure the state delegations. In this work the administration did a full share ; the legislatures and conventions of the South instructed their delegates to vote for the Yancey program and nothing else. He had visited the important centres or secured his ends through devoted adherents, and one by one the legislatures endorsed his plan. He was successful beyond expectation, and when the time came for him to appear in Charleston, he thought his victory certain. Older and shrewder politicians like Slidell were never sure of anything.

Their plan of campaign was prepared in Washington. On February 2, 1860, Davis introduced into the Senate his well-known resolutions, designed to express the opinion of the Democratic organization. These were accepted by his fellow Southerners, changed somewhat, and re-presented on March 1st as the ultimatum of the political party to which he adhered. There were seven of them. The first three recited familiar doctrines of the states' rights party, bearing on the slavery disputes; the fourth declared that Congress had not the constitutional power to limit the rights and privileges of slave-holders who might settle in the national territories; the fifth insisted that it was the duty of the United States courts to protect slave-owners in the enjoyment of their property in the territories, and added that in case of a failure to do this, Congress must intervene on behalf of slavery; the sixth affirmed the doctrine that no territory ready for statehood could be lawfully denied membership in the Union, because of the existence or non-existence of slavery; and the seventh reasserted the validity of the Fugitive Slave Law of 1850, declaring that state laws contravening the purpose of this "great national act" were hostile to the Constitution and *revolutionary* in character.[1] It is likely that the last article was not Davis's; but that it was intended to represent the views of the upper South.

The caucussing of Democratic senators on the Davis resolutions aroused much unfriendly remark in the press of the country. It was asserted, for example, by the Washington *States and Union*, a paper established by Pryor and Heiss, the latter of New Orleans, that leading senators meant to bind the party to a program of their own on the eve of the national convention, and such, in fact, was the aim. The organization did not fear criticism, but continued its work up to the day of the meeting of the delegates.

[1] *Cong. Globe*, 36th Cong., 1st Sess., Feb. 2d, March 1st.

In the midst of these untoward circumstances, the only political body still bearing any semblance of nationality, met in Charleston on Monday, April 23, 1860. It was a gathering of serious men to do very serious work. There was little drinking or loud and unseemly conduct. Prayers were said in the churches of this intensely disunion city, as well as throughout the country, for a happy issue of the threatening conflict. The faces of these visiting politicians were sad and earnest as they moved among the resolute Huguenots of the Palmetto metropolis; men behaved as though they were buckling on the harness of war.[1]

Yancey reached the city some days before the opening of the convention, and doubtless conferred with Rhett and his powerful following. He held meetings of the sympathizers with his program and persuaded or bulldozed the neutral or luke-warm as occasion seemed to require.[2] Slidell, too, was there, plying the art of Talleyrand with a deft hand. The lower South had come to Charleston to dictate the platform and also to choose the candidate. The Northern and Eastern delegates inclined to yield to its demands, but the progressive Western Democrats had now united for Douglas, and they would not think of any other nominee or of any platform which he could not accept and defend to his constituents.

The senatorial caucuses had determined what should be done in Charleston. It was to endorse the Davis resolutions and leave the Douglas men to accept them

[1] Rhodes, Vol. II, pp. 444–445.
[2] Trinity College Historical Papers, 1899, p. 60 ; So. Hist. Soc. Papers, Vol. XXI, pp. 154–156.

or bolt. With this scheme the Yancey men were pleased and the committee on platform, "packed," in two cases at least, would likewise agree. However, the chances of defeat were so many that the organization feared the outcome. The Northern Democracy was too strong to be treated with contempt, and besides they represented the "old line" party forces, who now for the first time since 1854 felt that their candidate was genuinely popular.[1] This growing favor with the people might work havoc with the schemes of those who "pulled the wires." Davis was intensely concerned, and as resolutely opposed to the nomination of Douglas on his now popular platform, as to the program of Seward, who was expected to be the candidate of the Republicans. He kept in the closest touch with the managers at Charleston. Slidell was his intimate supporter and Caleb Cushing, the president of the body, his devoted admirer. The committee on platform reported according to his wishes, though after a long and bitter fight; and now all the official influence of the party, combined with that of the administration, was used to secure its adoption. Thus far had able planning and shrewd intrigue brought the enemies of Douglas; but the convention was contrary-minded. Its angry majority immediately rejected the work of a year's thought and pains and the fight for a fair and open decision was begun. The minority report, which declared for squatter sovereignty, was accepted by a decided vote. The nomination of Douglas would have been the next step, but, according to the usage of sixteen years, this required two-thirds of all the delegates present, which

[1] Rhodes, Vol. II, p. 445.

rendered the assembly helpless in the face of a great crisis.

After some wrangling and much excitement, Yancey obtained the floor and delivered one of the epoch-making speeches of history in defense of the majority report, after which he and his followers withdrew from the hall in dramatic fashion. They reassembled the next day in a separate building, and, upon the advice of Slidell and other representatives of Democratic senators in Washington, with the enthusiastic approval of the lower South, planned for the nomination of a radical slavery ticket.

The convention proper, composed now of Douglas or Union men, was nevertheless unable to come to an agreement. It adjourned to meet in Baltimore two months later. The bolters, persuaded undoubtedly by Davis and the senatorial leaders, likewise decided to reassemble at the same time, not in Baltimore, but in Richmond. Both parties were evidently desirous of awaiting events, in the hope of getting into closer touch with the political managers in Washington. But Democratic senators and representatives were as much at sea as the members of the sundered convention. What Davis and the secessionists desired was patent to all ; what the nomination of Douglas meant was equally plain. There was no way of uniting these warring factions except through the surrender of one party to the other.

Could Davis, the most powerful Southern senator and the most potent figure behind the scenes in Charleston, have secured the nomination for himself or calmed the warring factions of his party ?

There is no documentary proof to sustain an affirma-

tive answer to these questions. It may be fairly argued
that he might have been the choice of the convention,
had the majority report of the committee on platform
prevailed. The Massachusetts leaders favored him;
the Pennsylvania machine was his for the asking; and
Mississippi and Arkansas had "instructed" for him.
B. F. Butler, years later, thought that such a course
might have solved the difficulty.[1] The Democratic
party might not have split, but its rank and file in the
North would have joined the Republicans and rendered Lincoln's victory overwhelming. As a defeated
candidate, Davis would have been in practically the
same position as he was in the November following.
He probably did not seriously desire the candidacy
at this time and contented himself with a less visible
control of the course of events.

The meetings in Baltimore and Richmond failed to
bring the Democrats together. Douglas received the
nomination of his party and John C. Breckinridge,
the Vice-President, became the choice of the South.
The border states, not satisfied with either of the candidates, put forward John Bell of Tennessee and Edward Everett of Massachusetts—both good and easy-
going Whigs of 1850. The Republicans named Abraham Lincoln as their standard-bearer, and entered upon
the race with all the advantages of a short party history, a strong moral appeal, and the promise of the
spoils of victory. Lincoln's election was treated as a
foregone conclusion, unless the various conservative
forces could unite on a single leader.[2]

[1] Letter of B. F. Butler in the Johnson Papers, Library of Congress.
[2] I say "conservative forces" because it seems clear that even the
Southern extremists desired the maintenance of things as they were.

The quarrel between Davis and Douglas, begun on the 9th of December, 1857, had come to a dramatic conclusion. The intense interest attaching to the two senators during these weeks and months of exciting discussion, was due to their representing so truly the aims and wishes of the great sections of their party, still in possession of the administration, and with many chances of success at the next election but for this threatening dispute. After the break-up of the Charleston convention, Davis urged a vote on his resolutions in the Senate. Douglas opposed them in a speech which lasted the better part of two days, and which was a severe arraignment of the Southern wing of the Democracy. He charged Davis with forcing the Yancey program on the party, which must either disrupt it or commit it to the expansion of slavery under the protection of the national government. This was a true indictment. Davis retorted, with unbecoming *hauteur*, that the South demanded only what the Constitution guaranteed it, and cited the Supreme Court's decision in the Dred Scott case as a final verdict in his favor. He also reviewed the history of the party and of the country since the introduction of the Wilmot Proviso in 1847. The issue had been joined, he said, on the question of dividing the spoils of war in 1847, had been temporarily settled in 1850, renewed in 1854 by Douglas himself, and now, he continued, "we are confronted again with it on the plains of Kansas and in every hamlet throughout the Confederation. It has now become the one subject of dispute in the Democratic party and it behooves us to say what shall be done." After two days of bitter arraignment of Douglas and his followers, Davis closed this, his most remarkable speech in the Senate.   His manner throughout was condescending and contemptuous, which not only did not injure his opponent, but did much harm to his own cause.   The influence of this discussion penetrated every social gathering in Washington during these last days of the old Congress. Ladies and gentlemen of the different sections were under constant restraint, when they happened to meet in polite society, lest they should refer to the one subject uppermost in the minds of all.   The representatives of the people of a common country mingled with one another as if under the rules of an armistice.

CHAPTER XII

THE issues of the campaign of 1860 were clearly drawn. Every intelligent man knew what Breckinridge and Lane desired; Lincoln and Hamlin demanded the restriction of slavery and in the end gradual emancipation; and all the other nominees plainly stood for compromise. In view of the almost certain success of the Republicans, Davis visited Douglas in the early summer of 1860, at the instance of Bell and Breckinridge, to suggest a withdrawal of all candidates and the nomination of a united conservative ticket with the sole purpose of defeating Lincoln.[1] Doubtless Buchanan, forgetting for the time the bitter campaign so long waged against Douglas, supported this scheme of Davis and Breckinridge. It was, in fact, a confession that the party organization had erred in its fight against the "Little Giant." He received the overture kindly, but refused to accept the suggestion to withdraw from the canvass, on the ground that his followers would then certainly vote for Lincoln and Hamlin. This was a proper estimate of the Northern Democracy. Douglas was the only man in the country who could have defeated the Republicans.

Davis must have seen this; but the Southern Democracy could not. No amount of persuasion could have induced the lower South to vote at this late

[1] *Rise and Fall*, Vol. I, p. 52.

day for Douglas. "Squatter sovereignty" had become as distasteful to them as the outspoken program of the Abolitionists. And their leader, Davis, entertained an ineradicable dislike for Douglas, which blinded him to all the man's good traits. "If our little grog-drinking, electioneering demagogue can destroy our hopes, it must be that we have been doomed to destruction," he wrote to Pierce in June.[1] Fully appreciating the gravity of the crisis which was involved, Davis remained in Washington during the summer of 1860, writing an occasional letter to his constituents or otherwise aiding his wing of the Democratic party;[2] he participated in a Breckinridge rally in the capital and heartily endorsed the "true National ticket." The President also lent a hand in early July by making a speech from the portico of the White House in which he announced that he would support Breckinridge.[3] But Davis was not satisfied or hopeful; he seems to have had a premonition of the fate that was in store for himself and his beloved South.

In the early autumn he returned to Mississippi, but he appears to have taken no active part in the canvass. A few days before the election he received a letter from Robert Barnwell Rhett, Jr., editor of the *Mercury*, asking his opinion as to the proper course for South Carolina to pursue in the event of Lincoln's success. His reply, dated November 10th, is not that of a revolutionist filled with the fires of innovation. There was little of the spirit of 1850; none of the zeal which

[1] *Amer. Hist. Rev.*, Vol. X, p. 365.
[2] Letter to W. M. Sloan, Vicksburg, Miss., July 8th. Published in Richmond *Enquirer*, July 30th, 1860.
[3] Curtis, *Life of Buchanan*, Vol. II, p. 291.

would urge a single state into secession.   He doubted whether South Carolina ought to withdraw from the Union without assurance from the tier of states reaching from Charleston to New Orleans; he feared that Mississippi could not wisely follow her, and he counseled delay if even one Southern state (Georgia) would not join the movement.   The only encouragement he gave the ardent revolutionist was in the fact that, in case South Carolina should act alone and an attempt be made by the United States to "coerce" her back into the Union, Mississippi and the other cotton states would support her.[1]

This was not the language the South loved to hear in 1860; in 1850 it might have been welcome.   The belief was that Davis had become a politician; that the love of power, such as he possessed under the Union, had seduced him from the bold but righteous course of earlier years.   Having cast his vote, like a good citizen, and lingered a few days at his beautiful home, he returned for the last time to his post of duty in the United States Senate.   He dreaded the issue and its almost certain outcome, and he hardly had the faith to undertake to stem the tide of certain revolution, even had he been the man to lead in such a work.

Soon after reaching the capital, he saw the President and was questioned by him as to some points in the coming message, relative to the crisis.   He took the ground which he had always taken when his ideas of national expansion failed of realization,—that of strict states' rights.   This was to be the ostensible basis of secession.   It was natural for him, and his people had been so taught since the days of Governor Troup of

[1] Alfriend, pp. 222-224.

Georgia and Judge Roane of Virginia, to believe that
the states might secede whenever their grievances justified it. Buchanan, though a Democrat and an adherent of Breckinridge, adopted the view that Webster
had taken in the debate with Hayne in 1833. With
the presidency leaning thus toward the Republican
side and the great majority of the North supporting
that policy, how could there be hope of satisfactory
compromise at this time? Davis was sorely disappointed when Buchanan took issue with him on this
matter. August Belmont, chairman of the Democratic
National Committee; Cushing of Massachusetts; Bigler of Pennsylvania, and the various Southern leaders,
with whom the President had been acting in the utmost
harmony from the beginning, all admitted the right of
a state to secede. How had Buchanan come to this
new position? The nature of his official station and
the atmosphere of the North had forced him to it.
But he did not, as the majority of the North did not,
say that the power to prevent secession inhered in the
national government. His position was a difficult one :
there was no right of secession ; there was also no
authority to prevent secession. Such reasoning as
this, while consistent with the clauses of the Constitution, was not apt to stay the hasty action of irate South
Carolina ; nor could it reassure the perplexed North.
Davis did his utmost to bring the President to his way
of thinking; the cabinet pulled the other way. The
result was a message that satisfied no one.

Congress assembled on December 3d. South Carolina had not seceded, but her senators and representatives had resigned, the legislature had ordered an
election for delegates to a constitutional convention,

and no one doubted that the breach was near.   Congress favored another compromise ; but the Republicans who had won in the recent election, in a minority, however, in both houses so long as the South remained in the Union, thought the time had come to say that slavery must henceforth be content within certain fixed limits.   The representatives of the lower South in Congress also thought the occasion for a settlement was at hand ; they would not be satisfied with less than the extension of the line 36° 30' to the Pacific, which had been the demand of Davis since 1850.

What could such a Congress, with such a President, do under the circumstances ?   Many propositions were made and some inflammatory speeches delivered before the telegraph brought the news that South Carolina had unanimously declared her independence.   Feeling that none of these offers could avail anything and that the administration could not be depended on to yield to South Carolina's demands, a group of Southern representatives and senators met on December 14th, in the rooms of Reuben Davis of Mississippi, and after discussing the all-absorbing subject, issued to their constituents an address in which they said :   " The argument is exhausted.   .   .   .   In our judgment, the Republicans are resolute in the purpose to grant nothing that will or ought to satisfy the South.   We are satisfied the honor, safety, and independence of the Southern people require the organization of a Southern Confederacy—a result to be obtained only by separate state secession." [1]   Seven senators, that is, a majority, from the lower Southern states, exclusive of South Carolina, signed this document, which came from the

[1] Rhodes, Vol. III, pp. 177–178.

press on December 15th.   Davis took part in the conference and his name, with that of his colleague, A. G.
Brown, appears among the signers of the manifesto,
which had a wide circulation North and South and
decidedly influenced the course of events.

The House was already forming its great committee
of compromise; the Senate, casting all its plans together, turned them over to thirteen members who
were for the time to supersede the House committee
of thirty-three.   These men represented all phases of
opinion and the best ability in public life.   If any
peaceable solution of the grave problems then pressing
upon every mind could be found, they would find it.
The country had confidence in the wisdom of Congress; and all moderate men and newspapers voiced
the sentiment that some satisfactory remedy must be
discovered.   Davis was chosen a member of the Senate
committee.   He declined to serve on the ground that
his participating in the meeting of December 14th,
and his view that there was no remedy which the incoming administration would accept, made it improper
for him to do so.   Over-persuaded by his colleagues
and by the chief advocates of compromise, he yielded
and took an active part in the sessions.   Five of the
thirteen members were Republicans; Davis, Hunter,
and Toombs represented the threatening South; while
the remainder were men from the border states who
favored compromise.   At the first session, Davis proposed that no report should be made to the Senate by
the committee in which a majority of the Republicans
did not concur.   Seward, Wade of Ohio, Collamer of
Vermont, Grimes of Minnesota, and Doolittle of Wisconsin were thus left to decide for their party and for

the country. This course was soon agreed upon and the important meetings of the committee took place from the twenty-first to the twenty-fourth of December. Crittenden, the most influential of the compromisers, the successor to Henry Clay, was chairman. His elaborate scheme, as now submitted, embraced the whole range of subjects in dispute ; but his first proposition, that of extending the line of 36° 30′ to the Pacific as a definite and final boundary between the slave and the free states, became at once the test question.

Davis, Hunter, and Toombs were ready to accept this proposal. The representatives of the border states, including Douglas, would have been delighted at such an adjustment. It remained for the Republicans to decide. And it was understood that whatever the committee agreed to would be satisfactory to the country at large. Indeed, all now looked to these tried and experienced statesmen for a settlement of the great national dispute.[1]

While the committee was in session, the news of South Carolina's withdrawal from the Union reached Washington. The gravity of the event was felt on the next day when it was seen that not only the cotton belt but North Carolina and other border states showed signs of approving the radical course. It was not a second nullification storm from the South that would soon blow over. Leading Republicans now began to weaken in their demands, and thousands regretted the votes they had given for Lincoln and Hamlin. The New York *Tribune* and Thurlow Weed's Albany *Journal*, added their voices to the demands of the *Herald*, the *World*, and the *Times* for a peaceable ad-

[1] Rhodes, Vol. III, pp. 15–1152.

justment of the differences.   Seward had been writing
letters to his wife for nearly a month, which show that
he was ready to abandon the "irrepressible conflict,"
and this change of heart on his part was vaguely understood among his followers.   If the New York senator gave his consent to Crittenden's plan, Grimes and
Doolittle would have easily added their votes and only
Collamer and Wade would have been left to protest
against the report.

However, the committee agreed upon no plan of
compromise and Crittenden was left to present his
scheme to the Senate himself when too late to get a fair
hearing.   What was the reason for this unexpected
disappointment of all the friends of peace?   On the
20th of December, the day the committee of thirteen
was named, Thurlow Weed visited Lincoln at his home
in Springfield to talk over the appointments and, perhaps, the policy of the new administration.   They
read together the dispatches from Charleston, and
Lincoln prevailed on the great politician and "boss"
to give up his plans of compromise.   Weed carried a
message to Seward which induced him to change his
view of the situation and to vote against a settlement.   Lincoln said, "No compromise on the question of slavery extension ; on that point hold firm
as steel." [1]   The popularity of the great War President has made students of the subject to overlook his
responsibility for this momentous decision, while Wade
and other less lovable Republicans have been regarded
as the causes of the failure of Crittenden's propositions.

[1] Rhodes quotes letters from Lincoln to John A. Gilmer of North
Carolina to this effect; he also wrote as much to Alexander
Stephens and even more to Horace Greeley.

The truth is, the Republican President-elect was almost alone in his firm stand on this point. His ground was, first that a compromise such as this would not satisfy the South and that in a few years the demand for the annexation of Cuba or another strip of Mexico would be made an ultimatum. Second, he thought to yield this contention would have been in effect to give up the results of the election. Contrary, then, to the judgment of the leading politicians and the omniscient editors, this novice from Illinois refused to sacrifice any of the principles on which the contest had hinged. Lincoln deliberately chose the horn of the dilemma, which meant war; but he did not then expect this result to ensue. He thought the South would not take the last step; indeed, few men of the North estimated at its true worth the revolutionary will and firm resolve of the Southern people.

When Davis learned that a majority of the Republicans on the committee of thirteen opposed compromise, he filed his vote, in accordance with his suggestion on the first day, against the opening clause of Crittenden's program; Toombs voted with him. This defeated the proposals by a majority of one. That Davis and Toombs were responsible for the war, as has been charged, is utterly untrue except in so far as their general influence during the ten years past tended to that result.

In the early part of January, various other plans were introduced into the Senate or the House, looking toward compromise. Crittenden procured a vote on his proposition in the Senate with difficulty. By this time the leading Republicans were informed of Lincoln's position on the question. The real opportunity had passed, the rôle of Henry Clay was outworn; yet, Corwin, of Ohio, introduced a similar scheme in the House, and the South now blocked the way to success. The only plan which really could have met the case passed the New York legislature, was advocated by the *Tribune*, and came before Congress early in February. It proposed to emancipate the slaves at national expense and colonize them in Africa. This was to be done gradually and in coöperation with the state governments; but the country was not ready for this step.[1]

Davis realized that when the committee of thirteen failed to agree, there was no chance for a settlement short of secession. He paid no attention to any of the schemes presented either in the Senate or in the House. Emancipation at national expense appeared to him the merest chimera. He would have pronounced it unconstitutional as well as insulting. Nothing shows better how far apart the North and the South were than the discussion of this, the only adequate proposition of the time. The *Tribune* debated the matter as though it were possible for the South to consider it, and the New York legislature seems to have thought such a solution would be acceptable to the Southern members of Congress. These believed, however, that nothing could be done which was not written in so many words in the Constitution; they also thought slavery to be a blessing and therefore not a subject of discussion. Their aim was to extend its area rather than to limit it. They desired to import fresh supplies of negroes from Africa rather than send those on

---

[1] *Cong. Globe,* 36th Cong., 2d Sess., Feb. 11, 1861; New York *Tribune,* Jan. 24, 1861; Rhodes, Vol. III, p. 270.

hand back to their original jungles. Could men of such widely differing ideals expect to live together in peace?

Meanwhile, the situation in South Carolina had grown infinitely more acute. On December 6th, by an almost unanimous vote, the people of the state returned the friends of immediate secession to the convention, called to assemble on December 17th. That body, composed of the well-to-do and the wealthy property-holders of the community, convened first in Columbia, but adjourned to Charleston on account of an epidemic of smallpox in the capital. Three days later the fatal ordinance was passed without a dissenting voice. A declaration of independence followed; and an address to the other Southern states was issued. The Gulf states were already moving toward the same goal.

Anticipating this action, the South Carolina members of the House of Representatives in Washington, on December 8th, called to see the President, in order to have an understanding about the status of Forts Moultrie, Sumter, and Castle Pinckney. Rumors had gone abroad that a cabinet crisis was at hand on the proposition to reënforce Major Anderson, whose men were few and whose supplies were running low. They left with Mr. Buchanan's written assurances that Major Anderson would not be attacked by South Carolina, provided the military status remained unchanged. And they went away satisfied that no aid or relief would be sent to the garrisons in Charleston harbor. A few days later Buell, an assistant in the War Department, went there to give Anderson verbal advice as to how to conduct himself in his dangerous situation.

The substance of the "instruction" was, to remain on the defensive; but not to permit himself to be surprised.

On December 26th, commissioners from the government of South Carolina appeared in Washington with credentials and formal instructions, authorizing them to treat with the government of the United States concerning the surrender of the forts then held by the latter, and in general to balance accounts between the two governments since the beginning of their partnership in 1788. Before the commissioners had had time to see the President, word came that Anderson had dismantled Fort Moultrie over night and concentrated his force in Sumter, a stronger place and out of reach of some shore batteries which he had seen put into position. Trescott, of the War Department, had been first to receive the information. He hurried to the commissioners, then to the Senate, where he saw Davis, and also Hunter of Virginia, both of whom accompanied him to the White House. There Davis, as spokesman for the party, broke the news to the President, saying : "I have a great calamity to announce to you." They insisted that he order Major Anderson back to Fort Moultrie. After some hesitation, Buchanan decided to make a cabinet matter of it. The decision of the administration a day or two later was that Anderson had not disobeyed orders and that he must be sustained.

On the following day the commissioners from South Carolina had an interview with the President, reminding him of his quasi-promise of December 8th to the South Carolina Congressmen, and demanding that Major Anderson be ordered back to Moultrie. The nature of the promise was not denied or disputed; only time to consider, to "say his prayers," was requested. But the die had been cast. Buchanan had decided to act with the Union section of his cabinet, and by this date all the Southern members, except one, had resigned, on one plea or another. Joseph Holt and Jeremiah S. Black, two strong-headed men of decided nationalist convictions, had gained the ascendancy with the President. The influence of Davis, which had all along been so great, now waned; for once in the last eight years his urgent advice had been positively rejected.

A few days later the cabinet decided to send reënforcements to Charleston and a fast side-wheel passenger steamer, *Star of the West*, was fitted out in New York and ordered to proceed secretly to the relief of Major Anderson. Men, arms, and provisions were put aboard and it was expected that the vessel would reach Fort Sumter in the night and steal in unobserved. Jacob Thompson, the last Southern member of Buchanan's ill-starred cabinet, permitted news of this move to reach Charleston in time for the state government to be on its guard. The *Star of the West* failed of its mission and was compelled to return to New York, the laughing-stock of half the country. On receiving news of this adventure, Davis again went, on January 9th, to the White House. He met a cooler welcome than ever before. His persuasive utterances on behalf of South Carolina had no effect. He returned to the Senate to hear read the special message of the President on the state of the Union. He no longer entertained a hope that peaceable secession was attainable.

The commissioners of South Carolina had been using their utmost endeavors to secure formal recognition. Personally they were well known to the President; they were among the best of South Carolinians at a time when culture in that state was at its zenith. Robert W. Barnwell, a member of an old colonial family, graduate of Harvard, and close student of religious and literary problems, college president and United States senator, headed the commission.   James H. Adams, a scion of Massachusetts stock, son of a college president, educated at Yale, and trained in public affairs, was the second member of the delegation.   James L. Orr, graduate of the University of Virginia, former speaker of the national House of Representatives, a leader of conservative opinion in his state, was the last.   Secession was not an affair of mere malcontents when such men as these appeared as its chosen representatives.   If they disputed with the President about the understanding of December 8th, it was not because of their disposition to be rude or to read into an agreement that which it did not contain; but because of an honest misapprehension on the part of the President of an exceedingly important matter.

On December 31st, they received his final reply ; he declined to meet them and refused also to change the military status in Charleston.   Indeed, news soon reached the South Carolinians that the relief expedition already mentioned was under consideration. Their rejoinder,[1] highly colored on account of their knowledge of the plan to reënforce Major Anderson and their pique at the failure of their mission, was sent to the White House on January 2, 1861.   It was,

[1] *Official Records*, Series I, Vol. I, p. 120.

nevertheless, a strong statement of the case for secession. Buchanan declined to receive this last document, and after some delay submitted the remainder of the correspondence to Congress in response to a call for information on the subject.

It was the message accompanying these papers that Davis heard read on January 9th, as he returned disappointed from his last visit to the President. He knew of the final letter of the commissioners and thought the case not fairly put before the country with that paper omitted. He therefore replied to Buchanan in a speech in the Senate, insisting on its submission. He sent a certified copy to the clerk, but King, of New York, objected to the reading of such a "treasonable" utterance. A spirited debate ensued; but Davis knew his ground and he succeeded in rebuking the President before the country and in getting South Carolina's justification spread on the records of Congress.[1] It was a shrewd stroke, but one that did not add anything to the Mississippian's reputation, nor tend to calm the angry feelings of the nation.

On the following day, January 10th, he delivered a formal and carefully prepared address, which he desired posterity to accept as his *apologia*.[2] In comparison with other defenses of great historic causes, it suffers incalculably. It is not permeated with that spirit of devotion to the interests of the weak which renders many a revolutionary manifesto immortal; it is not an appeal to the enlightened sentiment of the world on behalf of a new and more rational religious faith, like the famous "harangue" of William of Orange; nor

[1] *Cong. Globe,* 36th Cong., 2d Sess., Jan. 9th.
[2] *Rise and Fall,* Vol. I, p. 219.

does Davis, like Jefferson in his undying Declaration, challenge the support of mankind on behalf of a wider individual liberty. It is, in fact, the reverse of all this that the great Southern senator asks; a plea for privilege, for the execution of "his bond," for "equality in the Union,"—an equality which meant nothing more nor anything less than the expansion of slavery. By "your votes you refuse to recognize our institutions," he repeats for the hundredth time. The other idea advanced in various forms is that of state sovereignty, the compact theory of the Constitution.[1]

From the date of John Marshall's decision in the case of Hunter *vs.* Martin, Virginians had been taught by their ablest politicians that the Chief-Justice was wrong and that state sovereignty was both right and practicable. In Georgia, Alabama, and Mississippi the doctrine dated back to the famous Yazoo land controversy. In South Carolina it had been the religion of most men since 1832. Calhoun blew upon these dry bones during the last twenty years of his life and convinced the great majority of Southerners that they were a part of a living organism ; that secession was a legitimate remedy for serious ills under the Constitution. Davis was a devoted disciple of Calhoun, and, like the Carolinian, he was a statesman rather than a politician. He would not dissolve the Union if it could be held together by any sort of arrangement which left the South intact ; it was only as a

[1] For the framework and growth of this doctrine, the reader is referred to the Virginia and Kentucky resolutions of 1798–99; to the rulings and decisions of the Virginia Court of Appeals and the writings of John Taylor, of Caroline, 1815–1821 ; and to the fine-spun theories of John C. Calhoun, after 1828.

dernier ressort that he would invoke the inalienable right.

He had come to this position reluctantly, since the failure of the Charleston convention. When he lost his hold on President Buchanan, he saw that the sands were running low. On January 5th, he entered into a caucus with the Southern senators and assumed his share of the responsibility for advising the cotton states once again to hasten out of the Union and form a new Confederacy. They further asked their state legislatures or conventions whether they should return to their homes or remain in Washington to impede, as best they could, the progress of the administration in any plans of coercion that might be resolved upon. They were authorized to remain at their posts and the South hastened on in its revolutionary course.

In full realization of these facts and having done what he could to get the new government on foot and ready to buckle on the war harness, Davis made this careful *apologia* for himself and the South. He remained yet ten days in Washington, though he was not an active participant in the affairs of the Senate. On January 20th, he wrote his friend, Pierce, the ex-President:

"I have often and sadly turned my thoughts to you during the troublous times through which we have been passing, and now I come to the hard task of announcing to you that the hour is at hand which closes my connection with the United States for the independence and union of which my father bled, and in the service of which I have sought to emulate the example he set for my guidance. Mississippi, not as a matter of choice but of necessity, has resolved to enter on the

trial of secession.   Those who have driven her to this
alternative threaten to deprive her of the right to require that her government shall rest on the consent of
the governed, to substitute foreign force for domestic
support, to reduce a state to the condition from which
the colony arose. . . .   General Cushing was here
last week and when we parted it seemed like taking
leave of a brother.   I leave immediately for Mississippi
and know not what may devolve upon me after my
return.   Civil war has only horror for me, but whatever circumstances demand shall be met as a duty and
I trust be so discharged that you will not be ashamed
of our former connection or cease to be my friend."[1]

On the following day, the Southern senators took
formal leave of their colleagues.   Davis had passed a
sleepless night, due to the pressing responsibility of
his present course as well as to illness.[2]   Nevertheless,
he appeared in his accustomed place.   The floor, halls,
and galleries were crowded with anxious and earnest
spectators, as they had been only on great occasions,
when Webster or Clay spoke.   Amid profound silence,
he arose to bid his adieu ; the whole world knew that
it was too late to expect anything but an adieu.   He
told his story in simple, chaste English, with here and
there a touch of rhetoric, but in such a sad and convincing manner that many a tear fell upon cheeks unaccustomed to the moisture of emotion.   What he said
was but a conclusion of the address of January 10th.
It was not difficult for that generation to understand
his doctrine.   The great mass of men did not then feel

[1] *Amer. Hist. Rev.*, Vol. I, pp. 366–367.
[2] *Memoir*, Vol. I, p. 696.   Letter of Joseph Davis, January 3d, in
the State Department, Collection of Davis MSS.

resentful toward him, but toward the incoming administration and the party which supported it.

It was suggested in intensely partisan Republican circles that Davis and his *confrères* ought to be arrested before they left the capital. Such an attempt would have produced a riot in Washington ; but had this been done without disturbance, no Federal court before which Davis could have been cited would have pronounced against him. The judges of the subordinate tribunals would have released him without serious delay. The Supreme Court would have ruled in favor of his cause. The judiciary, since the death of Marshall, had constantly leaned toward the states' rights view ; the country at large, however illogical it may appear, believed that any state had the right to secede when its special interest seemed to be in imminent peril.[1] Unmolested, Davis went his way to Mississippi, to play a part yet more conspicuous than hitherto in this saddest drama of modern history.

A theory has been advanced, and was once generally accepted outside of the South, to the effect that this sundering of the Union was the result of a conspiracy in which Jefferson Davis was the principal character ; and the fact that he was the champion of South Carolina, a leader in the caucuses of the Southern senators, and that he remained at his post for some two weeks after Mississippi had seceded, giving aid and advice to the promoters of the Southern revolution, has been taken as sufficient proof of this contention. But the truth is that Davis did not desire to see the South secede except in last resort ; he was no

[1] See attitude of Northern states on Fugitive Slave Law ; the South was well-nigh unanimous in this opinion.

longer the extremist of 1850, though he believed the
conditions culminating in the election of Lincoln were
worse for the South than those of that year. Mr.
Rhodes has well said that, if secrecy is a condition of
conspiracy, the Southern leaders of 1861 were certainly
not conspirators, for they did everything publicly.
The newspapers printed all the " resolves " of their
" secret " caucuses; and the *Congressional Globe* is
filled with their warnings and their threats. Davis
was a leader in these meetings and a promoter of secession, because he had long been the trusted mouthpiece
of his state, whose people had been talking about it as
an alternative in certain contingencies, since the opening of the Mexican War.

The character of the movement of 1861 was, however, unique. The shifting of the centre of Southern
civilization to the lower South has been described.
The vitality of the slavery system was no longer in
Virginia and her neighboring states, but in that tier
of commonwealths stretching from Charleston to New
Orleans. The wealth was also largely found there.
This system and the opulence and culture which grew
out of it were based on the monopoly of cotton growing and to some extent on sugar culture. As has
been shown by Mr. Phillips, of the University of
Wisconsin,[1] the lords of this region lived along the
river fronts or in the neighboring lowland counties;
that is, wherever the cotton plant flourished. The
law of the survival of the strongest, which applied to
planting, just as it does to petroleum production in our
day, forced the small planter and farmer to the poorer

[1] *Amer. Hist. Rev.*, Vol. XI, p. 798; *South Atlantic Quarterly*,
Vol. II, p. 231.

lands or away to the West, where there were better chances of his becoming a large proprietor. During the three decades immediately preceding 1861, this evolution found in the cotton belt, now the "black belt," its full and rapid realization. The opportunity of the time was offered in the lower South, and Northern men of means as well as the younger sons of the old South flocked there by the thousand. The wealthy men, the millionaires of 1860, lived on these great plantations or in New Orleans, Mobile, and Charleston, leaving their hundreds of slaves to the management of thrifty overseers.

If any one doubts that the South was rich in 1860, let him consult the census of that year. South Carolina stood far above Massachusetts in the assessed values of property, and New Orleans was one of the large centres of commerce and a city of semi-European culture. Still the extent of this wealth was limited. The great plantation lords lived in two small areas, one embracing about a fourth of the state of South Carolina, the region about Charleston and Beaufort; the other, a little larger, reaching from Wilkinson County, Mississippi, to a point about one hundred miles above Vicksburg. In these confined but fertile regions dwelt the monopolists of 1860, who were ready for war at any time to avoid a surrender of their privileges, or franchises,—to use a more modern term. Their allies and lieutenants in the coming conflict were the next lower class, made up of less wealthy planters who lived in the "black belt," beginning about Washington City and extending to New Orleans, a region on the average less than a hundred and fifty miles wide. Thus something like one-tenth of the area of the South controlled the political action of the remainder ; while less than one-twentieth of the population belonged to this ruling, monopolistic class. It was the power of concentrated wealth, the value of lands and negroes devoted to the production of the staples—cotton, tobacco, and sugar—that dominated the thought of Southern men. In these princes of the plantation, the small planter saw his *beau ideal* in life ; and it was, therefore, not difficult to bring such men to the support of the larger masters, as it was also not a rare thing for a small planter to become a great slave-holder. The charmed circle of Southern aristocracy, like that of the English nobility, was not rigidly closed ; and aristocracy here as in England was therefore popular.

What made this obedience to or acquiescence in the program of Davis and his compeers in 1861 still easier was the general acceptance of the principle of state sovereignty—a doctrine, as already noted, sedulously taught since cotton-growing became the business of the South. The state had become, long before 1850, the idol of the Southern man's heart; it was a fetich, a sovereign as potent over the people as was Frederick II or Louis XIV.

It was a situation similar to that which we observe in the industrial system of the United States at the present day, untrammeled in the main by the power of a central government, and licensed by the individual states to do its will on the people in general. The lords of industry and transportation of the year 1906 are as loth to surrender any of their monopoly rights as were those of 1861 ; and, according to the view of many acute students, there is as much slavery connected with the later as with the earlier system, and far more hardship and suffering. So that when a great Southern senator, worth a half million dollars, equivalent in political power to several millions in our day, threatened to break up the national government, he was doing the same kind of thing, and he afterward assumed the same dictatorial mien, that the great Northern senator does when he defies the power of the nation to fix laws which shall regulate the railway traffic of the country. If there were treason in the extreme demands of privilege in 1861, there is treason in the same demands now presented to the people. Jefferson Davis was the champion of vested rights; the advantage he had over his younger brother of the present time consisted in the then unexploded doctrine of state supremacy.

The people of the South, in 1861, had made up their minds on secession. It remained for them to execute the inexorable decree. They were absolutely sure that they were right and that their interests were at stake. The other and sometimes greater question of expediency they were not prepared to answer. They looked to their leaders to determine this. These leaders, of whom Davis was the foremost, must be held responsible for the results of a premature or a too long delayed contest for what may be acknowledged to have been their chartered rights.

One frequently hears the remark from the common man of the South that 1850 was the time for secession. That was the opinion of Davis, Quitman and even Calhoun. In 1860 the North had grown immensely; her railways bound her varied interests together; it was easier for her to fight than it would have been ten years earlier. In this view one forgets that the South had also grown and what was more she had had time to prepare European opinion for the novel spectacle of a new government among the nations resting on the "fundamental" principle of African slavery. The changes in the political thought of France which took place after 1850 were favorable to her ; the free trade alliance between France and Great Britain was also propitious. But Germany was a new factor ; and as for Russia not much was expected to come from that strange country in aid of the democratic North. These things must be kept in mind when we estimate the responsibility resting on Davis for leading a willing people into what he knew would be an awful revolution. He studied the European situation, and had correspondents in France, who since 1854 had reported to him the idiosyncrasies of Louis Napoleon as well as the phantasies of English noblemen.[1] He knew England and her aristocracy well, and counted on aid from that quarter.

Indeed when one carefully notes the trend of opinion in England and France, one is forced to the conclusion that there was much better reason for the South to expect recognition than there had been for the American colonists to hope for aid in 1776. And the Southern leaders kept the situation of 1776 constantly in mind. As to resources, there was no comparison between the seceding states and the thirteen colonies, so far superior were those of the former. As to unity of feeling and harmony of action, the South had a great advantage over their ancestors. On the question of right, which

[1] Letter of E. B. Buchanan to Davis, La Rochelle, France, August 1, 1854, State Department papers.

always profoundly influences men in such crises, the slave-holders of 1860 were not worse off than their famous predecessors of 1776. The right of a sovereign state to secede from a voluntary union was much clearer in the eyes of Europe than that of a colony to break away from the mother country.

In the matter of economic interest the South—the one cotton producing region of the world—had more to offer than the North. And as to the opening which this break-up of the threatening power of united North America would make for the aggrandizement of land-hungry foreign states, it was evident that Europe would be the gainer. Besides English jealousy was still a factor to be thrown into the scale. Indeed, does it not seem strange that the South was not recognized? The astute Bismarck said a year or two before his death that the failure of Europe to take advantage of the Civil War and destroy the power of Anglo-Saxon America was the mistake of the age. And looked at from the viewpoint of European interest alone, the Iron Chancellor was right.

Beyond all this, there was the reasonable hope that the people of the North would not sustain the Republicans in the event of war. It was only by narrow margins that Lincoln had won in the great states of Pennsylvania and New York, and the Middle West was by no means a unit against the South. There were also Cushing, Butler, Seymour, Fernando Wood, Bigler, Douglas, and even ex-President Buchanan, leaders of much influence, who would certainly not support a war policy or persuade men into battle against the South. The Democrats, timid commercial centres, and the unwarlike tastes of an industrial society would

combine to weaken the arm of coercion. The resistance of the Northern people to their government was
relied on by the South and not unnaturally. On the
other hand, the South expected that slavery would
prove a valuable asset in the game of war, for the
negroes could produce an abundant supply of provisions as long as they were required. The white males
would have only the work of superintendence. This
would leave a large number of the population free for
military service. So long as the war was conducted
along the border, this system would operate without
serious break-downs. These considerations tended in
the eyes of thoughtful men to equalize the resources of
the prospective combatants.

When Davis presided over the Southern senatorial
caucuses of early 1861, he must have laid bare all these
facts and conditions. When he saw the Southern governors or other makers of opinion in person, both
before and after this date, surely he recited to them
these chances of success. The outlook was exceedingly
promising. Is it not a mere excuse to say that the
"lost cause" was doomed from the beginning? Still
the unexpected event often proves the undoing of great
undertakings and this was the case with Davis and
the South. We shall see what that unexpected event
was and how the North's chances increased because
of Southern blunders. While the Mississippian profoundly regretted the necessity of secession, as may be
seen in his speeches and in his private correspondence,
it was not because he thought he was leading a forlorn
hope.

CHAPTER XIII

THE FORMATION OF THE CONFEDERACY

THE various constituent conventions of the lower Southern states chose delegates to a general convention which was called to assemble in Montgomery, Ala., at a time when feeling ran high and anger at the Republicans was on the increase. Yet during the month of January, these excited people took pains to formulate a unique policy with regard to the new government. Intensely "secession" legislatures had called together the various state conventions in December; when they met, it was everywhere found that they were decidedly "conservative" in character. Few outright opponents to the revolution had been chosen, but the men who had favored delay—representatives of the Bell and Everett, and Douglas parties, small as they had been—now found themselves pushed to the front by their fellow citizens.[1] In Georgia, the party of delay was very strong; in Alabama, Yancey was a member of the state convention, but he was purposely defeated for the general convention. In South Carolina, Rhett was chosen, but the remainder of the delegation was opposed to him in sentiment, most of its members having at one time or another resisted the extreme policy of the *Mercury* group.

This plan of sending to the general convention of the

[1] *Life of Stephens*, pp. 380–381.

South, men who had either opposed secession or favored compromise was designed to enlist all classes of the people in the cause. The universal acceptance of states' rights as a political truism made the realization of the scheme easy. Secession was a doctrinaire movement, resting for strength on local patriotism and the important principle of the inviolability of property rights. Its leaders were not, as has been thought, mere office or honor hunters; they were, with a few notable exceptions, willing to retire when the work of agitation was done, leaving their opposing brethren and neighbors to reap the rewards and distinctions which, in 1861, were looked upon as great and certain.

The conservatives, like Stephens of Georgia, accepted the friendly and unselfish overture. This, however, put the convention in the power of those who had but recently loudly proclaimed the whole movement unwise if not unlawful. It was a strange spectacle—a revolution led by its opponents.

Yancey resented the policy as a repudiation of himself and he thought it could not be followed without injury to the cause. From the beginning, Rhett of South Carolina, railed at this "politicians'" scheme. It looked to him like turning the revolution into a reaction. Yet he had no more reason to complain than Yancey, whose state sent only one "original" secessionist to Montgomery, leaving the great head of the agitation at home. Stephens, who had been in correspondence with Lincoln; who had done all he could to prevent secession in Georgia, was rather surprised at the conservative influence in Montgomery, as he had been at his own election. But he liked the prevailing atmosphere of the new capital and soon reconciled himself to his rôle. He said of his co-workers : "Upon the whole, this Congress, taken all in all, is the ablest, soberest, most intelligent, and conservative body I was ever in." [1]

As a result, the Southern constitutional convention or Congress, as it was called, reënacted the laws of the United States and proclaimed anew the old Constitution, making a few changes which provided for the safety of slavery as an institution, for the dogma of states' rights, and for a less democratic administration. It is clear enough in all the proceedings of this Montgomery convention, that the revolution was henceforth to be conservative, paradoxical as this may appear. It was provided that the Confederate President should hold office for six years and not be reëligible ; members of the cabinet were to speak on the floor of Congress, like English ministers, in behalf of their reports and recommendations.

So marked was this aristocratic tendency that a long-term Senate was proposed, some going so far as to suggest that members should be elected for life. In Georgia and South Carolina a constitutional monarchy was discussed ; [2] and Mrs. Pryor says in her *Peace and War* that Southern ladies who left Washington with their husbands to seek their fortunes under a new *régime*, spoke of going South where a kind of empire was to be established. There was probably no wide-spread disposition of this kind ; but the natural feelings of the Southern aristocracy prompted these

[1] Johnston and Browne, p. 392.
[2] Columbus (Ga.) *Times ;* Augusta *Chronicle* and *Sentinel*. Sentiment expressed in the South Carolina legislature as reported to the Baltimore *American*.

individual aspirations and dictated the decidedly conservative tone of the new constitution and government.

This re-adoption of the Constitution of the United States was also regarded by the strong Rhett and Yancey influence not only as a repudiation of their doctrinaire teachings on free trade, but as a reaction in favor of the old political managers. It was the senatorial or "Yankee" party that seemed to them to cling so closely to Washington tradition that they could not frame a new constitution and make "brandnew" laws to suit the changed conditions. The establishment of the former mail routes and judicial districts was to the *Mercury* an "aping" of that filthy, reeking government which the noble South had now shaken off. The conciliatory policy toward the border states was likewise very distasteful to these extreme secessionists. It is all a "beg to the border states," said a reporter of events at Montgomery, "and they beg the Abolitionists. There will be no war; not even South Carolina can give it to us, the only war there being relegated to the poet's corner of the *Mercury*." [1] This cajoling of the wavering, this failure to declare free trade with Europe, and the ascendancy of conservative influences in the convention, meant to the ardent South Carolinians that a representative of the old senatorial junto would be elected President and that "reconstruction" would follow without war, or a trial of the strength of the new and righteous cause.

A more disheartening thing than the failure of free trade, or the election of a distasteful man as President

---

[1] Montgomery correspondence of the Charleston *Mercury*, Feb. 6–13, 1861, which the senior Rhett supervised when he did not directly inspire it.

was the declaration by these pro-slavery extremists that the importation of African slaves was to be forbidden forever and that those detected in violating this decree would be treated as pirates. A stricter law than that which Yancey and Davis had protested against in 1858 was thus enacted in the name of slavery itself. The policy of this action will be treated later. The South Carolina revolutionists declared it the severest blow their institution had ever suffered. The *Mercury* of February 12th, said that "while Arizona and the teeming states of Mexico lie open to us," and England and France set the example of employing coolies to do their work, "we preclude forever the formation of the one policy which can enable us to subdue and civilize those lands."

The paper which voiced these and other even severer criticisms of the convention and its work, was the largest in the South. Its circulation was increasing daily; new and improved machinery had to be installed [1] to enable the management to supply the demand. "Nearly forty years we have advocated the Southern policy now reaching a conclusion in an independent government," it boasted, a fact which lent the more influence to the journal and its owner, who was now beginning to oppose the very government he had done so much to establish.

From what has been stated, it will be seen that there was decided opposition to Davis as a candidate for the presidency even before his name was mentioned in Montgomery. It was well known that Rhett thought himself the logical candidate, just as Seward had been regarded as having the best claim to the nomination

[1] *Mercury* of February 18, 1861.

at Chicago in May, 1860. But South Carolinians, while they followed Rhett's teaching, were unwilling to entrust to such an enthusiast the destinies of their new-born government. They had protected themselves against this by electing a delegation to Montgomery more or less closely affiliated with the so-called "senatorial" influence. James Chestnut, William Porcher Miles, R. W. Barnwell, Memminger, Keitt and Boyce had all been prominent in Washington during the past decade. With Rhett, they composed the list of deputies. Their first choice for President was, to the disgust of Rhett, Alexander H. Stephens. This proving inexpedient, they willingly supported Jefferson Davis. Rhett perceived the coming defeat of his own ambition as early as February 3d, the day before the formal opening of the convention. He wrote to his newspaper: "The convention means to elect Senator Davis President." This he at once dubbed the "Washington-politician" scheme.

If such a plan as this had been mooted in Washington, Davis had discouraged it, for he went home in January, 1861, to receive high military appointment, which it was confidently expected the nascent Confederacy would endorse. This would be more important than civil service. He wished to command an army for the new nation and this desire of his was seconded by the Mississippi convention. His position was regarded as settled before the delegates came together at Montgomery. The presidency was thus to be given to some other commonwealth. Why the representatives from the several states decided to change this plan and confer the first office upon one who did not wish it, thus disappointing a half-dozen able Southern politicians, has not yet been fully explained by any of the writers of memoirs dealing with this epoch.[1]

Rhett's surmise proved correct. On February 8th, the convention was to elect a President and Vice-President. On the night of the 7th, the various delegations discussed the subject afresh. A plan agreed upon soon after the 4th, between the South Carolina and Georgia members to make Toombs President, which seems to have been acquiesced in by Mississippi and other states, was changed. The Georgia men met at 10 A. M. on the 8th formally to propose his name. They learned, however, that Florida, South Carolina, Alabama, and Louisiana had agreed to support Davis. Toombs, who was present, manifested surprise ; he had already said that he would accept the office. But the Georgians yielded and no opposition was offered to the nomination and election of Davis in the regular meeting of the Congress. Stephens was at once proposed as the candidate for the vice-presidency. He was likewise unanimously elected, the convention thereby putting itself on record again, as in favor of a conservative policy.[2] Rhett gave in his adherence ; but a few days later he voiced in the *Mercury* the charge that "Jefferson Davis will exert all his powers to reunite the Confederacy to the Empire." On February 14th, he wrote : "Here the convention is at sea ; and vague dreads of the future, and terrors of the people, and in some degree want of statesmanship,

[1] Possibly the account of the proceedings of the Montgomery convention by Rhett, now known to be in existence, may explain this.

[2] This account is substantially that of Alexander H. Stephens : Johnston and Browne, pp. 389–390. See also letters of Thomas Cobb in *Publications of Southern Historical Association*, for June and August, 1907.

paralyze all useful and essential reform. Let your people prepare their minds for a failure in the future permanent Southern Constitution. For South Carolina is about to be saddled with almost every grievance, except Abolition [against] which she has long struggled and [on account of which] she has just withdrawn from the United States government. . . . The fruit of the labors of thirty odd years, in strife and bitterness, is about to slip through our fingers. This is only the beginning of our ills."

This high and responsible honor came to Davis as a surprise, for we may believe him when he says that [1] "adequate precautions" against such an event had been taken. He manifested, too, a becoming sense of the dangers and disasters which might lie ahead. However, he could not decline such an office conferred under such circumstances. He set out for Montgomery, crossing the states of Mississippi and Alabama, and seeing a little of Georgia on the way. The people flocked to the railway stations to greet their new President and to hear from him as much of his future policy as he was disposed to communicate. He spoke to large gatherings at every stop of the train, and sought, as he tells us in his *Rise and Fall of the Confederate Government*, to disillusion the minds of those who thought there would be no war. The newspapers of the day, both Northern and Southern, make him fulminate against the North on every occasion. Davis undoubtedly uttered threats at Opelika, Ala., in case the South should be invaded. On the other hand, it was entirely unlike him to have indulged in the empty braggadocio, attributed to him in the New York

[1] *Memoir*, Vol. II, p. 18.

journals.   He appeared in Montgomery on February
17th, and heard from the portico of the historic
Exchange Hotel a warm address of welcome from
William L. Yancey, who closed it with the declaration : "The man and the hour have met."   On the
following day he received the welcome of the Confederate Congress from Rhett himself, the gods of compromise intending thus to force a new "era of good feeling."   A strange fortune it was that here assembled
these three ardent friends of "Texas", all warm
disciples of Calhoun, who had worked together in
Congress in 1845.   It was impossible for them to be
more than outwardly cordial on this celebrated occasion.   They were each destined to have a share in the
undoing of the cause for which they had so long
striven.

The inaugural of the President-elect was temperate,
wise, astute ; few could find fault with what he proposed and none could decry the calm, resolute dignity
with which he started upon the untried way.   Davis
stood on the portico of the antique capitol, which
looks down from a noble hilltop upon the fine old
Southern town, within whose bounds this everlasting
slavery question had been hotly discussed for twenty
or more years.   Montgomery was the heart of the
slave country and well it was that this great experi-
ment in a slave-government should begin there.

Davis did not mention the subject—an omission
he had hardly ever made since he entered public
life in 1844.   He discussed the tariff and agriculture
very much as Thomas Jefferson would have done.   An
army and navy, he thought, ought to be created.   In
the event of war "there would be no considerable

diminution in the production of the staples which have constituted our exports, and in which the commercial world has an interest scarcely less than our own." Upon the possibility of the reconstruction of the Union he could not have safely spoken in that presence; but he let it be clearly seen that, in his opinion, such a thing could never be, and that if coercion should be attempted, "the suffering of millions will bear testimony to the folly and wickedness" of those who inaugurate the policy. He closed most appropriately:

"It is joyous in the midst of perilous times to look around upon a people united in heart, where one purpose of high resolve animates and actuates the whole; where the sacrifices to be made are not weighed in the balance against honor and right and liberty and equality. Obstacles may retard, but they cannot long prevent the progress of a movement sanctified by its justice and sustained by a virtuous people. Reverently let us invoke the God of our fathers to guide and protect us in our efforts to perpetuate the principles which by His blessing they were able to vindicate, establish, and transmit to their posterity. With the continuance of His favor, ever gratefully acknowledged, we may hopefully look forward to success, to peace, and to prosperity." [1]

This address fitly expressed the feelings and aspirations of the sober second thought of the Southern people, as they reviewed the work of their representatives "in Congress assembled." All hearts warmed to the resolute and high-minded gentleman whom they had elevated to the place of responsible leadership.

[1] *Rise and Fall*, Vol. I, pp. 232-236.

Even the fiery young writers for the Charleston papers, for once in their lives, felt called upon to be pleased. Yancey consoled himself with the assurance that, after all, the Confederacy would succeed, and supported it warmly.   In Virginia, and other border states, there was a strong yearning for this virtuous government which had been formed by brethren in economic and social bonds.   Most men expected the new nation to move on for centuries in the path just marked out for it; none expected the direful future which lay immediately ahead.   There was, nevertheless, much underlying regret of the necessity of breaking up a great nation, a fear even that both politicians and people might have gone too far.

CHAPTER XIV

THE CONFEDERATE ADMINISTRATION'S POLICY

AMERICAN statecraft has departed widely from the British in the formation of cabinets. In England the leader of a successful reform or revolution is called upon by the monarch to take charge of administrative affairs. This man becomes the responsible head of a new cabinet and he brings to his assistance in the various departments his ablest co-workers and sympathizers. Unity of purpose and policy ensues. In the United States, for a reason which cannot be explained here, the opposite course is followed. The sovereign people refuse to choose for their President the leader of a successful political revolution ; and no better illustrations of this can be cited than the defeat of Seward in the Chicago convention of 1860 and the absolute ignoring of Yancey and Rhett in the Montgomery convention of 1861. Davis, the counselor of delay, the semi-conservative of the last two years, was chosen the first President of the Confederacy. He was selected because the opponents of secession and the conservative Virginians could unite upon him.[1]

When Davis came to choose his official advisers, he carried further the rule of compromise. Not content with the coöperation of the conservatives of the radical states with the radicals of the border states, clearly manifested in his own election as well as in

[1] Du Bose, *Life of William L. Yancey*, p. 586.

that of Stephens, he still more alienated those who had borne the brunt of the long agitation by filling the high positions in the new government with men who had at one time or another publicly opposed secession, some of whom had been competitors with himself for the chief position, while others were the open personal enemies of Rhett and Yancey.   Robert Toombs, disappointed at the sudden turn of things on February 8th, which defeated him for the presidency, was placed in charge of the State Department; C. G. Memminger, a lifelong opponent of the South Carolina revolutionists, took the Treasury portfolio; L. Pope Walker, from the Union section of Alabama, was made Secretary of War; Mallory, strongly opposed in his own state—Florida, took the Navy; Benjamin, of decided Whig proclivities, became Attorney-General; and Reagan, of Texas, another conservative, was given the Post-Office Department.   The purpose of these appointments was evidently the composing of differences and disagreements, not the securing of harmony in administration or the ablest talent for the work in hand.

The justification for this policy in the mind of Davis consisted in the belief that the revolutionists, who had fought hard and long for the cause, were above the lust of office and willing to retire, allowing their opponents to enjoy the emoluments and the honors of responsible administration.   The same idea found expression in the appointment of the commission to negotiate with the Washington government for the recognition of the Confederacy.   It was composed of two anti-secessionists and one Breckinridge man.   The single exception to this general policy was the appointment of William L. Yancey, Pierre A. Rost, and A. Dudley Mann, commissioners to Europe. These had all been ardent Southern rights men, firm advocates of secession for several years. Was it possible that Davis believed their ardent zeal and flaming eloquence would prove as effective in breaking down the indifference of the European chancelleries as they had been in "firing the Southern heart"? Neither Yancey nor Rost was in the remotest degree fitted for the delicate and all-important duties of Confederate diplomacy.

While these backward steps were being taken in Montgomery, the rivalry between North and South waxed warmer in Virginia, North Carolina, and Tennessee. The Virginia convention, called in the early winter to consider the grave situation of the country, had only thirty secessionists among its membership; an election in North Carolina about the same time went against the radical leaders; and Tennessee was in the firm grip of the Unionists, led by Andrew Johnson and "Parson" Brownlow. President Lincoln, like Davis, carried the deft hand of compromise into these states, offering responsible cabinet positions to such men as John A. Gilmer, of North Carolina, and Robert E. Scott, of Virginia. Still, the powerful influence of a common economic interest was on the side of the Confederacy.

In the vain hope of composing the radical differences between the lower South and the Republicans, who came into full power on the retirement of Davis and his followers, the famous Peace Convention was brought into being on the initiative of Virginia. From February 4th, till near the close of the month, the anxious and patriotic members of this extra-constitutional body did what they could to bring the Republicans to a recognition of the chief clauses of the Crittenden Compromise which Lincoln had caused to be defeated in the committee of thirteen. But the President-elect, supported now by the "stiff-backed" leaders of his party in the Northwest, was immovable. Though the convention represented a majority of the people of the country and a still greater preponderance of the wealth and influence, the control of affairs had fallen into the hands of minorities whose interests led in opposite directions. Davis could not have yielded, even though the Peace Convention had succeeded in moving the Washington authorities. Neither could the border states have escaped the inevitable, now that the Confederate government had been formally organized. The only choice left them was that of taking sides, and this decision could not be postponed beyond the firing of the first gun at Fort Sumter. The Peace Convention adjourned without accomplishing anything.

On March 16th, Yancey, Rost and Mann received their instructions [1] and soon thereafter set sail for London. These instructions betray another important line of Confederate policy. The commissioners were, first, to set forth the unimpeachable right of the South to sever its connection with the Union. In the next place, the immense importance of trade with the Confederacy was to be emphasized. The maxim, "Buy where you can buy cheapest, and sell where you can sell dearest," was to be openly proclaimed. The cot-

---

[1] Richardson, *Messages and Papers of the Confederacy*, Vol. I, pp. 1–10.

ton trade alone was estimated to be worth $600,000,-
000 annually to Great Britain. This would be cut off,
it was shrewdly suggested, in case war was permitted
to be waged against the cotton states. The question
of slavery, which Davis only too well knew to be a
great obstacle to recognition, was barely mentioned,
and the clause of the Confederate constitution prohib-
iting the slave trade, was accented. But there was no
hint that emancipation might finally become a feature
of Southern policy.

On the subject of advantageous treaties, a dispute
had arisen between the President and Rhett, the free
trade leader in the Congress. The latter, as chairman
of the committee on foreign relations, outlined a
treaty which Yancey was to offer to Great Britain.
It proposed absolute free trade between the two countries for a period of twenty years as a reward for
recognition. This was not unlike the scheme which
Franklin was instructed to press in Paris in 1776. But
the Confederate Congress was not ready to adopt
Rhett's plan, especially since the President did not
agree to it. This did not mean, as Yancey's and
Rhett's followers maintained, that Davis was unwilling
to make such a concession, but that he thought it best
to leave all matters of this nature to negotiation. It
must be remembered, too, that a majority of the men
in the Congress were in favor of a moderate tariff.

But with the instructions as outlined above, Yancey
had ample opportunity to enter into the making of
treaties, if once the greater question of recognition
could be settled. The powers of Europe knew that
the warring Confederacy would not higgle about the
terms of a treaty of commerce. England was irri-

tated by the passage of the Morrill Tariff Law at Washington.   Mr. Gladstone asserted in so many words that
the United States had long squeezed the Southern
orange and that a leading motive for forcible reunion
was just this advantage of a protective tariff to which
the South contributed immensely, but in whose benefits
she did not share.   France was hardly less interested
in this side of the controversy ; and Germany, though
the Confederacy, much to her undoing, did not recognize the fact, was decidedly free trade in opinion and
was becoming a more important factor daily.   It is
entirely probable that President Davis did not estimate at its true value the European desire for free
trade ; yet it does not follow that his own view limited
Yancey in negotiating or proposing treaties looking to
that end on the simple condition of recognition.

The great difficulty lay in the repugnance of European opinion to African slavery.   Even the suffering
cotton mill operatives, a year after the beginning of
the war, appreciated this hindrance to British intervention on behalf of the South.   The power of Cobden
and Bright rested as much on their sympathy for the
lower classes as upon their advocacy of free trade, and
the influence of these two noble men, thrown into the
scale of the high-tariff North at the crucial moment,
caused the failure of the movement for Southern
recognition.   Yancey, the apostle of slavery, was
among the first to perceive what a chasm thère was
between those who believed, with himself and Stephens, in a nation based on human slavery, and the
liberal doctrinaire leaders of European opinion.   He
could not think of promising emancipation and he
would not have done it had he been so empowered.

Besides to have yielded to this "fancy" of Europe would have removed the *raison d' être* of the Confederate government. Yet even this was to be offered before the final collapse.

It was foreseen, as already said, that the issue of the quarrel about Fort Sumter would force the border states to take sides ; it would also settle the question of peace or war. The Confederate commissioners, Roman, Crawford, and Forsyth, appeared in Washington in the early days of March and received a hearty welcome from fashionable society there.[1] They found the new cabinet as much divided on the matter of evacuating Fort Sumter as Buchanan's had been. Northern public sentiment, instead of rallying to the "stiff-backed" views of the new President, was still inclined strongly to peace, even if it meant final separation. Mr. Lincoln himself seemed to regret his attitude of the preceding December ; he allowed Seward to think that Sumter would be speedily given up. A majority of the cabinet favored such a solution ; and the organ of the administration, the *National Republican*, announced on March 9th, that Anderson and his men would be withdrawn. This was doubtless intended by the President as a "feeler." It stirred the Republicans to opposition, while the Democrats rejoiced. Lincoln saw how sentiment was turning and the administration veered its sails again to the popular breeze. Yet he himself pretended to be amazed when General Scott, on March 28th, recommended evacuation.

Meanwhile, the commissioners had found an influential mouthpiece in the able and patriotic Justice

[1] W. H. Russell, *My Diary, North and South*, Vol. I, pp. 92–95.

Campbell of the Supreme Court. Campbell was an Alabamian who, in the hope of a peaceful issue of the crisis, had not yet resigned his commission under the United States government. He went to Seward and received the assurance that Sumter would be turned over to South Carolina. A second visit to the Secretary of State, when the suspicions of the commissioners had been aroused, evoked the most positive assertion that the fort would be yielded to South Carolina before a letter could reach Montgomery. However, a relief expedition had been ordered and it can hardly be questioned that Seward knew this. He deceived both Campbell and the commissioners, though Davis denied that he had been misled or that he had ever expected any other course of events.

On March 15th, Seward had filed in the State Department a memorandum which the Confederate agents were informed they could get whenever they desired. When it became clear to all the world that they would not be received in any capacity, they called for the paper. It was a formal refusal to give them an audience, but they remained in Washington watching events until the fall of Sumter closed the last door of negotiation.

South Carolina was of course a part of the Confederacy and Davis held the threads of the situation in his firm grasp. General Beauregard, a brother-in-law of the senior Rhett and an able military commander, had been given immediate oversight of Fort Sumter and the surrounding neighborhood. The South Carolinians eagerly awaited the arrival of reënforcements for Major Anderson, who was reduced by this time to a state of semi-starvation ; the first appearance of an armed vessel at the mouth of the harbor would be a signal of war. Beauregard asked for definite instructions. Davis called his cabinet together on April 9th and placed before them the disappointing information that the United States not only refused to give up the fort, but would send reënforcements and supplies forthwith. The decision of the cabinet was that the Confederate commander must demand the surrender of Anderson and his men before the arrival of the expected relief.

At this meeting Toombs first manifested his disposition to oppose the President. He declared that it would be folly to take this step, since it would "lose us every friend in the North. You will wantonly strike a hornet's nest which extends from mountain to ocean, and legions now quiet will swarm out and sting us to death. It is unnecessary; it puts us in the wrong; it is fatal." [1] He failed to see that Davis could not listen to such advice. The purpose of his office was the defense of the Confederate states at every point. He authorized Beauregard to attack Fort Sumter at once, unless he could obtain its surrender by negotiation. Feeling the heavy responsibility of inaugurating war, the Southern general gave Major Anderson, who also dreaded the outcome, a chance to capitulate without bloodshed. This the latter could not do without proving untrue to his government. At 2 o'clock A. M. of April 12, 1861, the order to surrender was sent. [2] At 4:30 A. M. the firing began. It continued all day and until 3 P. M. on Saturday, April 13th. Then the garrison surrendered, and the

[1] Stovall, *Life of Toombs*, p. 226.
[2] *Official Records*, Series I, Vol. I, pp. 297–306.

first scene of the tragedy was over. Had it been possible for the Confederacy so to manœuvre as to force
the United States to fire the opening shot, a great
tactical advantage would have been gained. Davis
fully appreciated this fact, but it is difficult to see how
he could have procured such a result without yielding
to the enemy the first point in the war.

The leading secessionists of the border states were
present when the attack on the fort began. Pryor of
Virginia urged in most dramatic fashion to a half-in-
toxicated throng of Charlestonians, that the first shot
on Sumter would force the secession of Virginia. He
was right. The Old Dominion only waited to pass her
ordinance of secession, until the call came from Washington on April 15th, to send her quota of troops to
aid in the suppression of insurrection. North Carolina, Tennessee, and Arkansas followed suit. The
boundaries of the Confederacy expanded from the
lower borders of North Carolina and Tennessee to the
Potomac, with Maryland, Kentucky, and Missouri
now halting between the two governments. The immediate aim of Davis's conservative plans and appointments had been attained ; the whole South would
now fight together. It appeared to the outsider that
the sacrifice of the extremists had been wise.

The easy capture of Fort Sumter aroused the South
as few peoples have ever been aroused. The long
pent-up wrath of these discontented states burst forth
like a mountain torrent, fed by the melting snows of
many winters. Before the end of April, 19,000 men
had volunteered to defend the forts of the Confederacy,
and 16,000 were on the road to Virginia. The proposition for a loan of five million dollars was immediately

answered by subscriptions to the amount of eight millions, every bid being at par or above. And as the news of Lincoln's call for 75,000 volunteers to suppress insurrection spread abroad, the Southern people hurried to their court-yards and drill-grounds in numbers surpassing all immediate need, actually embarrassing the administration. An army of 100,000 men was at once provided for; Congress was called to meet in extra session on April 29th; and a proclamation was issued, offering commissions to privateers to prey upon the commerce of the United States.[1] Alexander Stephens was authorized to negotiate with Virginia on the subject of her entrance into the Confederacy, and the removal of the capital to Richmond.

With an accession of territory which doubled the area of the Confederacy; a response of the financiers to every call, which kept bonds well above par; and with the whole adult male population clamoring to be led to the front, it is not surprising that Davis was elated, or that his Secretary of War, in a speech to a hurrahing crowd, predicted that the Confederate government would occupy the city of Washington by May 1st. Davis, considering his painstaking efforts to procure the adherence of the border states, his guarded conduct and conservative policy, felt for once that the cause would surely triumph. Even his enemies joined in the chorus of praise. The Charleston *Mercury* ceased to criticise and abuse him and paid the following tardy tribute : " As to the object of the President's hastening to Virginia, we are convinced that it is the success of our cause which has attracted him. His presence will infuse additional life and vigor

[1] Richardson, *Messages and Papers*, Vol. I, p. 60.

among our troops. Finding him willing to run any personal risk, they will emulate his example and defeat the hordes of Abolitionists Lincoln has arrayed against us." [1]

With the almost unanimous good-will of the lower South, the Confederate government moved the capital to the ancient commonwealth of Virginia. An outpouring of loyal sentiment and devotion to the new cause characterized the journey of two days from Montgomery to Richmond. Old and young volunteers greeted Davis at every stop; they bought tickets in order that they might ride on the same train with the new and beloved President. Amidst all this adulation, he maintained his calm and quiet dignity. He traveled in the simplest style. There were no sleepers, no special cars, no extra trains. He occupied a seat in the rear coach of the ordinary train and conducted himself so unostentatiously that his presence was not known to the other passengers until the cries from without led to his recognition.

But these loyal Southerners manifested their devotion in other and more substantial ways. The government recommended that the usual crop of cotton should be decreased, and corn and wheat planted instead for the support of the armies. Almost every one heeded the admonition. There was rumor of a scarcity of saltpetre, an indispensable constituent of gunpowder: thousands of householders began to dig up the moist earth under their houses and in their cellars, from which to extract the precious commodity. Men who had never known how to be generous emptied their pockets, and women of the highest social standing

[1] *Mercury*, May 30, 1861.

worked day and night making clothes for the soldiers.

All this zeal and enthusiasm did not cause Davis to lose sight of the aims which he had already set for himself and his people. In the border states as in the lower South, the extreme secessionists were clamoring for an attack on Washington; for the raising of the Confederate flag on the old Capitol. But Robert E. Lee, who was now at the head of the Virginia troops, did not favor such a venture. A conservative by nature, he lent great force to the conservative policy of the new President. The solid and substantial element of the Virginia people agreed with Davis and feared that to invade the North would put the South in a bad light before the world. An aggressive, warlike, and conquering slave state would repel whatever friends the Confederacy might have in Europe; it would force the Democrats of the North to join the Republicans in support of the administration; and it would have belied the oft-repeated assertion of the South that she only desired to be let alone.

The long line of defense stretched from the Chesapeake Bay through middle Kentucky to the upper corner of Kansas, a distance of fifteen hundred miles. The crossing of this line was to be the signal of attack. To defend this frontier, and in support of the positions already taken by the border state military leaders, there were 360,000 to 400,000 available men, most of whom were still at their homes or on the drill-grounds of the various states.[1]

The organization of such a force in the face of an

[1] General John B. Gordon's *Reminiscences*, p. 17; and Davis's message to Congress on July 20, 1861.

enemy even more numerous was a large undertaking ;
and the difficulty was heightened by the desire of
each state to have its quota of field officers.   Regimental officers were appointed by the states, while the
captains and lieutenants were chosen by the private
soldiers.   Davis recognized the weakness of this
system, but he did not seek to interfere with any
of these established customs of the country.   In the
appointment of generals of high station, he en-
deavored to do away with the rule, which had applied in the United States Army since its organization,
of allowing, under all circumstances, seniority to
determine rank.   He knew well the officers of the old
army, and he was convinced that Albert Sidney
Johnston was the ablest of those who had joined the
Confederacy.   Others who gave up their commands
to "go with their states" into secession, and who
were naturally looked to as prospective leaders of
the Southern Army, were Joseph E. Johnston and
Robert E. Lee of Virginia, and P. G. T. Beauregard
of Louisiana.   All of these men, except Lee, seem
to have been jealous of their rivals and personally
hopeful of receiving the first place.   It was no easy
task for the President to fill the high offices according
to the rule of merit without offense to some of these
able volunteers.   To add to his perplexities, he was
too sensitive on the subject of his own prerogative and,
even as early as the summer of 1861, he manifested a
disposition to advance his personal friends, especially
the members of his class at West Point and others
whom he had known there.

Favoritism was inherent in the Southern system.
Aristocracy was acknowledged in every way but on

the statute books.   The great South Carolina families
expected to receive high stations and special rewards ;
the "first families" of Virginia could not be neglected ; and the large slave proprietors demanded in
thousands of cases special exemption from military
service in the open field.   The majority of the population of military age, however, were willing and anxious
to meet the enemy ; in fact, so impatient were they to
begin the fight, that they could not be induced to see
the value of thorough drill and complete subordina-
tion to discipline.   Every man thought himself a
leader and none loved restraint, especially those who
were the masters of slaves.   Under these circumstances and with the country absolutely certain that
success had already been won ; with officers clamoring
for precedence, and politicians wrangling for their pet
schemes ; with insufficient means of transporting
armies over great distances, and he himself beset by
his own preferences and favoritisms, it was indeed a
difficult thing for President Davis to will, to see, and
to do the right thing.

CHAPTER XV

DAVIS reached Richmond in the early morning of
May 29th, and was received with a salute of fifteen
guns. A carriage drawn by four horses took him to
the Spotswood Hotel, where handsome apartments had
been fitted up. The city was in gala attire and received its "first and only President" with every mark
of delight. The famous old hostelry stood at the
corner of Eighth and Main Streets and, up to the
close of the war, was one of the most important land-
marks of the place. Doorways, halls, and windows
were decorated with Confederate colors, and the
President's apartments were draped with the flags of
his new government, though the reader may pause to
remember that Davis was so attached to the "old
flag" that he had recommended its adoption by the
South, making changes only in the one used in battle.
Having reached his temporary quarters, he bade an
appropriate adieu to his escort of thousands who filled
the streets and waved handkerchiefs from the windows
of the houses in the neighborhood. He spoke words
of encouragement without threats against the enemy
and received the heartiest applause.

The permanent home of the Confederate President
had been selected and was now undergoing repairs. It
stood, and still stands, at Twelfth and Clay Streets, a
beautiful location in what was then the equivalent

of the "West End"; it had long been the
home of the Brockenborough family and was one of
the handsomest private residences in the city.   It was
entirely worthy to become the White House of the
Confederacy, and the sympathetic tourist of to-day
who lingers there is irresistibly drawn to the stirring
times when Lee, Johnston, Longstreet, and the Hills
called it the "Executive Mansion" and planned, within
its stately walls, the campaigns of Manassas, Seven
Pines and Gettysburg.[1]

The life of Davis now merges to a considerable extent with that of Robert E. Lee, his schoolmate at
West Point, and friend of the years just preceding the
outbreak of the war.   Lee was one of the conscientious, sober, and thoughtful officers of the "old army"
who lamented in April, 1861, the oncoming "revolution" as unnecessary,[2] but who felt within him the
force of state loyalty so deeply that he could not
continue in the national service, even though the
dazzling honor of the chief command was tendered to
him.   There is no stronger tribute to the cause of
secession as a righteous and just one than this decision
of Lee; for his family, unlike most others in Virginia,
had long been stanchly attached to the Union.[3]   His
home came down to him from Washington himself;
his father had been a Federalist leader and had suffered
at the hands of a states' rights mob in Baltimore in

[1] It is now the home of the Confederate Memorial Association
and as the Confederate Museum contains many valuable papers
and relics of the Civil War.

[2] *Letters and Recollections of Robert E. Lee*, by his son, p. 26.

[3] See a most interesting discussion of Lee's relations to the Confederacy by Charles Francis Adams—*Constitutional Ethics of Secession*, 1903, a pamphlet.

1819, shortly before his death ; while he himself had been engaged in the national service for thirty-five years and had won distinguished honors under the flag of the Union. Against the wishes of his personal friend, General Scott, and the entreaties of a favorite sister, and knowing that his handsome family estate, " Arlington," would be confiscated, he, nevertheless, set his pace toward Richmond when the irrevocable step had been taken. His sacrifices were appreciated. The convention offered him the sword of Virginia and he took his place at the head of the state Council of War.

Before the Confederate President took up his residence in Richmond, he had ordered eight regiments to move as fast as possible to Lynchburg, from which point they were to coöperate with the Virginia troops wherever they would be of the most service. General Lee had control of the local forces and had raised small volunteer armies at Hampton, Norfolk, Fredericksburg, Culpeper, Winchester, and in West Virginia. There were probably 30,000 of these troops, inexperienced, of course, poorly armed, and unaccustomed to discipline. Lee's chief assistants were Brigadier-General Joseph E. Johnston who, as we shall see, rather strangely held command under the Confederate authority, while at the same time operating in Virginia under Lee, and having the direction of the forces about Harper's Ferry ; Brigadier-General Beauregard, who had brought some 6,000 South Carolinians via Lynchburg to the defense of the common frontier ; and the state Brigadiers John B. Magruder, Hampton ; Philipp St. George Cocke, T. H. Holmes, and R. S. Garnett.

The deplorable weakness of the military situation in

Virginia was the distance between the points of attack and the entirely inadequate supply of wagons and horses for the movement of the impedimenta of war. The state was threatened by way of the peninsula from Fortress Monroe as a base; at Manassas from Alexandria, already in the hands of the enemy; at Harper's Ferry; and in West Virginia. Each of these points was more than a hundred and fifty miles away from the others and there were no direct railway connections and no good country roads, except one or two in the Shenandoah Valley and the upper counties. The need for wagons, horses, and drivers was imperative. Ammunition and other necessary supplies were deficient. Yet Virginia was looked to for aid in Baltimore where the first outbreak had occurred and Davis had telegraphed Governor Letcher, as early as April 22d, to reinforce the Southern party there if possible. Missouri had also sent to Richmond for arms to aid them in their fight against the Union party in that state.

While these events had been taking place, President Lincoln had ordered a strict blockade of all Southern ports, increased the navy by 18,000 men, raised the regular army of the United States to 42,000, and suspended the writ of *habeas corpus* along the roads leading from Washington to New York. On April 24th Alexandria was occupied and about the same time the region around Fortress Monroe was seized, and in some instances houses were burned and stores of provisions destroyed. General McDowell was steadily increasing his army, with headquarters at Arlington Heights— Lee's home; General Patterson threatened Harper's Ferry with twenty thousand men; and Major Anderson was raising troops in Kentucky and West Virginia who were a little later to aid General McClellan in the conquest of northwestern Virginia. More than 100,000 soldiers, including volunteers, had been put in motion by the North when Davis reached his capital. The armies of the South were equally numerous but not so well trained, though five or six thousand South Carolinians had been drilling since early in the previous winter. The nucleus of 20,000 regulars of the old standing army served the Union to good purpose, though this number was somewhat lessened by the loss of many capable officers who followed their states into the Confederate camp.

This war against the "Yankees" was no longer a "holiday excursion"; as Davis had insisted from the beginning, it promised now to be a tedious and bloody struggle. He set about his work of organizing and drilling the new recruits as they hurried on from the South. The present West End of Richmond, the "Fair Grounds" and the Grove Avenue neighborhood became the Southern *Champs de Mars;* there the ex-West Pointers, Virginia Military Institute cadets— the drill sergeants of the South—reigned supreme. Squad drill, company drill, skirmish line and order of battle were given from morning till night, much to the sorrow of the unwarlike recruits panting for a fight and impatient of this painful preparation to meet an enemy who would surely "run away at the first onset." Davis and Lee took hearty interest in these details of war and rode out daily to see the work well done. They also entered, with the utmost harmony, into the larger plans to repel the enemy already on the "sacred soil of Virginia."

General Beauregard had been strengthened at Manassas until he commanded a force of some 20,000 ; Magruder was fairly safe at Hampton and Norfolk ; but Johnston was in danger at Harper's Ferry. Before June 15th, the first crisis of the war was at hand, and Manassas was the point of danger. General McDowell with an army of 30,000 clamoring to be led against the enemy and urged " on to Richmond " by Northern public opinion, threatened Beauregard. The latter was extremely uneasy, being almost entirely unsupplied with wagons, so needful in the event of retreat. Davis ordered him to hold his ground and Beauregard asked for reinforcements from Johnston, who was, however, almost as closely pressed as he. The President, relying on the fine judgment of Lee, held back Johnston until McDowell had moved too far into Virginia to withdraw without danger. He then ordered Johnston to come to the relief of Beauregard just in time to give the South a fair chance to gain a victory. On July 21st, the two raw and unseasoned armies came to blows on Manassas plains ; after some hours of doubtful contest, Beauregard and Johnston, chiefly on account of the unexpected bravery of Jackson and his corps, saw the tide turn in their favor. McDowell's men, panic-stricken, threw down their arms, their knapsacks, even their coats, in the eager and senseless flight to Washington. A momentous victory had been gained by the young republic ; the North had lost a battle which well-nigh brought the recognition of her enemy, until now held in the utmost contempt. The losses in men on the Union side were 2,896 ; on the Confederate 1,897.[1] In the all-important matter of

[1] Rhodes, Vol. III, p. 450.

military supplies, the victors were fortunate indeed :
they carried away twenty-eight pieces of artillery,
5,000 muskets, 500,000 cartridges, sixty-four artillery
horses, twenty-six wagons, with camp equipage and
other valuable property.   The most urgent wants of
Beauregard's army were now at last partially supplied.

Davis had intended to appear on the anticipated
field of battle two or three days before the fight began ;
but the needs of the army were so great and the regular duties of his office so pressing that he was compelled
to remain in Richmond.   Since the whole work of
the Confederacy was to conduct the war, the President
very properly threw himself into the details of the
War Department as completely as if he himself had
been the Secretary of it.   Every telegram, every important order for supplies or reinforcements, or the
movement of troops in the field passed through his
hands.   Yet during this very period his harassing
malady came upon him again, and he was compelled
to conduct this business from a sick-bed.   The council
in which the plan of Manassas was decided upon was
held in his bedroom.[1]

Notwithstanding this, Davis hastened to the battle-
field on July 21st, and reached headquarters in time to
witness the retreat of the enemy.   He held conferences
with all the generals, discussed the feasibility of a
prompt pursuit, and gave directions as to the position of the wounded and prisoners.   He saw the importance of an immediate march to Washington and
wrote out a tentative order to General Bonham of Virginia to make his forces ready for the movement.
But on learning that his reports concerning the condi-

[1] *Official Records*, Series I, Vol. II, p. 510.

tion of the enemy were unreliable, he decided, Generals Johnston and Beauregard concurring, to leave this matter open for the night. Next day a heavy rain fell and the roads were rendered impassable for an army.

Davis was elated at the results of the first great encounter; on the night of the 21st, he telegraphed Congress, which had just assembled, that an important victory had been won, immense stores captured, and the enemy driven from the soil of Virginia. When he returned to Richmond on Tuesday, July 23d, he said in a short speech to the people at the railway station, who called loudly for him : "I rejoice with you, this evening, in those better and happier feelings which we all experience, as compared with the anxiety of three days ago. . . . Your little army has met the grand army of the enemy, routed it at every point, and it now flies, in inglorious retreat, before our victorious columns. We have taught them a lesson in their invasion of the sacred soil of Virginia; we have taught them that the grand old mother of Washington still nurtures a band of heroes; and yet a bloodier and far more fatal lesson awaits them, unless they speedily acknowledge that freedom to which you were born." [1]

Throughout the South the people indulged in the confident belief that the war would be short; that there was no doubt about the outcome; that short terms of enlistment were sufficient to replenish the armies already in the field. The President reviewed in his message to Congress on the eve of the battle the events of the last two months, calling attention to the steady extension of the area of hostilities and of the plans of the United States. The Federal Congress, in the early

[1] Alfriend, p. 306.

days of July, had authorized the enlistment of 500,000 men and provided an increased income of nearly $300,000,000 per annum. To meet these gigantic preparations, the Confederate Executive urged an equivalent increase in the Southern armies. Two days later came the news of the great victory and the Congress at Richmond relaxed its energies. Davis and his advisers, while they did not for a moment think the work ended, seem to have felt secure. No recommendation to enlist "for the war" was urged, and the preparation to meet the demands of the Treasury for a series of years was sadly deficient. Indeed, it was confidently thought that the value of the cotton crop, though this was decidedly decreased, would be equal to the burdens of the contest.

The wave of warlike enthusiasm which had followed the fall of Fort Sumter and the secession of Virginia, reached the cabinet about the time of the removal to Richmond. Walker gave up the War Department before the end of the summer for a command in the field, and Toombs, daily growing more displeased with his chief, asked for a place in the army. Benjamin succeeded to Walker's place and a little later R. M. T. Hunter was made Secretary of State. Yancey becoming at the same time dissatisfied with the outlook in London, had given up his European mission and ran the blockade into New Orleans. His position was filled by James M. Mason, of Virginia, a cousin of Robert E. Lee. Slidell, the arch-intriguer of the South, was deemed a fit appointee for the court of Louis Napoleon.

The next most difficult and trying task of this sum-

mer for the President was the appointment of the
chief generals of the army.   There was a group of able
and ambitious men, all West Point graduates, from
which he could choose; and most of these he knew
well personally.   Two, Samuel Cooper and Albert
Sidney Johnston, had been friends of his for many
years.   The oldest of them all was Cooper, Adjutant-
General of the United States Army, who had resigned to take service with the Confederacy soon
after its organization in Montgomery.   He was also a
cousin of Robert E. Lee and a grandson of George
Mason.

The second oldest candidate for the chief command in
the new army was Albert Sidney Johnston of Kentucky.
Having graduated two years ahead of Davis at West
Point, he entered the regular army in 1826 ; after a term
of eight years on the western frontier, he resigned his
commission and migrated to Texas, where he took the
remarkable step of enlisting as a private soldier in that
state's war for independence from Mexico.   Rising
rapidly to the highest position in the Texan army, he
had an active part in the organization of the "Lone
Star Republic."   On the outbreak of the conflict between the United States and Mexico, he raised a regiment and led it to the front, where he repeatedly distinguished himself.   In 1849 he became a paymaster in
the United States Army ; and in 1855 Jefferson Davis,
at that time Secretary of War, gave him command of
one of the new regiments of cavalry then being organized.   From 1855 to 1861 he served in the Southwest and
rose to the head of the Department of the Pacific, having been in California when hostilities broke out in the
South.   He resigned promptly and began his famous

overland horseback ride, chased by the authorities of the United States, via New Orleans to Richmond. He was known to be on the way to the Confederate capital, when the President was making out his list of appointments.

Robert E. Lee graduated at West Point in 1829 as second in the class of which Joseph E. Johnston was a promising member. Lee won signal honors in the war with Mexico, was superintendent of the Military Academy from 1852 to 1855 when Davis appointed him second in command of the cavalry regiment of which Albert Sidney Johnston was the chief. This troop of horse was kept busy on the Texan border until the outbreak of the great war. While on furlough in the autumn of 1858, Lee was sent by the United States government to suppress the John Brown raid, which he did with much discretion, thus bringing his name prominently before the nation.

The second member of this class of 1829 who had risen to high rank before the beginning of the war was Lee's classmate, Joseph E. Johnston. He had been in the active service of the country on the frontier until the beginning of the Mexican War when he, too, had an opportunity to show his great ability. He was promoted to the rank of brevet-colonel for gallantry at Cerro Gordo ; in 1855 he was appointed second in command of the First Cavalry by order of Jefferson Davis ; and he accompanied Albert Sidney Johnston on the expedition to Utah in 1859 as inspector-general. In 1860 General Scott was asked to recommend a suitable officer for promotion to the position of quartermaster-general. He sent in the names of Joseph E. Johnston, Robert E. Lee, Albert Sidney Johnston, and G. F. Smith.   Joseph E. Johnston received the coveted honor.

Thus had these young friends and classmates from Virginia run parallel courses for many years.   Lee had stood higher in the Military Academy ; but Joseph E. Johnston rose faster in the army and reached the rank of colonel a few weeks before Lee.   Both received advancement under Secretary of War Davis in 1855, and their relative positions remained the same.   But Johnston became a brigadier-general first, simply because his name stood above Lee's on General Scott's list of recommendations.   The wheel turned once more : when both Lee and Johnston resigned to take service under Virginia in April, 1861, the former was given the higher command—the chief direction of all the forces of the state.   Johnston was appointed a general, but he did not at once enter service under his successful rival.   Receiving a telegram from Montgomery offering him the command of the Army of the Valley of Virginia, he promptly accepted.   The issue of this long and friendly contest between able and aspiring men was not yet adjusted ; for it was not decided whether Lee as the head of the Virginia forces was to give orders to Johnston of the Confederacy or *vice versa*.   Lee was chary about issuing instructions to his subordinate, and Johnston before the battle of Manassas resented "orders," saying that he himself was the ranking general.[1]   A nice question of states' rights *vs.* Confederate authority was thus presented for settlement.

The fifth and last of these promising West Pointers whom Davis was expected to promote to high place,

[1] *Memoir*, Vol. II, p. 139; *Official Records*, Series I, Vol. II, p. 960.

in the Southern army, was Pierre G. T. Beauregard of
Louisiana, an engineer of distinction in the Mexican
War, a connection of the Rhetts of South Carolina, and
the first popular hero on account of his reduction of
Fort Sumter. Up to Manassas he was proclaimed the
great general of the war and that battle had not
dimmed any of his laurels.

The Confederate President was fortunate in having
so many able soldiers at his command ; but to one who
so keenly appreciated all the points of the rivalry involved, it was no easy thing to decide which of the
Johnstons should receive the higher station or whether
Lee should not outrank both. Lee was probably more
popular in the border states than any other and he was
the favorite of the great state of Virginia, though
Joseph E. Johnston stood almost as well. But Davis
loved Albert Sidney Johnston as a brother, their
friendship dating from the old Transylvania days.
They had fought together under Taylor at Monterey,
while Lee and Joseph E. Johnston had stood side by
side under Scott at Cerro Gordo. With Lee there had
been an intimacy since 1851 when Davis recommended
him to the revolutionists of Cuba as commander-in-
chief of their army,[1] which dangerous and questionable
position the Virginian declined. He did not lose any
ground with Davis while the latter was Secretary of
War at Washington, and later was a frequent visitor
at the house of the distinguished senator from Mississippi. Toward Joseph E. Johnston, Davis's relations
had been almost as close, and after the beginning of
the war, now at hand, they had steadily grown intimate. All these brilliant commanders had the utmost

Rhodes, Vol. I, p. 217.

respect for the Confederate President, whom they associated with the important events in their own lives and whose ability they greatly admired.

Weighing the cases carefully and long, Joseph E. Johnston having already begun to complain of his wrongs, the President sent, on August 31st, his list of recommendations to Congress for approval. The rank of each was indicated in the order of the names as follows: Samuel Cooper, Albert Sidney Johnston, Robert E. Lee, Joseph E. Johnston, and P. G. T. Beauregard. Joseph E. Johnston and Beauregard at once allowed signs of their disappointment to appear in the newspapers and one of the most acrimonious, as well as most fateful of all Southern controversies arose.

Albert Sidney Johnston was assigned to the command of the Department of Kentucky, including whatever Confederate forces might be raised in Missouri. Lee took the dangerous and difficult field of West Virginia at a time when Joseph E. Johnston's friends were beginning to call him the "dress parade and parlor general"—a slur on his position as adviser to the President. Joseph E. Johnston remained at Manassas in charge of the main army of the Confederacy; and Beauregard coöperated for the time with Johnston, with headquarters at Centreville. Cooper was appointed adjutant and inspector-general of all the Confederate armies.

In the organization of the army as in the appointment of officers, Davis steadfastly pursued the policy of employing experts rather than popular political leaders or orators. This he did while President Lincoln was following the opposite course: witness B. F.

Butler and John C. Frémont as early commanders of
Federal armies. There was nevertheless a decided and
foolish opposition in the South to the employment of
"West Pointers" in so many of the responsible positions. Men of influence in all the states felt that
"distinguished" civilians would lead an army better
than the "scientific plodders" of the United States
Military Academy. "General" Toombs was a type
of these political commanders; Floyd and Wise, of
Virginia, were others. Fortunately they were not entrusted with large armies as were Butler and Frémont,
and the Confederate President ought to have been
thanked for resisting the thousand and one claims
from this class of aspirants.

As the days and weeks of 1861 wore away and the
area and the magnitude of the war steadily expanded,
the Southern people realized what a gigantic revolution had been precipitated. The five hundred thousand "Abolitionists" whom Lincoln had "turned
loose" were pouring into Washington, where they were
gradually organizing for another march to Richmond.
In the late autumn General Lee was defeated in West
Virginia and that great mountain region became a
stronghold of the Union. The blockade closed in on
the Confederacy, trade became hazardous, gold and
silver took flight, and prices began to rise. The
clouds were settling down over the new government and
upon the people of a troubled country.

CHAPTER XVI

A GLOOMY WINTER

THE general elections were held throughout the Confederacy before the rejoicing over the victory at Manassas had waned. Davis was unanimously chosen for the presidency for the constitutional term of six years. Stephens met with some opposition on account of his former anti-secession convictions; but this was of only passing significance. In the choice of members for the first regular Congress, the spirit of compromise, which had been manifested from the beginning, found ample expression. R. M. T. Hunter, a quasi-rival of Davis who feared the unpopularity of longer remaining in the cabinet and who even thus early aspired to the succession, entered the Senate from Virginia; William Ballard Preston, of strong Whig tendencies, was his colleague. South Carolina, divided between the friends of Davis and the extremists, sent, as senator, Robert W. Barnwell, whom Stephens declared to be the ablest member of Congress, and James L. Orr, a counsellor of delay in 1860. Georgia's opposition was well represented in Stephens, the Vice-President and chairman of the Senate and a little later in Herschel V. Johnson, the Douglas candidate for the vice-presidency in 1860. Alabama sent Yancey, the most dissatisfied man in the Confederacy after Rhett. Mississippi, Louisiana, Texas, and Tennessee were more friendly in the general average of their representatives, with the notorious exception of the irrepressible Henry S. Foote, now of Tennessee, and the famous Louis T. Wigfall, of Texas. If ever a people attempted to bridle their Executive, the Southerners did so in their choice of civil representatives during the war. The first Confederate Congress under the Constitution contained all the elements of discord and disagreement it was possible to assemble under one roof in the South at this time.

The Provisional Congress was called together for a final session on November 18th. Foreshadowing the already anticipated desperate struggle, Davis said in his message on the first day:[1] "If we husband our means and make a judicious use of our resources, it would be difficult to fix a limit to the period during which we could conduct a war against the adversary whom we now encounter." And by way of inspiring an everlasting hatred and contempt for the North he added:

"If instead of being a dissolution of a league, it were indeed a rebellion in which we are engaged, we might find ample vindication for the course we have adopted in the scenes which are now being enacted in the United States. Our people now look with contemptuous astonishment on those with whom they had been so recently associated. They shrink with aversion from the bare idea of renewing such a connection. When they see a President making war without the assent of Congress; when they behold judges threatened because they maintain the writ of *habeas corpus* so sacred to freedom; when they see justice and law

[1] Richardson, *Messages and Papers of the Confederacy*, Vol. I, p. 140.

trampled under the armed heel of military authority, and upright men and innocent women dragged to distant dungeons upon the mere edict of a despot; when they find all this tolerated and applauded by a people who had been in the full enjoyment of freedom but a few months ago—they believe that there must be some radical incompatibility between such a people and themselves. With such a people we may be content to live at peace, but the separation is final, and for the independence we have asserted we will accept no alternative.''

These references to the manner of waging the war, to the treatment of civilians by the government of the United States, were designed to show the faint-hearted and hesitating in the Confederacy the utter futility of hoping for a restoration of the former conditions, as well as to justify the course of the South. The President now saw plainly what lay before him and his devoted people. He sought also to explain in a dignified way the failure of the mission to Europe which had been expected to return with assurances of the coveted recognition. '' We have sought no aid and proposed no alliances offensive and defensive abroad,'' he said ; ''we have asked for a recognized place in the great family of nations, but in doing so we have demanded nothing for which we did not offer a fair equivalent.'' He then foretold changes in the pursuits of the Southern people which would greatly reduce the size of the cotton crops, increasing the amount of cereals grown and bringing manufactures to the very doors of the people. This, he thought, would give economic independence, though it might entail privation and suffering for a time ; it would also seriously threaten the stability of the English cotton manufacturers. He continued :

"While the war which is waged to take from us the right of self-government can never attain that end, it remains to be seen how far it may work a revolution in the industrial system of the world, which may carry suffering to other lands as well as to our own. In the meantime we shall continue this struggle in humble dependence upon Providence, from whose searching scrutiny we cannot conceal the secrets of our hearts, and to whose rule we confidently submit our destinies."

From the tone of the message, it could hardly be predicted that Davis, before the end of another six months, would be following the course of Lincoln. Even in this document reference was made to an extension of the powers of the Confederate Executive. The two railway systems connecting the upper with the lower South—the line extending along the seacoast from Washington to Charleston, thence through Georgia and Alabama to New Orleans; and the road running from the same point through southwestern Virginia, east Tennessee, and Alabama to Mobile— were seriously threatened, the one by the enemy in eastern North Carolina, the other by the Tennessee Unionists. A third and much less exposed route might be established by building a connecting link between Danville, Va., and Greensboro, N. C. This would bring the Richmond and Danville road of Virginia into touch with a Southern road connecting Greensboro, Charlotte, and Atlanta; and there was little danger of its falling into the hands of the enemy so long as the Confederacy had an existence.

It was the plainest dictate of common sense speedily

to build these forty miles of railway. But the North
Carolina authorities, always jealous of their constitutional rights, objected to the undertaking. The old
Richmond and Danville corporation had proposed
to lay down this road some years before the war,
but that state had thrown obstacles in the way.
Davis brushing away constitutional difficulties with a
stroke of the pen, now urged Congress to begin construction under the war powers of the Confederate
government. The leading Richmond papers took up
the President's recommendation with zest, declaring
that trains would run over the new tracks before the
end of six months. Davis gave Congress opportunity
to take the initiative ; but he would not have hesitated
to order the work to begin under his own authority as
the commander-in-chief of the armies of the Confederacy. The road was built without great delay and
the fleeing Confederate President passed over its lines
southward in 1865.

The time had already come when Davis felt constrained to hold in check the discordant elements in
the "republic." If men had gone off to war in the
preceding spring as on a picnic excursion they were
now disposed to hasten back to their homes with even
more eagerness. Congressmen yielded to the im-
portunate requests of their constituents and twice
enacted legislation which would have put into the
hands of irresponsible physicians the authority to
grant furloughs to any one and all who thought camp-
life not conducive to good health. The first of these
laws would have depleted the army by 30,000 men in
a short time ; the second, passed a little later, was
equally bad. The President promptly vetoed both

and reminded Congress that an army could not be
administered by statute. The conduct of military
affairs must be left with the War Department, in
reality with the Executive himself. At that time an
overwhelming force was pressing Albert Sidney Johnston at every point of his long line. The passage of
this measure at so critical an emergency, showed
clearly enough what sort of men made up the majority
of the Provisional Congress. The fact that Stephens
and his friends did not by their great influence prevent
such foolish legislation goes far to disarm their bitter
criticism of Davis a few months later. Members of
Congress were then, as since, seeking popular applause
at the expense of the President, who was expected to
do his duty and protect the country by means of a
veto. Davis was equal to the responsibility. He went
a step further and said that Congress ought to keep
within the bounds of law and common sense.[1]

During the late autumn and early winter, when the
Southern armies were daily being depleted by deser-
tions, furloughs, and the expiration of the terms of
enlistment, General McClellan was organizing the
grand army that was to move with irresistible weight
upon the Confederate capital in the coming spring.
And Generals Halleck and Grant were not less hopeful
of breaking through the defenses of the West. The
North, putting forth her strength like a mighty
giantess, expected to crush the South in a few short
weeks. Recognizing the danger, the Richmond papers
began a campaign for the passage of conscript laws sufficiently drastic to put 750,000 men in the field. Supported in these advanced views by intelligent public

[1] Richardson, *Messages and Papers*, Vol. I, pp. 158, 162.

opinion, the press, a little later, urged the assumption
of the powers of a dictator by Davis. Let martial law
be proclaimed, cried the *Examiner;* let the cities and
towns be cleared of loafers, gamblers, and other
"birds of evil omen." And to stimulate the President
to the full realization of the dangers and disasters
promised in the near future, the news came in early
February that Halleck and Grant would probably
break through Albert Sidney Johnston's lines even in
the dead of winter. Before February 20th, it was
known in Richmond that all Kentucky was lost and
that it would require a mighty effort to save Tennessee.
The railway through the Southwest would be captured
when the Confederacy would be cut off from the
rich grain fields of Tennessee, Kentucky and West
Virginia.

On January 1, 1862, gold sold in Richmond at a
premium of fifty per cent. Articles of daily use had
risen in price more than a hundred per cent. Salt
sold for $20 per sack, a "trust" having been formed
for the control of the trade in this indispensable commodity. Men wore their last winter's clothes and
ladies appeared in church with bonnets patched up
from pieces of discarded ones of the last season. The
railways were breaking down from a lack of iron
for repairs; schedules could not be maintained, even
when the success of army movements depended on
regular service. Beauregard called on the churches
of Tennessee and the lower South to convert their bells
into cannon, and the President hastened forward his
scanty supplies of arms. To relieve these pressing
economic conditions and to procure the purchase of
arms and provisions for the soldiers in the field, the

Confederate Treasury offered merely paper "promises-to-pay," in the event of a successful issue of the war. They were convertible on demand into Confederate bonds bearing eight per cent. interest; but the interest was payable in paper, while the principal was secure only on the return of peace, and a peace favorable to the South. It was estimated that there was $60,000,000 in gold in the Southern states at the beginning of the war; but this took to flight or was hidden away in strong boxes before the first half-year had passed.

Meanwhile, the hope of recognition in Europe had vanished. The blunder of Captain Wilkes in the preceding November in seizing Commissioners Mason and Slidell, then in the custody of the English mail steamer *Trent*, and the consequent elation and boasting of Northern papers, caused Southerners to think for awhile that war between Great Britain and the United States would ensue. But Seward was shrewd enough to see that such a policy would be fatal; and Lincoln decided without delay that the commissioners must be given up to England, however distasteful to himself and the great public this might be. Before the Christmas season was well over, it was known that war would not follow and the South would have to fight out in sweat and blood the bitter and unequal struggle.

In the midst of these depressing events and surroundings, the provisional prepared to give way to the regular government. The inauguration was set for February 22d, a day which states' rights men of earlier times affected to despise. The procession and ceremonies were simple but dignified, the functionaries of the governments, both state and Confederate, taking their appropriate parts in their right places. At twelve o'clock a vast concourse assembled on the appointed ground, at the foot of the Washington monument in the Capitol square. The sky was overhung with clouds and a cold, penetrating rain fell all day. But the people were resolute if discouraged; they remained, many of them uncovered, to greet their President-elect and to hear what words of cheer and inspiration he might speak. A few minutes afterward, Davis appeared at the head of the procession pale, thin, ill, as one could have foreseen; Stephens followed and soon the platform was full. Bishop Johns of the diocese of Virginia offered a touching invocation. Then Davis rose and delivered his second inaugural address.

After a fitting reference to the birthday of Washington and the suggestive surroundings, he explained once again the course of events which led to secession, defending the right of leaving the Union and of independent state action in all vital matters. He referred to the military despotism of the North; the withdrawal of the right of *habeas corpus;* the barbarous brutality of "our enemies." The speaker was aware that all the world would carefully read what he had to say on this inauspicious occasion; his words were consequently well chosen and his real thoughts were expressed with precision or left unspoken with even greater art. He said:

"A million men, it is estimated, are now standing in hostile array, and waging war along a frontier of thousands of miles. Battles have been fought, sieges have been conducted, and, although the contest is not ended, and the tide for the moment is against us, the final result in our favor is not doubtful. We have had our trials and difficulties. That we are to escape them in the future is not to be hoped. It was to be expected when we entered upon this war, that it would expose our people to sacrifices and cost them much, both of money and blood.

"But the picture has its lights as well as its shadows. This great strife has awakened in the people the highest emotions and qualities of the human soul. It was, perhaps, in the ordination of Providence that we were to be taught the value of our liberties by the price we pay for them. The recollections of this great contest, with all its common traditions of glory, of sacrifice and blood, will be the bond of harmony and enduring affection amongst the people, producing unity in policy, fraternity in sentiment, and just effort in war." [1]

He closed with a touching prayer : " My hope is reverently fixed on Him whose favor is ever vouchsafed to the cause which is just. With humble gratitude and adoration, acknowledging the Providence which has so visibly protected the Confederacy during its brief but eventful career, to Thee, O God, I trustingly commit myself, and prayerfully invoke Thy blessing on my country and its cause."

The people dispersed silently and in meditation, as though they had attended Divine service. They were not enlightened, as the newspapers lamented next day, on the great subject of the Western army or the means of defeating McClellan. Not a word was spoken as to the future policy of the government ; no hope as to raising the blockade, already burdensome to all classes,

[1] Richardson, *Messages and Papers*, Vol. I, pp. 183-188.

was given ; only a solemn, earnest exhortation to persevere in the holy cause, a prayer for the blessings of High Heaven on the noble men and women who were laboring so faithfully in behalf of the new nation.

It was well that Davis did not dwell upon the subject of the Western campaign, for all the signs were against the South ; nothing could be said of foreign affairs that would add to the hopes of the people ; and still less could be published abroad as to his plans for the future, knowing, as he did, that every word would be read in Washington before the setting of another sun.

Three days later he sent a message to Congress, stating that Fort Donelson and Roanoke Island were, as the papers had already made known some days before the inauguration, in the hands of the enemy ; that the resources of the War Department under the volunteer system, though ample at times, were too uncertain for permanent reliance. There were 400 regiments in the field and probably 300,000 men under arms. These were scattered along the border from the Chesapeake to the western boundary of Missouri, from Columbus, Ky., to New Orleans and from Norfolk to Galveston, Tex. He did not now directly recommend the passage of a conscript law, but whoever read carefully might have foretold an early resort to some such measure.

The leaders of Southern opinion were already seriously discussing the formation of a standing army modeled after that of Prussia. To read the editorials of the Richmond papers of early 1862 is an entertaining exercise to-day, because it shows how inconsistent Anglo-Saxons are prone to become under pressure. If there ever was a section of the world that made a perfect fetich of its militia that section was Virginia. And up to the very outbreak of the Civil War the most dangerous thing any public man could have done in that state would have been to suggest the formation of a standing army. Virginians read Macaulay, swore by John Hampden, and declared that the day which saw a standing army on American soil large enough for any but police purposes, would mark the end of liberty. Indeed the whole South from the beginning had maintained the popular English theory that any but a citizen soldiery was the height of political folly. Yet John M. Daniel, the best of Southerners, now seriously urged the Confederate President and his Congress [1] through his famous newspaper to establish a regular army and order a universal conscript to supply it with men. The proposed army was not intended as a temporary makeshift to be done away with as soon as the independence of the South was secure, but as a regular "National" organization ready for any emergency. Not only the *Examiner* but the *Dispatch* and other conservative Southern journals joined the call for a conscript law, though they were for a while non-committal on the subject of a permanent "National army." Public opinion, pressed by repeated reverses in Kentucky and Tennessee and the ever-increasing danger of direct invasion along the Atlantic seaboard, was speedily educated to the necessity of a compulsory military system.

Davis watched these signs of change as closely as Lincoln studied the undercurrents of popular feeling in the North. He had never been an extreme adversary of regular armies; he had increased the United

[1] *Examiner*, January 30, 1862.

States Army in 1855 and had been the "military" senator during all his career in Congress. The steady pressure on Albert Sidney Johnston in Tennessee, and on Beauregard at Island No. 10 ; the impending danger to New Orleans ; the actual weakening of the Confederate forces in face of the enemy, with the beginning of ugly conflicts between the Confederate and the various state governments, forced him to recommend the passage of a law calling out all able-bodied men between the ages of eighteen and thirty-five.

Yet this message was made the signal for the opening of a strife which was to outlive the Confederacy itself. The one-year men whose terms were about to expire felt naturally that they had been treated badly by the passage of a law which compelled reënlistment "for the war" ; state volunteers for special local emergencies were not pleased to find themselves subject to the call of the Confederate War Department ; and the timid but well-to-do slave-holders whose services were, in fact, much needed at home, loudly resented what was declared to be an encroachment on their constitutional rights. Stephens, who always saw flaws in whatever the President recommended ; Rhett, the irreconcilable ; and Joseph E. Brown, the war Governor of Georgia, began a course of opposition which must be pronounced a most important, if not the greatest, cause of the final collapse of the Confederacy.

But Davis had already taken other steps in the government of the country which seemed to certain members of Congress a gross usurpation of authority. In view of the dangerous situation of Norfolk, Congress, early in the winter, had given the Executive the power to declare cities similarly situated under martial law, and with this came the abrogation of the privilege of the writ of *habeas corpus*. On February 27th, Norfolk had accordingly been put into the hands of the military authorities there, only five days after the solemn inaugural charges against President Lincoln for doing the same thing. Two days later the city and vicinity of Richmond were likewise taken in charge by the military arm. General John H. Winder became the military governor of the city, and a little later suspected enemies of the Confederacy, such as John Minor Botts, a distinguished politician and opponent of secession, were brought to trial and imprisoned for offenses not enumerated and not cognizable under the regular process of law. Thus the Confederate President followed fast in the footsteps of the Federal President along the road to military despotism. Justification for acts of severity was easy enough then as it is now : the state, either Northern or Southern, could not, in the midst of a desperate struggle for existence, allow powerful domestic enemies to move about freely, doing what harm they could. Besides Richmond had fallen into the hands of thieves and brigands who were preying upon the vitals of society almost unmolested by an overawed police. Winder closed the bar-rooms, forbade the sale of intoxicating liquors, disarmed the population and put a stop to the general lawlessness. While disgruntled politicians complained and good citizens who lived in comparative safety never ceased to rail at the Southern President who essayed the rôle of a despot, the people in the immediate vicinity of Richmond were thankful for the restoration of order and for the protection of property which at once ensued. But Winder and other temporary military governors learned to abuse their power and Davis later incurred some just criticism for supporting their pretensions.

The spring of 1862 was crowded with events : McClellan, pushed out of Washington by the urgency of the administration, reached Yorktown on April 2d, with an army of 100,000 men on his way to Richmond ; he began regular siege operations, advancing slowly but surely, after the fashion of the engineer, toward his goal with the least possible loss of life. The skilled eye of Davis saw what this much maligned Union commander meant to do ; he became exceedingly apprehensive for the safety of Richmond, as the myriads of trench-diggers advanced mile after mile, stretching their wings to the James on the left and to Hanover Court House on the right. On April 6th and 7th the bloody battles of Shiloh were fought and Albert Sidney Johnston was killed ; at the same time Island No. 10, a strong Confederate fortification in the Mississippi off the northwestern corner of Tennessee. fell into the hands of the enemy, with an immense amount of military stores and 7,000 prisoners, the Southern line of defense being immediately deflected to upper Mississippi and Alabama. On April 20th Farragut opened the lower Mississippi to New Orleans, and on May 1st Norfolk and the whole lower Chesapeake Bay became Northern territory. These losses, with eastern North Carolina, West Virginia, Kentucky, and Missouri already in the firm grip of Union armies, were enough to dampen the enthusiasm of more zealous secessionists than Jefferson Davis.

The only rift in the darkening cloud of reverse was the success of the iron-clad *Merrimac* over her earlier antagonists in the lower Chesapeake; but this soon closed when the famous *Monitor* came on the scene. The *Merrimac*, or *Virginia*, as she had been rechristened, was forced to retreat and she was blown up by order of her own officers soon after Norfolk surrendered, lest she should fall into the hands of the victorious enemy. Bitter indeed was the feeling of the Southern public upon hearing that this, their only hope at sea, had been destroyed by Southern hands. Davis thought it not wise to explain to them that their boasted iron-clad was outclassed and rendered useless as a means of aggressive warfare; he long bore the blame of the newspapers for this "panicky" act.

An entirely unexpected piece of good fortune now came in the successes of "Stonewall" Jackson in the Valley of Virginia from May 9th to June 8th. The dull-looking Virginia school-teacher proved himself a master in the art of war and the movement of men at a time when Davis was sorely pressed, daily fearing that Richmond would have to be evacuated. But McClellan's mud-turtle policy was bearing fearful fruit, though the Union general did not half know how much consternation he was causing. Mrs. Davis fled with the family to Raleigh, N. C., where they remained for a period of two months; the archives of the government were packed and placed on cars ready for removal to Lynchburg; Congress in fear of capture, unlike the ancient Roman Senate, made haste to adjourn; and Davis, according to the Richmond *Examiner*, stood telling his beads in St. Paul's Church. Even the cool-

headed Lee, who succeeded to the chief command
when Joseph E. Johnston was severely wounded on
May 31st, was sore-pressed for a plan of checking Mc-
Clellan before he could bring his "long guns" to bear
on the capital.

But the President was not so panic-stricken as the
papers intimated. He and Lee concerted elaborate
arrangements for the defeat of the invading army.
Jackson was reinforced from Richmond and notice of
the event was ostentatiously paraded in the papers of
the city, in order that McClellan might be misled as to
the number of Confederates, and mystified as to their
designs. The real aim was to have Jackson fall upon
his right flank near Ashland, and coöperating with the
Confederate left under the two Hills and Longstreet,
double up the Union lines. At the same time the
Confederate right and front, under the supervision of
Lee, were to attack the Northern forces at every point.
Davis was all the while in close proximity to the field
of battle and in constant consultation with Lee. Jackson failed, for reasons unexplained, to get his army
into place and A. P. Hill attacked, unsupported, late
on the afternoon of June 26th. The result was an initial failure ; but the first great conflict between Lee
and McClellan had begun. It closed seven days later
at Malvern Hill and with the comparatively safe retreat of the Union army down the James. Twenty
thousand Confederates were lost in this slow repulse of
the powerful Federal army ; half of these were sacrificed at Malvern Hill, because of mismanagement or
indifference on the part of Lee's subordinates. Jackson for once in his brilliant career had failed to act with
vigor on June 29th and 30th at Glendale and White

Oak Swamp, when he might have caused McClellan's ruin.[1]

With the failure of Lee to surround and capture his antagonist while extricating himself from the swamps of the Peninsula, the Confederates suffered an extraordinary opportunity to slip through their fingers. A truly great general would have completely destroyed McClellan's army if he had not led its commander captive into Richmond. Davis rightly indulged in no censure of Lee and Jackson, and on July 2d issued an address to the army of eastern Virginia, congratulating officers and men on the splendid victories of the last ten days.[2] The city rejoiced at the deliverance and lionized the soldiers who had wrought the apparent miracle. The greatest tide of invasion up to that date had indeed been rolled back, but not finally, for President Lincoln called on the states of the North for 300,000 three years' men and with surprising unanimity he was obeyed. Davis might well close his address with the admonition : "But duty to a suffering country and to the cause of constitutional liberty claims from you yet further effort."

[1] Rhodes, Vol. IV, p. 46 ; E. P. Alexander, *Military Memoirs of a Confederate*, pp. 121–129.
[2] Richardson, *Messages and Papers*, Vol. I, p. 229.

CHAPTER XVII

THE PROGRESS OF THE WAR

AFTER the failure of the Peninsula campaign, the authorities in Washington became disgusted with McClellan's conduct of the army and even doubted his patriotism. General Halleck, under whose supervision Grant, Buell and Pope had gained important victories in the West, was summoned to Washington to take charge of the armies of the East. He recalled McClellan from the James late in August and ordered him to station the major part of his troops at Acquia Creek near Alexandria. General Pope, a self-centred man of West Point training and Abolitionist antecedents, was also brought from the scene of his success at Island No. 10 in the Mississippi to take charge of the forces then operating under McDowell and of a large portion of the men drawn from eastern Virginia. Pope was expected to march direct to Richmond over the road made famous a year before by Joseph E. Johnston and Beauregard. He began his movements by breathing out threats of dire vengeance on the "rebels." Supported by the combined influence of Secretaries Chase and Stanton and given a free hand by the bureaucrat Halleck, it was confidently expected in Washington that something would at last be done toward the reduction of Richmond.

On July 13th, Lee sent Jackson's corps to the neigh-

borhood of Gordonsville to watch the operations of
McDowell, whom he had left in northern Virginia
when he had marched so rapidly to the aid of Lee in
the Seven Days' Battles. Toward the end of July,
A. P. Hill was dispatched to Jackson's assistance.
Lee himself remained in Richmond until the purposes
of the enemy became clear. When he learned of
Pope's appointment, he sent for Longstreet who had
been the former's classmate at West Point, to know
what sort of a man they had to deal with. Together
they made a fair estimate of their chances which were
favorable to the South. On August 13th the bulk of
the Confederate army was converging in the neighborhood of Manassas, and two days later Lee held a
council of war at Pisgah Church, near the scene of the
coming battle. Pope, who now had an army of
70,000, supported by half as many more in reserve, had
advanced the larger portion of it into a position invit-
ing attack, and left his line of communications with
Washington exposed.

General Lee commanded only 55,000 men all told,
but his army was in excellent spirits. The Union
general, on the other hand, as Lee was doubtless aware,
had managed to offend every important corps commander who was to take part in the conquest of Virginia; and McClellan, who was now practically removed from control, was none too well disposed toward
an upstart rival. Under these circumstances, Lee
planned boldly. He sent Jackson on a two days'
march around the Federal right to seize Pope's supplies and break his communications with Washington;
Longstreet was to support Jackson and when the toils
were fully set, Lee intended to attack in force. All

together they would isolate Pope and compel him to surrender his entire army as prisoners of war.

But on the night of August 17th, Stuart's adjutant-general, who carried a letter from Lee to Jackson, was captured and conveyed to the Union headquarters. Pope thus learned that "Stonewall" was approaching his right in force and withdrew his exposed divisions. The attack was then postponed until the 26th and 27th, when Jackson carried out his part of the original plan and seized the enemy's stores. On the second day a vast bonfire was made at Centreville of the captured supplies and the wily Confederate retreated to a safe place, whence he could coöperate with Lee and Longstreet near Manassas. Pope, with his whole army at hand, issued orders to move against Jackson at early dawn and "bag the whole crowd." But the Confederate strategist misled Pope and kept him marching and countermarching 60,000 of his troops all day, within gunshot of his own position yet without discovery. Late on the 28th, Jackson attacked the Union forces, while Longstreet and Lee were twelve miles away, and lost heavily, though he still further confused and mystified the foe. He continued to be strongly stationed in a piece of dense woodland on Pope's right. The next morning Lee hastened Longstreet to Jackson's support, but Longstreet, for some reason, moved slowly, and did not get into position till late in the day. This delayed Lee's plans until the enemy again came to a realization of their peril. On the 30th, the combined Confederate attack was made and Pope was badly defeated, losing thirty guns, 20,000 rifles, 7,000 prisoners and 13,500 in killed and wounded. The tardy movements of Longstreet the day before saved the Union army from complete disaster and caused the loss of many thousand Confederates. Pope retreated as rapidly toward Washington as McDowell had done a year before. He was the laughing-stock of his army until his removal a short while afterward. The 80,000 men who entered the fortifications of Washington in the first days of September, 1862, were almost as badly demoralized as their predecessors had been in 1861. They called loudly for McClellan. But Chase and Stanton were bitter in their denunciation of that general. A cabinet meeting was held, with the result that the President was almost unanimously advised not to return the commander of the Army of the Potomac to his old place. Lincoln did so, notwithstanding, and McClellan, who began speedily to revive the *morale* of the troops, prepared to strike a blow at Lee, whose movements now became the cause of growing consternation in the North as well as at Washington.[1]

Meanwhile Braxton Bragg, Beauregard's successor in Tennessee, balked Buell in his purpose of wresting the eastern portions of that state from the Confederates. Kirby Smith advanced into middle Kentucky with fair prospects of reëstablishing there the power of the South, gaining a victory at Richmond, and Bragg hastened forward at the end of August to aid in the great work. On September 2d he read to his army the news of Lee's victory over Pope. There was every reason for Davis and his generals to put forth superhuman efforts to continue this tide of victory until it should sweep beyond the Ohio River.

A comprehensive plan was outlined and agreed upon.

[1] Wood and Edmonds, *Civil War in the United States* : 2d Manassas ; Rhodes, Vol. IV, p. 137.

Lee, collecting his full strength, between 40,000 and
45,000 men, was to enter Maryland near Frederick ;
cause the surrender of Harper's Ferry on his left ; draw
McClellan away from Washington ; issue a proclamation
to the Confederate sympathizers in eastern Maryland ;
and fight a decisive battle near the borders of Pennsylvania.   A happy result was confidently expected, with
probably the annihilation of the Union army.   At
this juncture Davis was to join Lee and together they
would offer peace to the North on the single condition
of Southern independence.   This would come at a
time when the Congressional elections were being decided ; if the Federal authorities should refuse moderate demands, the North would very likely return the
Democrats to power in such numbers as practically to
force the hand of Lincoln.

The North was thoroughly frightened.   The thrifty
farmers of Pennsylvania, the merchants and manufacturers of Philadelphia, even the brokers and money-
changers of New York, trembled when they looked at
their morning papers lest it be announced that Lee,
whose army was always estimated at twice its actual
strength, had captured McClellan and was thundering
along the great highways to the Susquehanna.   Valu-
ables were hidden away in the ground ; women and
children were packed off to the mountains ; while
Governor Curtin called loudly for the militia to come
to the aid of the distressed state.   President Lincoln
and Secretary Stanton were exceedingly restive ; they
were not sure of their generals and the sentiment of
the soldiers was not such as to augur certain success.
The proposed Emancipation Proclamation, which had
been before the cabinet as a final appeal to the

radicals of the North to rally now to their favorite cause, the freedom of the negro, was laid away till a more convenient season. Both sides were convinced that a single great battle might decide the issue. Even the cool-headed Lee felt that the defeat of the Union army would bring the war to an end.

Let us turn now from astute plans and anxious expectations to actual execution. Lee crossed the Potomac during the early days of September and occupied Frederick on the 7th ; on the 9th, he noted that the Union force of 11,000 had not evacuated Harper's Ferry as he had expected. He at once ordered Jackson to that point, and Longstreet was to coöperate by stretching out his corps toward his extreme left. Lee remained comparatively inactive, watching the movements of McClellan's army of 85,000 men, as it advanced slowly along the roads from Washington toward Frederick. On the 13th, McClellan was nearing the Southern position. On that day the Confederate plan of invasion and attack, lost by the carelessness of D. H. Hill, was found and given to him. Knowing at once that Jackson was many miles away and that Longstreet was near Hagerstown, he hastened to capture the Confederates by piecemeal ; but speed to the Union commander was quite different from what it was to "Stonewall." He did not reach Lee's position until the 17th, when even Longstreet was ready for the conflict and Jackson was returning from his distant work, flushed with victory and complete success. Lee had brought together the major part of his army after some losses, taking a stand behind Antietam Creek but in front of the Potomac River into which he might be driven if the battle went against him. He was outnumbered two to one [1] by an army devoted to its leader and hopeful of victory. The battle would have occurred on the 16th, but for the constitutional sloth and petty carefulness of McClellan. On that day Jackson put his corps into place. After some changes of the positions in line of his chief lieutenants, the Union general attacked. The bloody work began about 5 o'clock A. M. on the 17th, and continued until late in the afternoon, without decisive result to either side except in the fearful loss of life. On the next day Lee was with difficulty dissuaded from renewing the fight, and on the 19th, the Confederates recrossed the Potomac without molestation. The first Maryland campaign had failed, a result due in the main to the "lost dispatch." Lee had sacrificed nearly 10,000 of the very flower of his army ; while McClellan's killed and wounded numbered 12,000.

The proclamation to the Maryland people had been issued and "Maryland, My Maryland" was added to the stock of Southern war songs. But the inhabitants of the western part of the state remained true to the Union cause to which they were closely bound ; and the Southern influence had not reached the eastern counties until after Lee's failure, when it was perilous to move. The offer of peace to the North by Davis and Lee was not made and the Northern people regained their composure, rendering fairly loyal support to their government in the ensuing elections. Lincoln, taking what courage he could from the drawn battle, issued his famous proclamation declaring slavery at an end in all portions of the country which were in insurrection against the United States.

[1] Wood and Edmonds, p. 128.

Before the end of September Bragg confessed his failure in Kentucky. He had permitted Buell to out-manœuvre him and reach Louisville, the true objective of both sides, in time to make useless further effort by the Confederates. Bragg had thrown away advantages which to Lee or Jackson would have been entering wedges for the conquest of the coveted line of the Ohio.

The interest of Davis in these large schemes of September, 1862, was intense. He wrote Lee almost daily after the second battle of Manassas. On the 2d of September he hastened the good news of victory to Bragg and encouraged him in his plans for the movement into Kentucky; on the 4th, he proclaimed to the country that the "Lord of Hosts had once more blessed our arms with victory on the plains of Manassas." He also added the news of Confederate victory at Richmond, Ky., and called upon the people to "bow down in adoring thankfulness to that gracious God who has been our bulwark and defense."[1] His original desire to serve the Confederacy as a commander in the field came to view again during these days of buoyant hope. He set out to join Lee at the moment the latter entered Maryland.[2] But on receiving word from the general that he had abandoned the line of communications leading direct to Frederick, which would render hazardous the proposed journey, he returned to Richmond, writing Lee in detail as to what he desired to be said in the address to the people of Maryland. These instructions were admirably drawn and presented a plausible apology for the invasion as well as for the war in general. The discon-

[1] *Messages and Papers*, Vol. I, pp. 268–269.
[2] *Official Records*, Series I, Vol. XIX, Part II, p. 602.

tent and sufferings of the Marylanders were referred to in the most propitiating language.[1]

In Lee's anxiety lest Davis should run too great a risk, he sent an aide, Major W. H. Taylor, to dissuade the President from the trip. This zeal for his safety has been taken to indicate that the commander-in-chief did not desire his presence at the front. There is no evidence to justify such a conclusion. Lee and Davis were intimate friends, they coöperated without friction and in no instance was the general hampered in his movements by his superior. Davis gave Lee an absolutely free hand and did his utmost to support all his plans with the necessary men and means.

The hopes of the army now fell. Soon after recrossing the Potomac, General Lee reported that from a fourth to a third of his army was dispersed, chiefly because of the straggling propensities of the men ; also that from 6,000 to 10,000 of his soldiers were barefooted and had been since the beginning of the march into Maryland. Wagons and horses for transportation were lacking ; and both officers and men, except those above the grade of brigadier, were insensible to the importance of discipline. To remedy the ills due to straggling, he asked for a permanent court-martial composed of men of high standing and clothed with authority to inflict the death penalty. Congress manifested no desire to conform to this request and began an inquiry as to whether officers of the armies had been allowed to impose capital sentences. Lee further urged an extension of the conscript law so as to include all able-bodied men between eighteen and forty-five years of age. This, he thought, would bring him a

[1] *Official Records*, Series I, Vol. XIX, Part II, p. 598.

sufficient number of recruits to enable him to confront the growing army of his opponent. A violent debate broke forth in Congress when Davis recommended the passage of such a measure. Yancey of Alabama was most offensive in his opposition; he believed, as was natural for such a doctrinaire, that a return to the volunteer system would bring the desired recruits. Stephens, who should have been a wiser man by this time, was as unreasonable as Yancey. North Carolina replied to the demand for more troops with the election of Vance, an avowed opponent of Davis, to the all-important position of governor, by a majority of 40,000 over the administration candidate. Joseph E. Brown, Governor of Georgia, had already refused to recognize the drafts under the former conscription. From this time he put every obstacle in the way of the administration.

These were not encouraging signs; but worse were to come. The ardent extremists of South Carolina who, from the beginning, had called for the capture of Washington, began to utter their complaints of mismanagement :—of extreme caution on the part of Lee, of incompetence on the part of others. To these criticisms the many adherents of the *Examiner* now joined their voices, and Yancey went so far as to declare in the Confederate Senate on September 16th, that he preferred conquest by the enemy to the despotism of Davis. He denied the power of the Confederate government to call upon the militia of the states for their defense. Even Henry S. Foote, now a member of the House from Tennessee, proposed overtures of peace. Instead of urging forward to Lee every man and every dollar that could be spared, these men entered into a bitter controversy about the unfair distribution among the states of the high military offices. It was "horrible" to Alabamians and North Carolinians that Virginia had so many generals.

Davis was sorely vexed at the stubborn resistance to his recommendations; and this spirit, coupled with the extravagance of some of his antagonists, led him to adopt more dictatorial methods than were wise. All his early fire and impatience of restraint were called into play. He carried his measures, but at the expense of some important former friendships which might possibly have been saved to him. Toward Lee, however, he manifested the finest spirit. He wrote to that discouraged general on September 28th, describing the difficulties he had with Congress and the apprehensions and distempers of those who criticised the movements of the army. He would do everything in the power of the Executive to relieve urgent needs in the field, and send forward as many fresh troops as could be collected. The kindly letter closed without a regret as to the failure at Antietam and assured Lee that no amount of outside criticism could weaken his faith in the commander-in-chief. "I am alike happy," said he, "in the confidence felt in your ability, and your superiority to outside clamor, when the uninformed assume to direct the movements of armies in the field."[1] Lee felt the force of these most welcome words and replied on the day he received them: "I wish I felt that I deserved the confidence you express in me. I am only conscious of an earnest desire to advance the interests of the country and of my inability to accomplish my wishes."

[1] *Official Records,* Series I, Vol. XIX, Part II, p. 634.

Such good-will and loyal support were not in store for McClellan, whose work at Antietam had had the effect of a signal victory. He was a Democrat, an opponent of the radical policy of the North on the subject of slavery ; he was popular, and the logic of events marked him out as the candidate of his party for the presidency at the next election. His recent practical triumph over Lee with an army of 100,000 men, as it was believed in the North, added to his laurels and intensified the devotion of his troops. There was now as much need of getting McClellan out of the way as there had been of breaking down the influence of General Taylor, in 1847.[1] He was curtly dismissed on November 7, 1862, and Burnside, the successful general in eastern North Carolina, a corps commander in the Army of the Potomac, was given the responsible position.

Burnside altered the plan of campaign arranged by his predecessor and set his troops in motion toward Fredericksburg, from which point the new march to Richmond was to begin. Lee was pleased with the change. He prepared to meet his opponent on the line of the North Anna River, thirty-five miles south of Fredericksburg. His aim was to draw the whole Army of the Potomac into the woodlands and swamps of eastern Virginia during an inclement season, surround it, and force a total surrender not unlike the victory of Von Moltke at Sedan in 1870. It is more than probable that, with Burnside in command, such a catastrophe would have befallen the Union army, had Lee been permitted to have his way. But Davis feared to take the great risk of permitting the enemy

[1] Cf. Wood and Edmonds, p. 143, on this point.

to come within twenty miles of the capital without an attempt to check him. The Richmond, Fredericksburg, and Potomac Railway officials and the citizens of the region to be traversed by the contending hosts added their earnest pleas. Besides, the affairs of the Confederacy in the Southwest were in a dangerous situation, since the failure of Bragg's movement against Kentucky ; and Davis justly feared that to allow Burnside to penetrate the very heart of Virginia after the failure of the Maryland campaign would work harm in Tennessee and on the Mississippi. The President took counsel of his fears for once and hoped for recognition or intervention from Europe.[1] Lee was not seriously disappointed on learning the President's suggestions, since he also was very loath to destroy the only railroad in this section and lay waste a loyal region.

The campaign of Fredericksburg now began. Longstreet took his position late in November on the south bank of the Rappahannock. Jackson was ordered to Orange Court House, where he could threaten the right flank of the enemy or at a moment's notice march to the assistance of Lee who was with Longstreet. In the face of an army of 113,000, the Confederate general deliberately divided his forces and was not uneasy. On December 12th, the bloody battle of Fredericksburg began. Jackson had reached his place on the right only the day before, while Longstreet had had time to entrench and render a natural stronghold impregnable. The Confederates had in line and near the field 78,000 men, half of whom had seen service from the beginning of the war. Burnside's men were the

[1] Col. G. F. R. Henderson, *Stonewall Jackson*, ed. of 1900, Vol. II, p. 302.

flower of McClellan's well-drilled army. The weak
place in Lee's line was on Jackson's right; the strongest was Longstreet's left. Burnside, for some unknown
reason, chose to make only a minor effort against Jackson and concentrated his best troops in an attack on
Longstreet. The result was what any good division
commander in the Union army must have anticipated
—disaster. More than 12,000 of Burnside's men fell,
while barely 5,000 Confederates were killed and
wounded, a majority of whom were in Jackson's undefended position. Lee was surprised to witness such
folly, though he was unable to profit by it on account
of the naturally strong ground beyond the river into
which the defeated army retired at the close of the
battle. Indeed, the Southern commander seems never
to have learned how to use a victory; he could beat a
great army with a small one but could not, like Napoleon, annihilate it.

It was known in Richmond since the early days of
December that a battle was to be fought near Fredericksburg. The government manifested no uneasiness. The
people of the city thought a victory would close the
war; [1] and General Lee wrote Davis that a complete
triumph at that time would probably have this result.
This expectation was wide-spread and affected the recruiting service; it accounts, in some measure, for the
rapid and surprising increase of Lee's army from
33,000 men on September 22d, to 91,000 by the 10th of
December, at a season of the year when the greatest
hardships were anticipated. [2] The soldiery of the South

---

[1] Jones, *A Rebel War Clerk's Dairy*; the Richmond papers, *passim*.
[2] *Official Records*, Series I, Vol. XIX, Part I, p. 621; *Ibid.*, XXI,
p. 105.

as of the North was still of a citizen character.   When important events were expected, and victory seemed imminent, they flocked to the standards ; but when depression and defeat reigned, they industriously ploughed their fields or minded their shops.   After the battle of Antietam, almost half of McClellan's men deliberately went home to attend to their private affairs [1] and Lee's nominal, as shown on the original muster rolls, was twice his real strength, even at the time of the battle of Fredericksburg.   This buoyancy of the public spirit, this popular and official expectation that the war was about to be brought to an end, shows that the people had not come to realize the meaning and magnitude of the struggle.

A cause of this cheerful outlook in the South, so different from the prevailing opinion during the preceding winter, aside from the signal victories in Virginia, was the favorable turn of things in Europe. Slidell had been received with marked courtesy in Paris.   Mason at first met with the proverbial British aloofness, but in September, Mr. Gladstone, then a powerful member of the administration, said in an address at Newcastle that the Southern leaders had created an army, a navy, and a nation.   A little later Mason was given to understand that Napoleon III had sounded the British government on the subject of intervention.   The French Emperor was then deeply involved in the scheme to put Maximilian of Austria on a Mexican throne.   He likewise had important commercial ends to serve.   To his mind there could never be a better time for France to make a move looking toward the increase of her influence and power

[1] *Official Records*, Series I, Vol. XIX, Part II, pp. 365, 374.

in America. On October 30th, he proposed to England and Russia a plan of joint intervention, calling upon the parties to the American war to submit to an armistice for six months, in which time they were to be persuaded peacefully to arrange their difficulties.[1] Another sign of European favor was the readiness of English and French financiers to underwrite Confederate bonds. It appeared to Davis at this time that it was only a matter of weeks or months when the new government would be formally received into the family of nations. And such an outcome was the nightmare of Charles Francis Adams, the Minister of the United States in London, during these autumn days. He read Gladstone's speech, hastened to Earl Russell with his earnest protests, and a little later played the bold game of threatening to ask for his passports, in case the French proposals were favorably considered in London.[2]

Here was a crisis of the utmost importance to the Confederacy. Russell yielded to Adams; admonished Gladstone for speaking his mind so freely; and delayed answering Napoleon's note for a half-month. Russia replied earlier and with a decided negative. The Confederate commissioners, once at the height of hope and expectancy, had now sadly to inform their government that recognition was postponed indefinitely. Thus the tide had turned in Europe, while at home the fearful battle of Fredericksburg did not end the war. Winter set in intensely cold and harsh; and the two armies went into camp to await the opening of spring,

---

[1] *Rise and Fall*, Vol. II, pp. 376–377 ; *Life of James M. Mason*, by his daughter, pp. 338, 349.

[2] C. F. Adams, *Life of Charles Francis Adams*, p. 278 on.

when they could again get at each other's throats.   But
Lee was not despondent though he had to pay $15 a
pair for shoes for his barefooted men, procured bread
with difficulty, and meat not at all.

CHAPTER XVIII

IT was not to be expected that the head of a revolutionary government on whom depended the lives and fortunes of millions of people could avoid criticism or even bitter hostility. And unfortunately Davis was not a man who could well compose differences. He was not a compromiser; and his military education and later political success, arising from the consistent pursuit of a definite line of policy, had only confirmed him in habits of self-confidence and command. He could not conciliate disappointed rivals like Rhett and Yancey, and he failed of course to appease Joseph E. Johnston and Beauregard, both of whom made tacit alliances with his opponents—Johnston with Stephens and Beauregard with the Rhett family.

But Davis was not indifferent to the personal liberty of his people nor forgetful of the rights of individuals. He was slow to suspend the privilege of the writ of *habeas corpus* and when he did finally yield to the needs of the situation, it was only under the forms of law and at the request of Congress and the people concerned. In this respect the contrast with President Lincoln is all in favor of the Southern leader. And when the need for martial law in a given locality had passed, Davis was quick to restore the authority of the civil magistrates. Few Southern opponents of secession suffered for their convictions at his hands. There were no "midnight arrests" in the South ; and the greatest freedom of speech prevailed. Congress set the example of criticism of the Executive, and the policy of Congress was in turn criticised by both Davis and Lee from the beginning of the war, though the President protected the popularity and influence of the commander of the armies by treating his opinions and letters as confidential. No newspaper was suppressed in the South by order of the government, and three of the greatest journals were from the outset hostile to Davis, indulging almost daily in the most unseemly abuse. Nothing he did pleased them and his acts were held up to ridicule by one or all of these from 1862 to the end of the contest.

One of the first difficulties in which Davis became involved arose in connection with the choice of officers of the army. Governors of states almost dictated the appointment of favorite supporters, and public sentiment required the pairing of a Democrat with an "original" Whig [1] in the nomination of field commanders. Davis sought to block this ill-advised game, as we already know, by giving preference to men of military training or experience. But in this he made the mistake of promoting too many of his friends. Thomas F. Drayton, whose removal from the Army of Northern Virginia was recommended by Lee, was one of these ; another was General John C. Pemberton, who, though he manifested decided ability, was never able to render the cause efficient service. On the other

[1] Isham G. Harris, Governor of Tennessee ; Joseph E. Brown of Georgia, and others in numerous letters and telegrams in June and July of 1861.

hand, political considerations, in some instances, forced him to raise influential civilians to high military rank. John B. Floyd was probably the most conspicuous example of this mistaken policy; but he failed ignominiously at the critical moment at Fort Donelson and was removed from his position without arousing wide-spread complaint, though his cause was championed by the Richmond *Examiner* and his many friends in southwest Virginia urged him for the Confederate Senate. This is but a single example.   There were many more, only less notable because the individuals concerned were of less prominence.

Another occasion of discontent was the differing views of the Confederate and the state governments with regard to the appointment of company, battalion, and regimental officers.   The traditional custom was to allow private soldiers to choose their own officers except those of regimental rank who were named by the governors of the states.   This practice Lee, with the support of all his generals, opposed, since it gave rise to a laxity of discipline, inconsistent with the safety of the army.   Straggling, shirking duty at critical moments, and the pillaging of the people who lived in the regions where the war was waged, could not be prevented when the lower officers recognized the will of the men as their only authority.   The commander-in-chief urged a change of policy in this regard in the autumn of 1862; and Davis adopted his entirely reasonable suggestions.   But the governors of the states refused to coöperate and in North Carolina and Georgia a spirit of hostility was aroused.

Still another and no less fruitful source of trouble was the demand of each locality for protection against invasion. In Tennessee complaint was made early in the war that the best soldiers were sent to Virginia; Missouri secessionists declared that Davis was opposed to their entrance into the Confederacy, because he could not forward men and arms for their protection against the Blairs and John C. Frémont, who sustained the Union authority in that great state; North and South Carolina charged the President with stripping them of troops for the defense of Virginia, when large naval armaments were thundering against their coast towns and breaking into their rich eastern counties by way of the undefended rivers and inlets. In anticipation of these complaints, Davis had scattered volunteers over the whole territory to be defended. But Joseph E. Johnston, whose influence was very great, insisted that all the forces of the Confederacy should be concentrated at two points—northern Virginia and west Tennessee. According to their interests, their prejudices, or the whims of the moment, the people adopted one or the other of these views and began their attacks on the President to secure what they desired. When reverses came, it was always the fault of the Executive who had wilfully refused to listen to popular counsel; when victories were won, it was by the bravery of the noble soldiers in the field.

Before the end of 1862 all these lines of criticism had been pretty well occupied and the President had decided to listen to none but his chosen advisers. To encourage the faint-hearted and to inspire the soldiery, Davis undertook a journey to the Southwest on December 10th, three days before the expected battle of Fredericksburg. He left Richmond *incognito*, lest his going cause a panic or give further occasion for remark

to his critics.   He traveled in a special car via Petersburg, Lynchburg, and Wytheville to Knoxville, where
he declared in a public address that the "Toryism of
east Tennessee had been greatly exaggerated."   On
Friday night he was serenaded at his hotel in Murfreesboro by a large and enthusiastic crowd.   He replied in an inspiring speech, calling upon Tennesseeans
to aid in the defense of their soil which he would hold
to the last extremity.   He said that he entertained no
fears for Richmond, and that if the people would but
arouse themselves and sustain the conflict a while
longer, foreign intervention would be offered which
would mark the close of the war.[1]

On the next day the question of forcing into the army
of defense the thousands of Kentuckians and west Tennesseeans who were "refugeeing" within the Southern
lines was presented to him.[2]   He disapproved the
plan, though some ill-feeling was manifested among the
soldiers in reference to men who refused to fight for the
common cause.   After a formal review of the army
under Bragg and earnest consultation with the commanding officers, he continued his journey south by
way of Chattanooga, where he had a long conference
with Joseph E. Johnston, whom he had recently put
in command of all the Western forces.   Here he received a telegram, announcing that Burnside was
crossing the Rappahannock.   "You can imagine my
anxiety," he wrote his wife; "if the necessity demands, I will return to Richmond, though already
there are indications of a strong desire for me to visit
the further West, expressed in terms which render me

[1] New York *Herald*, December 17th, 1862.
[2] *Ibid.*

unwilling to disappoint the expectation." [1]   From Chattanooga he went to Mobile, and thence into Mississippi where he made an address to the legislature. The outlook was discouraging : all western Tennessee was in the hands of the enemy ; New Orleans, Baton Rouge, and both banks of the Mississippi, including the Davis plantations, "Brierfield" and "Hurricane," were held by Commodore Farragut. Vicksburg alone remained a Confederate stronghold on the great river. The importance of this point could hardly be overestimated, for with its fall the connection between the far Southwest and the old South would be broken.

General Joseph E. Johnston had journeyed with the President from Chattanooga, and had preceded him from Richmond by only a few days, though he had hardly recovered from his wound received at Gaines' Mill. He was not pleased with his position : he disliked Pemberton, the general in charge at Vicksburg ; and he entertained a very low opinion of General Bragg. When he received his appointment to the West, which was next to his rival's the most responsible command in the Confederacy, he remarked that "with Lee's army I could do something" ; [2] and the *Examiner*, a sort of Johnston organ, said there was no chance for him to succeed where he was ; that he had organized the army of Lee and Jackson—leaving the reader to infer that he ought to have superseded Lee before Fredericksburg. [3]   Still, he had been in long and friendly conversation with the President about the condition of the Southwest and he remained in Jackson to hear

[1] *Memoir*, Vol. II, p. 367.
[2] Mrs. Davis, personal letter.
[3] Editorial of December 4, 1862.

what was looked forward to as the apology of the administration to that portion of the country.

Under these unpromising conditions, Davis rose to address his former constituents, who but two years before had bidden him farewell when he set out for Montgomery to take up the responsibilities of his dangerous office. It was indeed an anxious assemblage. He began by emphasizing his former love for the Union. Then he rehearsed the extraordinary changes of the preceding year, admitting that the war had proven far more serious than he had expected ; "but we can never, never reunite with the North, a people whose ascendants," he unworthily said, "Cromwell had gathered from the bogs and fens of Ireland and Scotland." He then entered into a dignified defense of his administration which most fair-minded men must have taken to be satisfactory. The failure to invade the North, the necessity for the conscript laws, the disappointing attitude of Europe were set forth with a frank manliness that his audience appreciated. On the vexed point of states' rights he said : "I hope no conflict will arise between the states and the common cause ; and if any state chooses to inflict such a blow by making conflicting military laws, I hope Mississippi will be the last to join such a suicidal policy." "Vicksburg," he concluded, "must not fall. Hold this valley [the Mississippi] and the Northwest will cease to support a war for the benefit of New England contractors."

When the President sat down, General Johnston was loudly called for. He responded in the following characteristic words : "Fellow citizens, my only regret is that I have done so little to merit such a greet-

ing. I promise you, however, that hereafter I shall
be watchful, energetic, and indefatigable in your defense." "Tremendous, uproarious and prolonged applause," says the reporter,[1] followed this short speech.
Judging from the demonstrations, the general was
more popular than the President even in the latter's
own state.

From Jackson Davis went to the towns along the
Mississippi River up to the neighborhood of Memphis,
where, according to one newspaper, he appeared *incognito* on December 27th.   He returned to Richmond
via Augusta, Charlotte, and Danville in the early days
of the new year.   The journey had been intended as a
stimulant to the patriotism of the Southwest, though
an equally compelling motive had been to get personal
knowledge of the conditions in that unfortunate part
of the Confederacy.   General Johnston maintains that
the purpose was to confer with the subordinate commanders on the state of the country and the army and
to set them against himself.   It cannot be denied that
Davis doubted the ability of the new general-in-chief
for that region, but he was still of the opinion that he
could not make a better appointment.

On December 30th, while the President was on his
return trip, Bragg was attacked by Rosecrans at Murfreesboro.   A bloody encounter ensued in which the
loss on the Confederate side was 10,000 men, on the
Union 13,000 ; but the result was a drawn battle.
Both armies bleeding from their wounds lay opposite
each other for two days when the Confederate general
was led to believe that the enemy was being heavily
reinforced.   This was untrue ; but he ordered a re-

[1] Richmond *Dispatch*, January 5, 1863.

treat, leaving the field and the rich region in the hands of his unsuccessful rival. A more alert commander with the same army, and in a friendly country, would have expelled the foe. Davis had trusted him and hoped that he would gain a victory. Twice he had let a fine opportunity slip and failed to meet expectations. Bragg disliked Johnston and the soldiers disliked Bragg. The day of his removal was not distant. Neither was Pemberton strongly entrenched in the public confidence; he was reproached for being a Northerner and a favorite of the President. He was also on bad terms with Johnston, who was, however, well liked by the people and the army, though as uncertain and slow in his movements as he had been in Virginia. On the Union side were the best of generals —Grant, Sherman, and Thomas—with twice as many men in the ranks as the Southerners had, and with storehouses filled with provisions gathered from the fields and barns of the Confederacy.

While Davis returned to his capital encouraged with the outlook in northern Virginia and possibly still hopeful of European intervention, he could not have expected much from the Southwest. He hoped that Pemberton might succeed; but with an army of 20,000, that commander could not expect to accomplish anything in a contest with Grant. The people along the way had not manifested enthusiasm and hope; quiet, undemonstrative, and in none too large assemblies they met him at the railway stations. Thus at the beginning of 1863 the commanders of the troops were at loggerheads; parties and cliques had grown up; and the President was not implicitly trusted by the people.

But this was not the worst. Joseph E. Brown, who had commenced his refractory course in June, 1861, had brought the state of Georgia to a condition of mind akin to open revolt. The legislature, which elected Herschel V. Johnson to the Confederate Senate on a program of protest, passed resolutions, expressing its disapproval of the conscript law. Johnson addressed its members in a tone of criticism and Alexander Stephens, who was present, publicly endorsed the speech and privately countenanced the most serious opposition to the President. In the preceding October Brown had written Davis that "no act of the government of the United States prior to the secession of Georgia had struck a blow at constitutional liberty so fell as has been stricken by the conscript acts. . . . The people of Georgia will refuse to yield their sovereignty to usurpation." [1]

In the more aristocratic portion of South Carolina the influence of Davis's opponents was still supreme. The *Mercury* continued to call for energy in the Confederate authorities. The senior Rhett was in Columbia doing what he could as a member of the state convention, still in session, to bring the President into contempt, even suggesting impeachment as the only way to rid the Confederacy of its incubus. The friends of Rhett had already planned a convention of the Confederate states to depose Davis. [2] The journey to Mississippi was not favorably regarded and the doubtful attitude of the public mind in the home of secession was very likely the reason he did not visit Savannah and Charleston according to his original plan.

[1] *Official Records*, Series IV, Vol. II, p. 131.
[2] Charleston *Courier*, May 22, 1862.

The Rhetts and Joseph E. Brown had been and were intense states' rights dogmatists ; they also had a show of excuse for their dislike of Davis. But Governor Vance of North Carolina offered an even more effective hostility to the administration of the Confederacy. Having made his reputation as an opponent of state sovereignty, he could not well stand upon another platform on this occasion. Neither had he been set aside in the early history of the Confederacy and left a stranded politician. He was ready now to fulfil the promises of his election and he resisted from the day of his inauguration many of the important and necessary laws of the Richmond government. In November, 1862, in his able address to the legislature he held up to scorn the "Confederate officer who refused to permit the execution of a writ of *habeas corpus* within his camp." He deprecated the President's power to suspend the sacred writ : "I can see but little good, but a vast tide of inflowing evil from these inordinate stretches of military power which are fast disgracing us equally with our Northern enemies." He struck a chord in the popular heart, although he must have known that Lee's opinion was to the contrary, when he said : "It is mortifying to find entire brigades of North Carolina soldiers in the field commanded by strangers, and in many cases our own brave and war-worn colonels are made to give place to colonels from distant states." [1] States' rights from this time forward remained the mud-sill of Vance's Confederate policy. A new convert always makes the best inquisitor-general.

He who but half understood the meaning of this dis-

[1] *Official Records*, Series IV, Vol. II, pp. 188–190.

affection and discontent in the early days of 1863,
when Lee's great victories were still fresh in the minds
of men, must have foreseen the final outcome. A
country with all its harbors blockaded and penetrated
by large and well organized armies, under the command of resolute generals, can hope to escape subjuga-
tion and ruin only by united and heroic resistance.
While there was heroism enough in the South at this
period, there was anything but harmony in counsel.
Davis did not admit, at least so far as the published
record shows, that he apprehended disaster from this
source or from any other. He entered at once into
conferences with Lee, looking to the expulsion of the
Union army from northern Virginia, knowing full well
that if success crowned his great plans and devoted
efforts, even his most bitter opponents would hasten to
congratulate him and claim a share in the glorious result. Thus had it been with Washington; thus will
it always be with men who lead forlorn hopes to
victory.

CHAPTER XIX

THE CRISIS OF THE WAR

DAVIS returned to Richmond to prepare his message to Congress, which was about to assemble. The hopes of the South were high, the news of Murfreesboro causing hardly any uneasiness to the great majority who were now becoming convinced that Lee was invincible. In the North the hopes of the extremists had been raised to a high pitch by the Emancipation Proclamation, only to be dashed to the ground by Fredericksburg. The Union army was ready to mutiny; Burnside prepared, nevertheless, to lead the soldiers in another hopeless charge against Lee's right, but was restrained by the anxious Lincoln. The general then went to Washington and recommended the removal of Halleck and Stanton, both of whom had, in his opinion, lost the esteem of the country. He himself proposed to retire to private life. A cabinet crisis was on. Congress was ready to vote a lack of confidence in the administration, but, after bitter discussion and many misgivings, it remained intact.

Under these circumstances, the recent proclamation was not apt to cause great uneasiness at the South. The North would have forgotten the ill-timed manifesto but for the revilings of its own discontented editors. Davis referred to it contemptuously in his message of January 12th, while the negroes continued their servile labor as though no proclamation had been issued.

President Lincoln's order of January 1st, designed to make effective the decree of the preceding September, fell flat for the time. All men recognized more fully than ever that the promises of both sides were dependent upon the armies in the field—and there Lee was the master.

As a last but not satisfactory resort, General Hooker was appointed to lead the march to Richmond. He had served well at Antietam and his corps had sustained heavy losses at Fredericksburg. He bore the sobriquet of "Fighting Joe," and he was the fifth general successively appointed to this task. Before the winter had passed, the discontented subordinate of Burnside had checked the demoralization of the army of invasion and reëstablished discipline and confidence. On the Confederate side, however, a change of policy in the War Department, approved by the President to satisfy popular clamor, deprived Lee of a large part of Longstreet's corps and D. H. Hill's division, which were sent to the defense of Suffolk, 120 miles away. This left the Army of Northern Virginia unable to carry out a plan which Lee had been revolving; namely, of opening the campaign a second time in western Maryland. He therefore quietly awaited the development of Hooker's strategy. This became evident in the last days of April. It was to turn Lee's left flank, seize his communications with Richmond and force another battle, or an "ignominious retreat" on the Confederate capital, as Hooker declared in his address to his troops at Chancellorsville. The Union general commanded 110,000 men; Lee 60,000 at most, and Longstreet was absent. Jackson, however, was closer than ever to his chief and right well did they work together on that fatal field. The Confederate leaders, on May 1st, entangled their antagonist in the Wilderness, where he held himself on the defensive, confident of victory. At 3:30 A. M. of May 2d, a private road leading to the extreme Federal right was discovered. This point had not been well fortified. Jackson proposed to go at once and fall on it unexpectedly. He took 26,000 men on the risky march, while Lee remained in front to entertain the enemy with the idea that the main onslaught was to be made there. Screened by the dense forests, Jackson was able to carry out his bold design. At 6 o'clock P. M., he struck with irresistible fury at Hooker's left and was doubling up the enemy's line after the fashion of Frederick the Great, when he fell mortally wounded at the hands of his own men who were acting in obedience to his orders. The battle continued, but not with Jacksonian vigor, and on the morrow the Federals recovered from their surprise. Hooker was, however, unwilling to take the offensive. Fighting and manœuvring for position continued until the 6th, when the Northern army retreated, leaving the field to Lee. The Confederates lost 13,000 men besides Jackson in this series of conflicts; the Federals, 17,000.

Without "Stonewall" and the many brave men who had fallen in these sad days, Lee and Davis arranged for a second invasion of the North. Longstreet returned and fresh recruits were put into the vacant places of this heroic army, which was now reorganized and divided into three corps under this general, Ewell, and A. P. Hill; each corps was in turn made up of three divisions under leaders, like Gordon, Pickett, and Pettigrew, who were scarcely inferior to their

commanders.   The *morale* of the troops was as good as
that which enabled Napoleon to gain so many victories ;
and the enthusiasm and confidence of the people
in the Army of Northern Virginia have never been
equaled in the history of American warfare.   Lee
himself felt a quiet assurance of victory which caused
him to expect eminent success on Northern soil, where
Northern citizenry would have to bear some of the ills
of contending armies.   Indeed, the commander-in-
chief was so confident and hopeful that his corps generals feared he might risk all in a rash attack, and
tried to exact from him a promise not to engage
the enemy except upon grounds of his own choos-
ing.[1]

When the plan of invading Pennsylvania was laid
before Davis by Lee in person about the middle of
May, he hesitated.   There were many considerations
to be reviewed.   In the Southwest, Johnston, Bragg,
and Pemberton were each and all outnumbered and
without prospect of reinforcements of a reliable character.   Vicksburg, the one connecting link between the
East and the West, was closely besieged ; and Jackson,
the capital of Mississippi, had already fallen.   Bragg
lay before Chattanooga unable to move with safety
against Rosecrans, whose headquarters were at Murfreesboro.   Davis inclined to the view that assistance
ought to be sent from Virginia, either to Bragg or
Johnston.   General Longstreet suggested to Lee the
feasibility of forwarding an army corps to Bragg,
which would enable him to defeat Rosecrans and
march toward Fort Pillow and Island No. 10, thereby
forcing Grant to raise the siege of Vicksburg and fight

[1] Longstreet, *From Manassas to Appomattox*, p. 331.

for his communications.[1] This would weaken Lee at Fredericksburg, leaving him to conduct a defensive campaign against an army almost treble his own in numbers; and it was feared that he might be beaten and Richmond fall as a consequence. The people of Mississippi and Tennessee were clamoring for relief and Johnston was urging on the War Department the concentration of the forces in the Southwest against Grant or Rosecrans. He declared that by sacrificing Mississippi, Tennessee might be saved or *vice versa*, but that both would be lost in the attempt to hold both. Davis was undecided what to do.

Finally, Lee's plan was accepted as an indirect way of saving both Vicksburg and Chattanooga, and there can be little doubt that the determining influence was the fact that on the shoulders of the trusted commander-in-chief would rest the great responsibility of success. The movement into Pennsylvania would draw the Union forces out of Virginia, cause Rosecrans and Grant to hesitate in their forward movements and at the same time satisfy the clamor of certain elements in the South for an invasion of the North. Besides Lee's presence in the Cumberland or Susquehanna Valley, it was falsely argued, would greatly aid the peace party at the North.

On June 3d, the Army of Northern Virginia began its march. Lee gave strict orders against the maltreatment of non-combatants and caused payment to be made for whatever supplies might be required for the troops. One of the chief purposes of the invasion would have been sacrificed if the people of the North were embittered by the ruthless conduct of a

[1] Longstreet, *From Manassas to Appomattox*, p. 331.

marauding army. Filled with the notion of forcible reconciliation, Lee wrote the Confederate President a long and carefully prepared letter which was little less than a sharp rebuke. Davis had said repeatedly that reunion with the North was unthinkable.[1] Lee wrote in effect that such assertions, which out of respect for the Executive he charged against the press, were short-sighted in the extreme. The South, he thought, should encourage the idea that peace *might* bring a restoration of the Union in order to increase the number of those in the North who were laboring for that end. "If we once receive overtures for a cessation of hostilities," he argued, "we can then fight as stanchly for entire and final separation as we have been doing with arms in our hands."[2] A week later Lee reëmphasized the importance of this worldly-wise policy. There is no record of a reply by Davis, though the Richmond newspapers ceased temporarily to declare the utter impossibility of reunion on any terms.

While the army concentrated in southern Pennsylvania, the various subsidiary commands in Virginia were instructed by Lee to march northward to positions which had been vacated. These movements greatly annoyed the Confederate authorities in Richmond, lest a sudden attack be made from Norfolk or Fortress Monroe. D. H. Hill, who was holding Petersburg and the James, and Whiting, who commanded in eastern North Carolina, refused to give up regiments in support of Lee's plans, fearing of course serious attacks from the enemy. President Davis did

---

[1] In the address before the Mississippi legislature and in recent messages to Congress.

[2] *Official Records*, Series I, Vol. XXVII, Part III, p. 881.

not compel obedience to Lee's wishes in these smaller details and strongly hinted both directly and indirectly that a regiment of cavalry should be detached from the main army and sent to Richmond. This suggestion was declined.

Anxiously the President watched the signs in the North and read the dispatches of Lee as the time for the great encounter approached. By the last days of June, the advance divisions had approached Harrisburg, producing the utmost consternation in that capital, in Philadelphia, and in New York. On the 28th, the news of Meade's coming[1] caused the Confederates to concentrate in the neighborhood of Gettysburg. But Stuart had failed to obey orders strictly and was out of reach. This seriously embarrassed Lee. On July 1st, the two armies began in a tentative way the greatest conflict of the war. The advantage remained with the Confederates; and Lee decided to continue the attack on the morrow, which was contrary to what Longstreet regarded as the understanding between the commander-in-chief and his lieutenants, as it was contrary also to Lee's preferences. But the latter was nervous because of Stuart's continued absence and a little annoyed at the hesitancy of Longstreet who proposed another plan of battle. Here was evinced at the crucial point the fatal error of allowing too much freedom to corps commanders. Lee's own limitations as a great military chieftain were also in evidence. Unlike Frederick the Great at Rossbach and Napoleon at Austerlitz, he attacked his enemy in a strong position when defeat meant disaster. With the advantages

[1] Meade had succeeded Hooker in the command of the Union army.

which Lee possessed over his less experienced antagonist, he ought easily to have drawn him from his
stronghold and defeated him. But this was not done.
The Confederates attacked with greater resolution on
the 2d, and were again fairly successful.

So the battle was renewed on July 3d, but without
coöperation and mutual support among the corps and
division commanders. The fighting was terrible in the
forenoon and the losses heavy ; but the decisive work
began when Longstreet moved against the Federal left
at 4 P. M. The artillery had been firing steadily since
one o'clock to no serious purpose but the waste of
ammunition ; when Pickett's division of Longstreet's
corps made its famous charge, the artillery ceased
firing and was not drawn up to support the movement ;
the big guns remained silent during the fearful carnage.
Night closed the scene and Lee withdrew, having sustained a loss of 20,000 men in the prolonged attack ;
Meade lost 23,000.

Retreat a second time from Northern soil was now
absolutely necessary. This was done in excellent order, although the rivers had risen on account of heavy
rains since the Confederate advance. Meade put no
obstacle in the way of his beaten foe, appearing to be
amply satisfied with the great results already attained.
President Lincoln was aroused to anger by this delay ;
but he did not remove his new general. The North
was elated and proud enough of Meade as he was.

They had occasion to rejoice on that Fourth of July,
for Grant telegraphed that Vicksburg was in his hands
and with it nearly 40,000 prisoners of war. With
Lee defeated and hastening back to Virginia, the
Mississippi moving on "unvexed to the sea," and

Chattanooga, the centre of the long line, in imminent peril, the war did indeed appear almost at an end. Mr. Rhodes says[1] that Gettysburg and Vicksburg ought to have closed the struggle.

The Southerners did not think thus; their newspapers and public speakers everywhere denied that a decisive blow had been sustained in Pennsylvania. Late in August the belligerent Charleston *Mercury* declared that a great victory had been won and advised the immediate seizure of Washington. In Richmond the resolute temper of the people was equally patent, though Confederate money was refused by Virginia farmers and gold was worth twenty times as much as paper currency. Lee was so discouraged with the results that he offered his resignation,[2] which Davis promptly declined. "Suppose, my dear friend," the latter wrote under date of August 11th, "that I were to admit, with all their implications, the points which you present, where am I to find that new commander who is to possess the greater ability which you believe to be required? I do not doubt the readiness with which you would give way to one who could accomplish all that you have wished, and you will do me the justice to believe that, if Providence should kindly offer such a person for our use, I would not hesitate to avail of his services. To ask me to substitute you by some one in my judgment more fit to command, or who would possess more of the confidence of the army, or of reflecting men in the country, is to demand an impossibility. It only remains for me to hope that you will take all possible care of yourself, that your

[1] Rhodes, Vol. IV, p. 319.
[2] *Memoir*, Vol. II, p. 393.

health and strength may be entirely restored, and that the Lord will preserve you for the important duties devolved upon you in the struggle of our suffering country for the independence which we have engaged in war to maintain."

With sorrowing but resolute heart, this man of iron will set himself to repair the almost irreparable losses. At each end of the long line of defense the Confederates had sustained crushing defeats. Lee retreated to the classic ground of northern Virginia with an army which, unlike Burnside's after Fredericksburg, still had the utmost confidence in its leader; "Joe" Johnston retired from the country around Vicksburg after the loss of the major portion of his troops in that region. The next blow was to be struck in the neighborhood of Chattanooga, where Rosecrans was receiving reinforcements every day. If the Confederacy failed here, its downfall was well-nigh certain.

Davis turned with more anxiety than ever to Bragg, hoping against hope that the god of battles might finally crown that uncertain general with victory. But Bragg was hardly sanguine himself. His prestige had received a severe blow by his failure, in September, 1862, to regain Kentucky, when the chances were so favorable. At Murfreesboro he lost still more, though his men fought like demons. Now his officers had little confidence in his ability to lead an army; and between him and Johnston, his superior in rank, there were jealousy and bitterness which must inevitably end in disaster. However, the Confederate President had not been influenced against his favorite. Many of Johnston's troops were hurried now to Chattanooga; Longstreet was sent on the long journey to have a hand in the inevitable conflict; and Buckner, of Kentucky, led his little army to the assistance of Bragg. The people met in their churches and prayed for victory; the clergy encouraged them to hope for deliverance.

On the Northern side there was also much interest in the issue. Sherman and Thomas were hurried forward to Rosecrans with their corps of well-seasoned troops, while Burnside with his Army of the Ohio, seized Knoxville as a preliminary to the attack upon the Confederates and to bar the way of Longstreet southward. Sixteen thousand men were taken from Meade, now at Culpeper Court House in Virginia, and sent via Wheeling, through Ohio and Kentucky, to Nashville, whence they hastened on to Chattanooga. Rosecrans—a general of the Joseph E. Johnston class —was slow to begin the dangerous advance, realizing the full weight of responsibility resting upon his timid shoulders. He moved cautiously toward the Tennessee River, which lay between him and the Confederates; he deceived Bragg as to his point of crossing and in the early days of September found his army safe on the east side of that difficult stream. He now had Chattanooga in his hands; with the defeat of the Confederates at this point, he could easily penetrate the very heart of the lower South.

Bragg was able by ruse and shrewd manœuvres to draw his opponent after him in detail and then give battle on his own ground, having been joined by Longstreet's veterans. The Federals were compelled to fight in the Chickamauga Valley some miles south of Chattanooga. On the 18th of September the issue was joined, and Bragg gained some advantage on his right. He expected on the morrow to break the enemy's communications with Chattanooga and the North and, holding his own left firmly in hand, surround Rosecrans and force a surrender. But Thomas, who was stationed on a ridge on the Union left, could not be moved; he held this strategic point with great tenacity and against the fiercest attack. The Confederates failed once more to act with promptness and the proper coöperation among the different commands was wanting. On the 20th, it was planned to open the assault on the Union right at sunrise, but both Polk and D. H. Hill, like Longstreet at Gettysburg, failed to be in place. Delay gave the advantage to the enemy, who had been expecting the battle to begin on their left. Yet at ten o'clock the work went forward and late in the day Longstreet swept the Federal right before him. A general and complete Union disaster was averted only by the steady bravery of Thomas and his corps. But even he would have been forced to yield or be captured had Longstreet and Bragg been able to coöperate cordially. The latter failed to act on the former's better knowledge of the situation and showed some pride of rank besides, thus enabling Thomas to save the major portion of his superior's army from destruction. He retired quietly at night from his exposed position and on the 21st, the Union troops were safe in Chattanooga. The Federals lost the field and 16,000 men, while the Confederates only held the ground they had never quite given up with a loss of 20,000.[1]

The Federal government was bitterly disappointed; and the people were losing faith in their President. Volunteering almost ceased; and in New York, Ohio,

[1] Wood and Edmonds, pp. 282, 285.

and Indiana, stern resistance was offered to the drafting system. Rosecrans's army was starving in Chattanooga, cut off as it was from the source of supplies in all but a single direction. Stanton grew uneasy ; sent for Grant, who met him near Louisville ; and together they planned for the safety of their depleted army of the West.

Davis saw the situation clearly ; he was not elated at the result. He heard that Bragg could not control his officers and men, to say nothing of taking the initiative against the starving enemy. He traveled once more to the seat of hostilities in the Southwest. Leaving Richmond on October 9th, he reached the general about the 15th. The President did what he could to compose the long-standing quarrels of the officers, but with meagre success.

Going southward from this point, he addressed the people in Selma, Ala., calling upon the "nonconscripts" to volunteer to do garrison duty and thereby release the necessary recruits for the armies in the field. "Thus we can crush Rosecrans and be ready with the return of spring to drive the enemy from our borders. The defeat of Rosecrans will practically end the war." But the enthusiasm of former years was conspicuously absent. A sort of apathy seems to have settled down upon the country. At Mobile, Davis was not more successful in arousing the war spirit than he had been elsewhere, though there was no lack of determination in the little army assembled for the defense of that important harbor. Returning through western Mississippi, Alabama, and Georgia, he decided to beard the lion in his den and address the people of Charleston. On the first of

November, he made an eloquent speech from the steps of the fine old city hall which, despite the absence of the Rhett sympathizers and the cold criticism of the *Mercury*, was not without effect on that ardent community.   He reached Richmond on November 6th, only to receive information that the bad temper and ugly wrangling among Bragg's subordinates continued as before.

Still Bragg held the key to Rosecrans's position— Lookout Mountain ; from which point he ought to have been able to force the evacuation of the city or the surrender of the entire army.   This advantage was not improved.   Late in October, Grant, on succeeding to the command of all the Union forces in the Southwest, visited Chattanooga and ordered the seizure of a portion of Lookout Valley.   He built a bridge across the Tennessee in the face of the Confederates which was held against all attack, and which enabled the Union army to procure supplies without serious difficulty. This occurred while Davis was still in the South.   It added greatly to the unpopularity of Bragg.   Three weeks later Grant and Thomas, after a prolonged struggle, drove the Confederate from his position and forced a retreat, which began on November 25th, to Dalton, Ga., thirty miles southward.   Here he remained until spring, when Sherman began his famous operations.

These reverses forced the President to remove Bragg. He offered the position to General Hardee, a successful corps commander in the battle of Shiloh in 1862, apparently without consulting Joseph E. Johnston, which only added to the personal animus of that general.   Hardee refused the dangerous honor and on

December 16th, Johnston was asked to take charge of the oft-defeated but still resolute army.   With Lee on the defensive in northern Virginia ; the Mississippi River open ; and the whole of Tennessee, with most of Mississippi state and part of Alabama and Georgia in Federal control, the outlook for the devoted supporters of the Confederacy was dark indeed.

The contemplation of such losses, with a full realization that his popularity was waning, furnished small consolation even to the stout heart of Davis.   The people had rejoiced for awhile after receiving the news of Chickamauga, only to realize in Missionary Ridge that they had "celebrated" prematurely.   The steady rise in the prices of the necessaries of life produced on Southern farms or in Southern shops is a fair barometer of the popular feeling.   Bacon sold in Richmond on December 1st, for $3.50 per pound, wheat for $15 per bushel, boots for $100 per pair ; a gold dollar was worth twenty-eight dollars in Confederate currency.[1]   Men took grim courage in the approach of winter, though firewood in the towns cost $19 per cord, and longed for foreign intervention or the powerful hand of a dictator.

[1] *A Rebel War Clerk's Diary*, Vol. II, entries for the early days of December.

CHAPTER XX

THE CONFLICT DRAWS TO A CLOSE

WITH the failure of Lee in Pennsylvania and the loss to the Confederates of the region around Chattanooga, the crisis of the war passed. From this time forward the chances of success for Davis and his lieutenants consisted in the possibility of wearing out the patience of the Northern people. Decisive military victory, such as Lee had hoped for at Second Manassas or Chancellorsville, was now out of the question; the struggle was to be concluded by the ablest strategists and military politicians in the country. Great blunders were unlikely now.

General Grant became commander-in-chief of the Union forces in November, 1863. After entrusting the affairs of the Southwest to Thomas and Sherman, both professional soldiers of wide experience, he took charge in person of the veteran Army of the Potomac at the beginning of spring in 1864. He had 120,000 men; Lee had 60,000. Both generals were popular in their respective sections and more popular in their armies, though in both these respects the Southern was superior to the Union leader. Each side expected to win; and the material in each army was of the best quality, the Confederates probably enjoying a slight advantage. When the weather became clear, the severest conflicts of the war would certainly begin.

Sherman, with 100,000 men, was confronted by

Joseph E. Johnston in northern Georgia with 53,000. Here, too, the soldiers were veterans and their commanders of the highest character. Thus the lifelong rivals, Lee and Johnston, held the strategic positions at the opening of the last year of the war. Was it possible for them to save their country at this late hour? The answer depended on the ability of the Confederate President to supply their needs.

On December 7th, after spending a month in the South, studying the condition of things, Davis addressed his Congress and the country in the most earnest and candid language. He admitted the crushing defeats of Gettysburg and Vicksburg; explained the failure of Bragg at Missionary Ridge, by asserting that a division of the army had been guilty of cowardice; and deplored the loss of east Tennessee. He took courage, however, from the successes of the various coast defense operations from Galveston to Norfolk. Reviewing the foreign relations of the Confederacy, he charged England with unfair and deceptive conduct, and complained bitterly of a neutrality which gave the enemy every advantage. Of France he said little, except to hint that the Confederacy would not object to the establishment of the Napoleonic power in Mexico in the person of Maximilian of Austria. But there was no hope of recognition anywhere—that fond delusion of the early days of the war; he made no appeal to the people to continue steadfast for a short while in the expectation that Europe would interfere.

To fill up the thin ranks of the armies of Lee and Johnston, he insisted that the conscript laws should be so modified as to bring into the service all who had formerly supplied substitutes. Negro cooks and

wagoners should be employed in order that the
fighting line might be strengthened by the men thus
released from less responsible duties. All those of
military age should be enrolled and drilled in the
various camps of instruction; however, skilled mechanics and others whose labor was essential for the
sustenance of their communities, were to be detailed
to do their special work. He complained of the prolonged absence of commissioned officers from their
posts of duty.

But for the greater evil, the demoralizing, irredeemable
paper currency, he was unable to suggest a remedy.
The Confederate finances were from the beginning badly
managed. Hoping for foreign intervention, reliance
was put upon temporary makeshifts. The Montgomery Congress emitted paper money to meet the
obligations of the nascent Confederacy. When military operations assumed huge proportions, bonds were
issued without security and disposed of at par to
wealthy planters, who had no thought but that their
new nation would soon be at peace and ready to redeem its obligations. When two years of the war
had passed, Southern statesmen saw how flimsy a
thing irredeemable paper was. They then undertook to issue bonds with interest payable in gold and
silver; but the blockade served to exclude the importation of the necessary precious metals, and these
bonds, like the others, depreciated in value, the government failing to pay the interest as promised. Men
then resorted to an increasing use of paper currency.
Bonds were less desirable than simple non-interest
bearing notes, which could be passed on to one's
neighbor without formality. By the end of 1863, the

Confederate Treasury had issued $700,000,000 in simple promises to pay; and depreciation had advanced until a pair of boots cost $50, while gold sold in Richmond at the rate of one to twenty-five. The various states and cities added to the inflation until men resorted to barter rather than accept the money of their government. In North Carolina tenpenny nails took the place of paper five cent pieces.

The bitterest recollection of all responsible leaders was the fact that in 1861 cotton could have been bought at low prices with paper money at par, exported to Europe in English ships and held there as a basis for the Confederate financial operations. In this way the greatest difficulty of 1864 in meeting the advance of the enemy—the easy exchange of commodities and the movement of foodstuffs—could have been obviated. It was a sorrowful result of sanguine hopes, of the belief on the part of most men that cotton was king. It was too late in 1864 to repair the ills of short-sighted statesmanship. The blockade now held King Cotton fast on the Southern plantation, where he fell into the hands of the invader and only added to the wealth of the powerful North.

Yet something had to be done. Davis recommended the forcible reduction of the volume of the currency, which was a confession of bankruptcy. The method was to compel the holders of notes to accept four per cent. bonds in their stead, or exchange them at the ratio of three dollars of the old issues for two of the new. Congress enacted the desired legislation, but the people refused to take the bonds, preferring the notes with the penalty which had been prescribed.

In this state of things, the farmers declined to sell

their produce, except in exchange for coin or the greenbacks of the enemy. Had they been willing to continue the use of the redundant Confederate currency, the salaries of government officials and the stipends of the private soldiers would not have been equal to the support of their families. With meat selling at three dollars a pound, a soldier with eleven dollars a month could not begin to supply his family with food. The government was the greatest purchaser of foodstuffs; but it had nothing except paper with which to buy. Impressment became essential; it was the only means in 1864 of keeping the armies in the field. This caused the alienation of the people for whom the war was being fought. The Georgia farmer hardly knew whom to dread the more, Wheeler's cavalry or the enemy.

In anticipation of this necessity, Congress had already procured the passage of a law levying a tax in kind upon farm products; the rate was one-tenth. In certain localities this was paid, but with reluctance. Hard-pressed and frugal Southern planters declared their readiness for a heavy tax in money but never in produce of their fields. The government could not fairly refuse its own currency, as the planter knew; at the same time he realized that any sum of worthless money was an easier tax than a small portion of his annual crops. Nothing better tested the loyalty of the farmer than this tax in kind. Mass meetings were held in Georgia and North Carolina, protesting against the iniquity of it, and Brown Vance had another grievance with which to ply the Richmond administration.

Before February 1, 1864, these disintegrating forces

and conditions became alarming to the Executive, who nevertheless hoped that if the Confederates would but rally to his support for one more year, the cause might be won.   He addressed Congress in a special message, calling its attention to the state of the country.   "The zeal of the people," he said, "is failing: discontent, disaffection, disloyalty are manifest among those who, through the sacrifice of others, have enjoyed quiet and safety at home ; public meetings of treasonable character, in the name of state sovereignty, are being held ; soldiers are taken from the armies on the eve of battle under the cover of writs of *habeas corpus ;* traitors in the city of Richmond give information to the enemy ; and when laws are enacted to prevent these abuses, the officials of states or localities contrive through litigation or other delays to nullify them."   " Desertion is frequent," he continued, "and becoming the order of the day ; and those who seek to arrest the evil are attacked by the citizens of the communities, in which the delinquents live, as public enemies.   Bands of deserters have organized and now systematically plunder, burn, and rob wherever they go ; so that the thin ranks of Lee must be made thinner still in order to find loyal men to protect our homes.   Must these evils be endured ?   Must the independence for which we are contending be put in peril by these people ?" [1]   Alarming symptoms indeed were these ; the dissolution of the Confederacy seemed imminent.

Davis suggested another remedy.   It was the suspension of the writ of *habeas corpus* in all disaffected districts, which would have been equivalent to putting the country into the hands of a supreme dictator.

[1] *Messages and Papers*, Vol. I, p. 395.

Only some such measure could have saved the Confederacy in 1864. But there was not patriotism enough in the South to entrust the President with such powers, though Congress did pass a law granting many of his requests. The enemies of Mr. Davis now hurried thick and fast into the arena against him. In North Carolina and Georgia the most formidable opposition was made; and these states, next to Virginia, were the chief reliance of the Confederacy after the loss of the region around Chattanooga. Georgia refused to send reinforcements to Johnston, who was fighting on her own soil, unless her recalcitrant governor—Brown —be allowed to appoint the regimental officers; and those farmers who resisted the impressment officers were protected by the state authorities. Able-bodied men subject to the draft were appointed in Georgia, North Carolina, and other states, to insignificant civil posts as a means of thwarting the recruiting agents of the Confederate War Department. The Rhett party in South Carolina and the followers of Yancey in Alabama were crying out against the Richmond despotism, which to them was far worse than that of Lincoln himself.

The two great duties of Davis in 1864, feeding the armies in the field and recruiting its depleted ranks, were, in the face of these obstacles, difficult to perform. There were, however, other hindrances which at times balked the most zealous endeavors. The railways, few as they were, were run down, poorly equipped, and managed sometimes by incompetent or disloyal officials. Schedules could not be maintained. The transportation of passengers had to be discontinued except in the cases of soldiers and government employees.   Freight could not be moved with safety and regularity.   Thus storehouses were bursting with army supplies in various sections of the country, while Robert E. Lee dined on a single cabbage head boiled in salt water, and his men and horses were starving for the lack of food.   Distances were too great to permit the hauling of these provisions on wagon roads ; and had this difficulty been less, the supply of wagons, as well as materials for constructing them, was insufficient.   To make these bad conditions worse, the Confederate commissary officials were unfit for the large duties of their positions.   Commissary-General Northrop, a member of a South Carolina family of prominence and a West Point graduate who had seen service in the United States Army, was from the beginning slow, uncertain, and impervious to suggestion.   Lee repeatedly complained of the inefficiency of this department and early in 1864, he suggested the removal of Northrop ; but Davis stood by his appointee.

Keenly appreciating all these difficulties of the Confederates' Grant matured his plans about May 1st, and prepared to advance against Lee and defeat him or hold him fast in the neighborhood of Spottsylvania Court House.   At the same time General Butler, who commanded 40,000 men at Fortress Monroe, known as the Army of the James, was to move against Petersburg, get possession of the railroads which pass through that city to Richmond, and, taking the Confederate capital in the rear, compel its surrender.   Lynchburg or Danville must then have become Lee's base of supplies.   General Burnside, with a force of 15,000 men, was to support Grant's movement by threatening the Valley of Virginia. Thus nearly 200,000 men were to be put in motion simultaneously against Richmond.[1]

Davis was profoundly impressed with the danger of the situation; he gave personal attention to the badly managed commissary and conscript departments. But it was mainly in devising means of defeating Grant and Sherman that he occupied himself. In the winter months he had summoned the generals from the field to consult with him about different plans. Lee was often in Richmond and once Longstreet came from his post of duty in east Tennessee to attend one of these conferences. There were two possible ways of thwarting Grant. One was to draw him into the dangerous region of the Wilderness and cut his army to pieces. For this purpose Lee's forces were too weak. A second scheme and a more feasible one was the defeat of Butler on the lower James.

This incompetent general held the key to the conquest of Richmond, for he could have seized Petersburg at any time before May 10th, without serious opposition. There were less than 3,000 men in his path. Beauregard was far away at Weldon with a force of 10,000 men, guarding the railroad against attack from Norfolk. Davis was now urged to reënforce him with one of Lee's corps, so that he could fall suddenly upon Butler, either capturing his entire army or dealing it such a blow as would render it useless in the coming campaign. A movement of this kind would have been easy under Jackson, but Davis distrusted

[1] Charles Francis Adams, *Some Phases of the Civil War*, in Mass. Hist. Soc. Proceedings, second series, Vol. XIX, p. 351,—a brilliant piece of military criticism.

Beauregard's ability, and Lee agreed with the President without giving other reasons than his own weakness. A crushing defeat or the capture of the major portion of Butler's forces would have produced a profound impression on the North in the early spring of 1864. Whether it would have led to negotiations for peace is open to serious doubt.

Longstreet favored the formation of a new Southern army, to be collected in the Carolinas and assembled stealthily in the neighborhood of Bristol, Tenn., whose purpose was to be the reconquest of the western portion of that state and of Kentucky, where there were thousands of Confederate supporters. This army was then to move rapidly upon the communications of Sherman and force a retreat. Longstreet thought that a few brilliant strokes would arouse the country and cause recruits to come in large numbers, thus enabling the new commander to meet Sherman with a fair show of success, while Joseph E. Johnston could at once take the offensive and regain possession of Chattanooga and the rich Tennessee Valley. Beauregard was suggested as the leader of this movement ; but Longstreet knew that the President's relations with this commander would preclude such an appointment. He himself would then have been the only logical candidate for the position. Whether this able subordinate of General Lee, with his corps in Knoxville at that time, could have performed such brilliant feats in the proposed field of operations is doubtful. But the greater obstacle in the mind of Lee, whose judgment was given against the scheme, was the impossibility of procuring the necessary men. Fort Fisher in North Carolina could not be stripped of its garrison, and Charleston was exposed to daily attack by superior forces. New recruits were very difficult to obtain in the territory still open to the Confederate authorities, and Lee, in whom every one felt the utmost confidence, stood in need of all that could be enlisted. Davis decided against Longstreet's plan but sent a brigadier's commission to Nathan B. Forrest, the erstwhile slave-trader of the Mississippi region, with instructions to raise an army of cavalry in west Tennessee, and break up the traffic along the great river. This illiterate but enterprising general gave promise at one time of accomplishing all that Longstreet had planned.

On May 3d, Grant moved against Lee's right; his march was not interrupted until the great Union army had penetrated the Wilderness on the very ground of Hooker's discomfiture a year before, when Lee fell with his whole strength upon the North's entangled corps. The Confederate generals thought that "the Lord had delivered their enemy into their hands." [1] In the two days' fight which followed, the Federal loss was 17,600 men, the Confederate over 10,000, with Lee standing firm, ready to renew the conflict. On the 7th of May, Grant moved toward Spottsylvania Court House, only to find his antagonist ready for him there. Heavy fighting occurred daily until the 12th, when a short respite was granted the Union army, which Lee welcomed as much as the enemy. On the 18th, and again at the end of the month, Grant renewed the fatal "hammering" which he thought was necessary to finish the war.

By this time the Northern commander had reached the North Anna River, the ground on which it had been

[1] Rhodes, Vol. IV, p. 440.

planned to capture Burnside's army in December, 1862. The Confederate position was found to be almost impregnable and Grant, having lost an army half as large as that of his opponent, public opinion at the North began to turn against his "hammering" process. He abandoned his frontal and flank attacks and moved his army toward Lee's right in the direction of Gaines' Mill, in Hanover County, where the best fighting of McClellan's army in 1862 had occurred, and where Joseph E. Johnston had been wounded, giving place to Lee. Here Grant fell precipitately on the Confederate front at a place called Cold Harbor and lost 7,000 of his best troops in a few hours without gaining any advantage whatever. On June 12th he began to move his forces toward the James River—the position from which McClellan had proposed, in August, 1862, to attack Richmond—having lost 54,900 men since May 4th. No army could long stand such depletion. The government of the United States began to waver in its support of the new general and the Treasury was threatening to give way under a strain of nearly two millions a day. Secretary Chase was almost daily declaring that he could not find the means for conducting such a campaign longer than three months. To supply recruits on this scale and apparently to no good end, was more difficult than at any previous time during the war. It was beginning to look as if Grant would go the way of McClellan, Burnside, and Hooker ; and then what? Would the North give up the contest?

Meanwhile Butler had remained idle, as though he actually desired to see Grant defeated. His demonstration against Petersburg, and the railways over which Lee's army was reënforced and provisioned, was so feeble that a single brigade which happened to be in the neighborhood drove him off. Beauregard was recruited from various points in the Carolinas and ordered to attack the Union general at Drewry's Bluff. On May 16th, Butler was repulsed and, in the language of Grant "bottled up" by an inferior force for the remainder of the campaign.[1] The latter reached the James in safety late in June, relieved Butler, who was henceforth to be his unwelcome second in command, and began to cast about for some less costly means of capturing Richmond; or rather of defeating Lee, who still confronted him and was now in touch with Beauregard.

Leaving the storm centre of the Confederacy for a moment, let us turn to Johnston and Sherman who began operations on the same day that Grant crossed the Rapidan. Joseph E. Johnston, whom Davis had distrusted since the fatal quarrel after the first battle of Manassas, now held the fortunes of the South in his hands; for a successful invasion of Georgia by Sherman's army was a more serious thing than the capture of Richmond would have been. Johnston, like all able engineer officers, had the full confidence of his men;[2] but he had never won an important victory unless First Manassas be placed to his credit. Besides, he felt that he had been badly treated, while his subordinates half doubted his devotion to the cause. The men, however, expected victory with the least possible loss of life. The line of the Chattanooga and

---

[1] Adams, *Some Phases of the Civil War*, Mass. Hist. Soc. Proceedings, second series, Vol. XIX, p. 351.

[2] Witness McClellan's unfailing popularity with the Army of the Potomac.

Atlanta Railroad was to be the bone of contention ; the country was rough and well adapted to defensive operations.

Sherman attacked the Confederates first on one flank, and then on the other, and gained his point each time, losing, however, as was foreseen, nearly twice as many men as Johnston. After each onslaught, the Confederate general retreated to a strong position in the rear, entrenched himself and awaited another encounter, never once taking the offensive with concentrated strength—a policy which he had urged upon Davis from the beginning—and attempting to capture the enemy. Before the end of June, Sherman, tiring of the hide-and-seek game among the Georgia hills, assaulted his antagonist at Kenesaw Mountain, less than twenty miles from Atlanta. His hope was to open the way to the Georgia metropolis at a single blow. He was defeated with a loss of 3,000 men and was forced to return to the slow but sure flanking method of the preceding months. On the 9th of July Johnston crossed the Chattahoochie River and thus entered upon the last phase of the contest.

The two sides now looked anxiously for the result of Sherman's bold invasion. In the North a Presidential campaign was on. Grant had practically failed in his plan against Richmond and the friends of the Republican administration trembled lest McClellan, the popular but mistreated Union general who had been nominated by the Democrats, should be elected. Such a result would have brought peace and Southern independence. John Sherman, then a powerful Republican member of the Federal Senate, wrote his brother that his success or failure before Atlanta would probably decide the fate of the Union, and the general realized the weight of responsibility resting upon him.

President Davis was greatly disappointed at the successive retreats of Johnston ; he knew that the fall of Atlanta would dishearten the South as nothing else had done. And he feared, too, that a great victory at that time would so encourage the people of the North as to make sure the reëlection of President Lincoln. Once more, as on so many other occasions, everything seemed to hinge on the work of a single day. Would Johnston retreat again ? Would he surrender Atlanta and elect Lincoln ? These were questions anxiously asked in Richmond in those fateful July days. Davis wrote Johnston for some plan, something to encourage the belief that the Southern stronghold would prove the grave of Sherman ; but he received no such assurance. Delegations of prominent Georgians went to Richmond to urge the removal of the retreating general. Senator Benjamin H. Hill attended a cabinet meeting to press the matter, though he was unable to answer the President's query : "Whom would you appoint to succeed him?" [1] After much hesitation Johnston was replaced by John B. Hood, one of the corps commanders of the Army of the Tennessee.[2] The change was made on July 17th and the deposed general left Atlanta for Macon at once, in order, as it was rumored, to prevent mutiny on the part of the soldiers. Hood gave battle and was badly beaten two days later, when Sherman was enabled to march around to the south of Atlanta as Grant was doing at Richmond. The Confederate con-

[1] Letter of James Lyons to Major W. T. Walthall, June 10, 1878, Confederate Museum Papers.
[2] *Rise and Fall*, Vol. II, p. 557.

tinued to confront the enemy, keeping the city in the
rear until at Jonesboro he was again defeated and
compelled, toward the end of August, to evacuate the
place. He moved southwest toward Palmetto, Ga.,
near the Alabama border, to await further instructions
from Richmond, while Sherman entered Atlanta.

The South was divided in opinion as to the wisdom
of this removal, and Davis was bitterly arraigned in
the following autumn, but this was after Hood had
failed to arrest the progress of Sherman.   There was
no very outspoken criticism at the time, for the people
were losing confidence in Johnston; even his own
soldiers feared the consequences of their commander's
policy.   He himself was sorely disappointed and in his
justification he at once thinks of Lee's failure to beat
Grant rather than of his own short-comings.   His jealousy of Lee, which had been nursed since 1861, finds
vent in the telegram of July 18th, in which it was declared that he had not been given as good a chance as
his rival, yet he had done better.   It was not the
spirit of Lee at Gettysburg, when he publicly assumed
all the blame for the disaster.

The failure of Hood caused Davis the greatest uneasiness.   He hastened via Danville, Augusta, and
Macon, to the headquarters of the defeated army.
There the outlook was discouraging.   Sherman had
60,000 men in Atlanta; Hood had 40,000, and the
Confederates were demoralized.   After inspecting
the soldiers, Davis and the general, in conference
with the division commanders, decided that their only
chance of success was to cut Sherman's communications with Chattanooga, tear up the railroads around
Atlanta, and raise a popular war in Georgia and Ala-

bama which would put the Union leader in the position of Napoleon at Moscow. Leaving Hood at Palmetto, Davis returned to Macon, a centre of as intense a Southernism as Charleston itself, to make one of his first great war speeches. He said: "Our cause is not lost. Sherman cannot keep up his long line of communication; and retreat sooner or later he must. And when that day comes, the fate that befell the army of the French Empire in its retreat from Moscow will be reënacted." [1] On September 25th, he met Beauregard, Hardee, and Howell Cobb in conference at Augusta, where it was decided to make the chief feature of the campaign against Sherman the breaking of the Federal communications with Chattanooga. In fact, it is difficult to see what other policy was open to him; for Hood's inferior force could hardly be expected to operate successfully against the enemy strongly fortified in Atlanta. The President, accompanied by the generals, was present at a great rally, where the utmost harmony seemed to prevail. He urged the people to sustain the sacred cause of self-government, to cast their gold to the winds, and leave their families behind for a while; for "if our Confederacy falls, constitutional government, political freedom itself, will fall with it." [2]

He then called upon Governor Brown and his people to rise up in their might and cast the insolent enemy from the sacred soil. "This Confederacy," he declared, "is not played out as the croakers tell you. Let every man able to bear arms go to the front and the others must work at home for the cause. Our

[1] Richmond *Enquirer*, September 28, 1864.
[2] *Ibid.*

states must lean one upon the other; he who fights now for Georgia fights for all. We must beat Sherman and regain the line of the Ohio. Let men not ask what the law requires, but give whatever freedom demands." [1]

Beauregard set out at once for Hood's headquarters, to arrange with him the details of the plan to "smoke Sherman out of Georgia." The militia of the state were to be rallied by Howell Cobb and G. W. Smith; Stephen D. Lee, of Mississippi, was to move his command of 10,000 into Alabama to support Hood and Beauregard; Joseph Wheeler and N. B. Forrest were to bring their cavalry commands into supporting distance. The farmers and planters were to turn out in force and block the roads, over which the Union army attempted to move, with fallen trees and other obstructions. It was indeed to be a people's war.

When Beauregard reached Hood, the latter had already crossed the Chattahoochie River on his way to cut Sherman's communications. The two generals disagreed, as was to be expected, and Hood, undoubtedly in accordance with the wishes of the President, to whom he gave the most respectful obedience, moved his army to Gadsden, Ga. Sherman hastened Thomas back to Tennessee with a force strong enough to defeat any army the enemy could bring against him, while he himself took up the march toward Savannah, much to the disappointment of the Confederate chieftains. On hearing that Sherman declined to follow Hood, Davis telegraphed the latter, on November 7, to change his plans; but the message was not delivered until it was too late and the Southern

[1] Richmond *Enquirer*, October 12, 1864.

army, now 44,000 strong, marched into Tennessee, where it was disastrously defeated by Schofield and Thomas before the end of the year. Sherman continued his journey toward Savannah.

But while Davis was firing the Georgia heart, Vice-President Stephens, who had not been at his post in Richmond for nearly two years, was doing what he could to break down the influence of the administration. Governor Brown, the faultfinder, Senator H. V. Johnson, and other influential Georgians coöperated with him. Together they had procured the passage of resolutions by the legislature,[1] which denounced the President and severely criticised the conduct of the war from the outset. The people were thus told by a large majority of their representatives that the Richmond administration was tyrannical beyond anything they had known under the old *régime* ; that they were unlawfully forced into the army, robbed of their possessions by the impressment acts of Congress, and deprived of their dearest rights. Davis's call to the militia of the state to aid in expelling Sherman, Governor Brown treated with contempt, and demanded that some of the Georgia regiments then with Lee, be returned to do the required fighting at home. On the day after Davis closed his campaign of encouragement, Stephens took up his residence in South Carolina and said to the people of Augusta, in passing through the town, that the resources of the South were exhausted and that peace ought to be made. He even talked of entering into a compact with the Northern Democracy to control the policy of the

[1] See Stephens' resolutions in Johnston and Browne's *Life*, *passim*.

Union.[1] If ever a man of mature years and high reputation talked and behaved like a child, it was Stephens in the autumn of 1864; the worst of it was that he was a favorite leader of the people and next in official station to the President himself.

In North Carolina the attitude of the state administration was not unlike that of Georgia. Vance had again been returned to the Governor's chair. He was a shrewd man, in conduct and character, the nearest approach to Lincoln the South had produced; his ears were constantly on the ground. Consequently he was never on the unpopular side of any question. He was the most difficult man Davis had to deal with.

A few points only will illustrate this: In 1863, when some of Longstreet's corps passed through Raleigh on their way to Chattanooga, a party of Georgia soldiers fell upon Holden's newspaper office[2] and demolished it, because of the editor's influence in breaking down the power of the Confederacy. Vance threatened to recall North Carolina's contingent in Lee's army to avenge this wrong; but a day later, when the anti-secessionists of Raleigh demolished the office of the pro-Davis *Journal*, he was so completely satisfied as to allow the regiments to remain in their places. Raleigh was reported in Richmond to be a centre of disloyalty to the "Davis government."

North Carolina was the greatest manufacturing state in the South having just half of all the plants of this kind in that section. Vance had no notion of permitting these factories to work for the Confederacy

---

[1] *A Rebel War Clerk's Diary*, Vol. II, p. 283.

[2] W. W. Holden, whose paper, the most powerful journal in the state, was advocating peace.

as a whole ; he arranged, during his first administration, to supply the North Carolina soldiers with clothing on state account, charging for the service. A little later, when clothing was scarce, he kept ten thousand uniforms in store in Richmond nearly a year, refusing to sell them to the government for the needy soldiers from other parts of the Confederacy. With his numerous weaving mills he was able to dress his troops well ; all the other states together had only twenty manufacturing textile plants, and their troops were necessarily poorly clad. Vance boasted in his many speeches that he could clothe the men who went into the army from North Carolina, and the people applauded him to the echo.[1]

In 1864, Wilmington was the most important port in the South. Through it nearly all the supplies from abroad entered the Confederacy. Vance claimed, as he had done in the matter of manufacturing, the precedence of state blockade runners over those of the general government, at times denouncing the Confederate administration for daring to use the port freely, in even more vigorous language than he was accustomed to abuse the Lincoln government.[2] He demanded that North Carolina's interests should be first satisfied ; then if anything remained, the Confederacy might have it. This was popular in this intensely states' rights commonwealth, and he grew in favor daily. The North Carolina legislature, under the influence of the Vance doctrines, joined Georgia in the protest against all the unpopular measures of the Confederacy, notwithstanding the fact that Lee was known to en-

[1] *Official Records*, Series IV, Vol. III, p. 691.
[2] *Official Records*, Series IV, Vol. III, p. 1056.

dorse almost everything Davis recommended to Congress.

North Carolina had entered reluctantly upon the sea of secession in 1861 ; but having embarked, her people labored valiantly for the common cause, furnishing their full quota of men, who fought like demons at Gettysburg and elsewhere, until political disagreement was fanned into a flame of discontent by the ambitious politicians at home. In 1864, however, Lee complained that his troops from this state were deserting in large numbers; he favored a more stringent enforcement of the conscript law. But when Confederate officials seized deserters and prepared to hasten them on to their places in the army, Chief-Justice Pearson interfered by releasing every one who applied to him for the writ of *habeas corpus*. The judge simply denied to the Confederacy the authority to suspend it under any circumstances. Vance sustained his chief-justice and proposed to the administration that all deserters and conscripts be left alone until, in the fulness of time, the State Supreme Court could decide upon the legality of Pearson's rulings.[1] Only in this manner, said the governor, could peace between the Confederacy and the state be maintained ! But Lee's army would have been decimated and rendered useless as a barrier against Grant's invasion, if Pearson and Vance had been allowed to have their way.

When Davis refused to recognize the force of these extraordinary proceedings, Vance sought another way to checkmate the Confederate President. He detailed 14,000 men, most of whom ought to have been with Lee, to insignificant positions in the local govern-

[1] *Official Records*, Series IV, Vol. III, p. 176.

ment. Citizens of means, who were physically able to serve their country in the field, sought to be "detailed" and their requests were granted. Davis insisted that every man should be put into the ranks, but Vance replied that he would then take North Carolina out of the Confederacy.

Realizing the meaning of the bitter discord in Georgia and North Carolina, with full knowledge that the opposition to himself was steadily increasing, Davis, after his return to Richmond, wrote to Stephens in a kindly but reprimanding tone, asking him if he did not think it would be more becoming for such an able man, in so high a station, to return to his post of duty rather than remain away to work up hostility against the administration.[1] Late in the autumn Stephens came back to Richmond, took up his residence only a few yards from the Executive Mansion and called on his chief. Stephens said at the time that Davis refused to see him and social intercourse ceased;[2] but he remarks in his book that socially they were on good terms to the end.

The opposition of leading men and the discontent of the masses increased after the disastrous movement of Hood into Tennessee in December. In Congress the feeling was intense and for a time it appeared to the friends of Davis that some attempt might be made to remove him from office. Investigation of the removal of Joseph E. Johnston was mooted; the general himself was present to urge his case. His cause was championed by a majority of Congress and the people, and

[1] Confederate Museum Papers.
[2] *Ibid.*, letter of James Lyons, an intimate friend of Davis to Major Walthall of Mississippi, 1878.

newspapers began to press for his restoration. Friends of Davis insisted that he be invited to appear in person before Congress to explain his policy; but a motion to that effect failed on the plea that the President must first signify his willingness to address the body.   James Lyons, the delegate from Richmond, reported the case to Davis, who declined to indicate any wish in the matter.

The closing months of 1864 brought the news of Sherman's successful march through Georgia and of the imminent peril of Savannah, Charleston, and Wilmington; Mobile had already fallen.   While Grant had not prevailed in his efforts against Richmond and Petersburg, a detachment of the Union forces in Virginia had invaded the Valley, with the aim of laying waste the farms and storehouses from which Lee still drew supplies.   David Hunter, of unsavory fame, did the work effectively, and late in December, when Early was detached by Lee to rid this strip of country of the enemy, Sheridan, who had superseded Hunter, defeated the Southerner at Cedar Creek and made his way toward Lynchburg with the view of joining Grant's left wing, already stretching out toward Farmville, Va., for that purpose.

The fortunes of the Confederacy were now nearly lost and every one knew it but Davis, who hoped against hope that some signal victory might yet be won to save the day.   The one weak point in the strategy of the Union at that time was the position of Sherman.   That bold general had long since ceased to maintain any communication with his government. His hope was in the fall of Savannah, which might become his base for a further march northward through the Carolinas. If that city held out heroically, there was reason to believe that Sherman could be surrounded and forced to surrender. Would not gallant South Carolina, with so much to fear, rise *en masse* to put down the invader? The destruction of the Federal army would have been a staggering blow to the North ; Grant would have felt more than ever his own danger ; and his government might have consented to treat. Furthermore, the success of Sherman and a victory over Lee would not have meant final disaster to Davis, who expected to maintain his ground with small forces after the manner of Washington in the Revolution, and wring recognition from the North even after defeat in the open field. In great anxiety Richmond watched the war bulletins as the year 1864 neared its close, while President Lincoln walked the corridors of the White House through long sleepless nights, fearing for the fate of the army in Georgia.

CHAPTER XXI

THE COLLAPSE OF THE CONFEDERACY

LONG before Congress met in Richmond in the early days of November, 1864, one member of Davis's cabinet had made up his mind what to do to avert the catastrophe which he foresaw. That member was Judah P. Benjamin, the hated Jew, whom the President had retained at his council table, despite the thousand and one protests of the Southern people and press. He favored the liberation of the slaves—the one thing the leaders of the South had always declared to be simply impossible. The astute Secretary of State saw two results which might follow such a step and he hoped for the third,—independence.

The first object of Benjamin's scheme was to secure foreign recognition by giving assurance of emancipation. He knew, even at the beginning of the war, that slavery was a great stumbling-block in the way of Confederate diplomacy; this obstacle he now proposed to remove. Had he been able to announce such a program in 1862, it is more than probable that success would have crowned his efforts.

The second object of this desperate manœuvre of the Confederacy was to give freedom to the negro on condition of his enlisting in the army and fighting till the close of the war. Such a proposition was utterly foreign to all Southern reasoning on this vital question; but under stress of a strong sea, the good captain

throws overboard many valuable possessions. The
argument and oratory with which Davis, Yancey, and
the Rhetts had for twenty years delighted their public
were now to be regarded as superfluous baggage. It
was hardly doubted that the negro would fight for his
liberty ; and if he did not prove as courageous as Lee's
veterans, he could be judiciously distributed among
companies of white soldiers and thus gradually be
brought to the point of standing and delivering his
fire. It is needless to outline the details of the plan,
for it was never put into force.

Benjamin found it difficult to convince his chief that
such a step was necessary, and if so, that the plan
could be made effective. It was indeed a bold thing
to propose to Jefferson Davis ; but the Secretary of
State had the full confidence of the President, and Lee,
in whom all men had implicit faith, was known to favor
the enlistment of negro troops. Davis yielded, therefore, and agreed to make tentative reference to the
subject in the forthcoming message.

Meanwhile, leading publicists had been plying the
editors of the more important newspapers with long
letters, looking toward the same change of policy.
Finally the Richmond *Enquirer* came out in favor of
the scheme and other papers spoke mysteriously of a
"last alternative." When Congress assembled, it was
the common talk of Richmond that the negroes would
be armed, if worse came to worse ; and the message,
surely enough, contained the recommendation. Though
but 40,000 of such troops were thought to be necessary
at the time, it was understood that the President
meant far more than he said ; only for consistency's
sake had he been reticent. Congress, made up as it

was of slave-owners, did not relish the bitter alternative ; R. M. T. Hunter, the President *pro tem.* of the Senate, was decidedly hostile to the plan and so expressed himself in the newspapers.   '' What did we go to war for, but to protect our property in slaves,'' was the gist of his almost sensational declaration. Many suggestions were made by anxious members of Congress, but the forward march of Sherman toward the sea brought unwilling lawmakers back to the unwelcome subject.   As is usual in times of stress, the remedy was postponed until, as Davis forcibly reminded his panicky Congress, it was too late ; and when a law was finally enacted, Hunter having been forced by public sentiment in Virginia to let it pass the Senate, it was such a lame one that only a few negro companies were ever organized under it, and none ever entered the Confederate fighting line.

But Stephens, having returned from the field of unrest and downright disloyalty to the administration, proposed stronger measures than that of arming the negroes.   In Georgia, North Carolina, and elsewhere, large peace meetings had been held ; and the politicians had begun to direct public sentiment toward the impossible goal of a convention of all the states, in which the long discussed differences of North and South might be arbitrated.   Farmers and mechanics of small means, who had never been enthusiastic on the subject of war and secession, came into unaccustomed influence ; they desired peace at almost any price. Reconstruction brought no nightmares to their tired spirits.   They encouraged every effort that looked toward that end but opposed any policy that gave promise of conferring citizenship upon the negro.

The newspapers also seized this new idea with avidity and steadily called for a general convention as though that matter did not rest with the now victorious Republicans of the North. The notion that Davis and the politicians in power desired a continuation of hostilities grew and spread. It was generally believed that he at any rate would never consent to any sort of compromise, because of his own feelings and personal situation ; and a majority of the people at the end of 1864 were convinced that he somehow or other had been the cause of the failure of the war thus far.

Stephens made a powerful speech in the Senate, arraigning the administration for incompetence, bad judgment, and a despotic tendency. He declared the war a failure and demanded either the removal of Davis or direct negotiations with the Washington government, ignoring the Executive altogether. Representative Atkins of Tennessee became his spokesman in the House and secured the reference of his resolutions to the Committee on Foreign Affairs, of which William C. Rives, still a very influential man in Virginia, was chairman. After much deliberation, and while the clamor against Davis was increasing daily, Rives was sent to confer with General Lee and find out if he would consent to assume the sole authority in the Confederacy, proclaim martial law, and carry the country through the present crisis. No one seems to have doubted his ability to save the state, if he would only consent to do so. The newspapers, at least some of them, seem to have been let into the conspiracy, for they called now for a dictator after the fashion of ancient Rome. Congress became well-nigh unanimous on the subject, though there was no constitutional authority for any such procedure.

The greatest blow to the plan of those who would have brought about a counter-revolution, was the categorical refusal of Lee to accept the dangerous commission ; and after a very disheartening interview, Rives returned from the general's headquarters to report his failure. Stephens now pressed for direct overtures of peace to the Northern administration. The Committee on Foreign Relations, by a vote of eleven to two, reported favorably to Stephens's plans and on the floor of the House the majority was almost as large, though a few stanch friends of Davis held out to the last and stated that if the President could not save the country, no one could. Such was Lee's view as well.[1]

The Virginia delegation in Congress called on the President to warn him against resisting the wishes of that body and asked him to reorganize his cabinet ; and the Virginia legislature, perhaps at the suggestion of Davis himself, most respectfully suggested to the Confederate Executive that he appoint Lee general-in-chief of all the armies. Speaker Bocock, of the House, wrote Davis confidentially that he must do something, else its members could not be restrained from voting a lack of confidence in him and his administration.[2] The President resented this attempt at intimidation, though he did not show his feelings to the public. As a result of the agitation, James A.

[1] Letter of Thomas L. Snead to Major W. T. Walthall, April, 1878. Snead was an efficient member of the Committee on Foreign Affairs and was present at all its meetings during this crisis ; see Confederate Museum Papers.

[2] *Official Records*, Series I, Vol. XLVI, p. 1118.

Seddon resigned from the cabinet. When Davis accepted the resignation, he protested against the interference of Congress in cabinet affairs, saying that it was unconstitutional.

It was at this critical moment that F. P. Blair, a former close friend of the Davis family, came to Richmond on his well-known peace mission. He spent a good deal of his time at the home of Mrs. William Stanard, a lady whose table was frequented by Stephens and other malcontents. Blair was certainly able to learn that Congress was engaged in a bitter controversy with the President, which could not fail to add to his impression that the South was tired of the war. He saw Davis on January 12th and sought his approval of a plan to compromise the difficulties between the parties to it, and unite the armies of both in an expedition to Mexico for the purpose of upholding the Monroe Doctrine and expelling the so-called emperor, Maximilian. Remembering the warm desire of the President to annex a large portion of Mexico in 1848, he suggested that Davis should lead the army, and that after the French were out of the way, the country should become a part of the United States.[1] But the wheel of time could not thus be set back to 1848. Davis, after a patient and respectful hearing, gave his friend a letter, saying that he always stood ready to receive any commission or commissioner whose purpose was the restoration of peace to the "two countries."

Blair returned to Washington and obtained a note from Lincoln, saying that he was always ready to receive without ceremony any overture for the restoration of peace "to the people of our one common country."

[1] Rhodes, Vol. V, pp. 58-59.

Clearly there was no meeting ground for the authors of these letters. Yet Blair hoped to accomplish something and visited Richmond a second time bearing the President's meagre message. He next returned to Washington and directed his efforts to securing a military convention, but Lincoln was not less opposed to concession in this form than by direct negotiation. Davis saw plainly enough that nothing but submission or a decisive victory would bring peace. Congress thought an effort to treat ought to be made; and the people with some of the state governments agreed with that body.[1]

Davis took advantage of this state of things to bring the machinations of Stephens and his friends to an end, as well as to convince the public that peace could not be obtained except on the hard terms of surrender or by heroic resistance on the field of battle. He appointed Stephens, Judge J. A. Campbell, and R. M. T. Hunter commissioners to meet representatives of the United States government and secure satisfactory terms, if possible, on the irreconcilable conditions stated in the brief notes of the two Presidents. Stephens was surprised at his nomination; he accepted, however, though the result ought to have been foreseen. He could not yield what the United States demanded without sacrificing his own popularity. If he failed, which was almost certain, an end must be made of all his agitation for a peaceful settlement and Davis would stand justified. Impeachment of the President and the appointment of another Executive could no longer be urged by the Vice-President. Even Governors Vance and Brown would have to seize one or the

[1] *Rise and Fall*, Vol. II, pp. 612–617.

other of the horns of the dilemma, and their criticism of the administration would fall to the ground. Congress now ceased for a season its war on the President and by way of relief created the office of general-in-chief of the Confederate armies, with the understanding that Lee was to be appointed to the place. Davis received the proffered olive branch and promptly tendered Lee the new honor, which was accepted by that popular man.

The controversy between Johnston and the Executive likewise came to a sudden conclusion. As Sherman moved northward through South Carolina, with only slight resistance from Beauregard and Wheeler, who had been hastened eastward on the fall of Savannah, the popular cry for the restoration of the old commander became well-nigh universal. Davis refused, but found a way to yield without humiliation by allowing Lee to order Johnston to the required position. The task was a delicate one, for the latter's animus against Davis had been caused by Lee's elevation over him; and the great chieftain knew only too well the character of his rival's telegram of July 18th. Lee generously insisted on Johnston's reinstatement, and took his place once again in front of that victorious general, Sherman, as the latter advanced into North Carolina.

The hopes of well-informed Southerners—especially of the soldiers of Lee's army—were now centred in the conference which was to take place between Lincoln and the Confederate commissioners. The people of the North were almost equally anxious to bring about a cessation of hostilities. The meeting took place April 3d, on a United States steamer in Hampton Roads; but no agreement could be reached, not even the armistice which the Richmond authorities had probably looked for. President Lincoln could not allow the South a breathing spell without jeopardizing the cause—complete reunion—for which he stood ; though he was entirely willing to do what he could to make surrender as easy as possible for his proud foe. He would recommend to his Congress the policy of paying for the slaves ; he would make easy the road to reconstruction. But Stephens and his *confrères* knew that the President often failed to carry his points with that body and they knew, too, that surrender and reconstruction were not what the Confederate Congress desired. Independence was as yet the *sine qua non* in Richmond. As the distinguished civilians passed back through Lee's lines and the whisper of failure reached the men, there was every demonstration of sorrow among those weather-beaten veterans. The two armies had learned to admire each other and warmly did they hope that the last gun had been fired, and that their ranks would soon be broken, never to be formed again.

The report of the commissioners was sent at once to Congress, accompanied by a message from Davis in which he said : "The enemy refused to enter into negotiations with the Confederate states, or with any one of them separately, or to give to our people any other terms or guaranties than those which the conqueror may grant, or to permit us to have peace on any other basis than our unconditional submission." [1] Stephens had opposed sending a written report to that body—it marked the close of all his efforts in negotiation ; but President Davis saw clearly that such a com-

[1] *Messages and Papers*, Vol. I, p. 519.

plete failure could only result in convincing the public
that he had not been in error when he avowed
that by successful war alone could success be hoped
for. His short message brought Congress to his feet
for the last time, Stephens himself promising to return
to Georgia to "fire the hearts of the people." What
contradictions does the life of this brilliant Southern
leader present! Davis attended a mass meeting of the
citizens of Richmond on the evening of the same day
and delivered what is called the greatest oration of his
life. Snow lay thick upon the ground and his health
was so bad that every one felt he was endangering his
life for the cause; but what had not this thin emaci-
ated form suffered in the great conflict? What mattered 'it now to him whether he lived or died, if the
Confederacy triumphed? He spoke to those who, in
their despair a few days before, had accused him of
being the cause of their ruin and who had talked freely
of impeaching him for high crimes and misdemeanors.
Now all was changed and most self-respecting men
sincerely regretted their language. Even the bitter
Examiner, whose great editor had been recently borne
to his last resting-place in Hollywood, paused a moment to hear the President's words.

This memorable speech began with a regret that
they were not celebrating a victory ; nevertheless, he
was always glad to meet resolute people, who would
lay all they had upon the altar of their country. He
had never from the beginning of the war expected
peace except through victory ; but the President of
the United States had given him reason to believe that
a conference might bring a cessation of hostilities, and
to that end he had appointed a commission. These

patriotic gentlemen were not to consider any plan not based on the independence of the South ; for he could never consent to give up the Confederacy.   With it he would live or die.   Repeating what Congress had recently declared to be a serious blunder—the assertion made at Macon in the preceding summer, that if only half the absentees of the Confederate armies would return to their posts of duty the country could be speedily saved—he showed that he realized his victory over Congress and that much injustice had been done him by that body.   He was right when he said that two-thirds of the men who ought to be in the ranks were at their homes.   " Let us then unite our hands and our hearts," he concluded ; "lock our shields together and we may well believe that before another summer solstice falls upon us, it will be the enemy who will be asking us for conferences and occasions in which to make known our demands." [1]

Every one who heard this address admitted that it was a great oration ; it aroused starving Richmond to new enthusiasm and set other gifted speakers to calling upon their people to rally once more to the great cause. Lee issued an address to his troops and the Governor of Virginia spoke to his legislature and people at the foot of the historic Washington monument in the Capitol Square.   But the new enthusiasm did not spread far and the misery of a starving army soon oppressed again the spirits of the high and the low.   Lee warned Davis that the physical strength of his men was failing and that he must not be surprised if calamity should befall the army.   On February 24th, the great general complained that his North Carolina

[1] Richmond *Examiner*, February 7, 1865.

soldiers, influenced by accounts of things at home and
by the assertion that the deserters there outnumbered
the home guards, were leaving in large numbers and
taking their arms with them.[1]   South Carolinians were
likewise deserting in squads of from twenty-five to
fifty.   Newspapers outside of Richmond encouraged the
soldiers to save themselves as from a burning building.[2]
There were perhaps 100,000 deserters scattered over the
Confederacy.   No amount of oratory could reanimate
the cause, for the people, as Joseph E. Johnston said a
little later at Greensboro, were tired of the war and felt
themselves beaten.

There was one faint hope that dimly flickered in the
Confederate State Department.   Congress had now
decided to call out 200,000 slaves on the promise of
emancipation.   The President had several times urged
such a step and Lee was advising as to the details of
the scheme.   Under these reassuring auspices Benjamin had sent a wealthy Louisiana friend and politician, Duncan F. Kenner, via New York to London, to
ask for European assistance on the basis of the abolition
of slavery and a liberal supply[3] of cotton for the hungry
manufacturers of Manchester.   When Congress was
about to adjourn on March 10th, Davis asked them to
remain awhile longer in the hope of favorable news
from the commissioner.   Benjamin wore his accustomed smile, and James Lyons, an intimate at the
"White House," seemed hopeful.   But a few days

[1] *Official Reports*, Series I, Vol. XLVI, Part II, pp. 1254, 1258,
1293.
[2] Raleigh, N. C. *Progress*, and *Standard*, February 10th, on.
[3] For an excellent account of Kenner's mission as well as of
Confederate diplomacy in general, read Callahan's *Diplomatic
History of the Southern Confederacy*.

later, no favorable reports from abroad having come, Davis asked Congress to confer upon him the authority to suspend the privilege of the *habeas corpus*, evidently hoping to hold out against all odds until Kenner's mission succeeded or failed. The reasonable request was denied and Congress finally adjourned in a bad humor and with only slight expectation that they would ever reassemble.

The Louisianian met with some success in borrowing money, but Lee was about to give up Petersburg. Davis received news on April 2d, while on the way from his house to church[1] that he would have to uncover Richmond; this rumor was confirmed by a telegram from the commander-in-chief, which was received during the services in St. Paul's. On the receipt of this message, Davis hastened from the building and called his cabinet together to make the final arrangements for the evacuation of the capital. These preliminaries having been arranged, he spent the remainder of the day and following night arranging his papers.[2] The next day, April 3d, a long train of cars, laden with the archives of the Confederacy and crowded with civil officials, from the President himself down to the anxious citizen who had forced his way into it, drew slowly across the James River. Since early dawn the people had been hurrying on foot or in cabs and wagons from their beloved but doomed town. Less than four years before they had joyously greeted this same President's happy party as it entered the city; now they spoke but few words and occasionally let fall the bitter tear.

[1] Confederate Museum Papers.
[2] *McClure's Magazine*, December, 1900.

Many could not leave ; these awaited with dignity the approach of the hated enemy, and women who had nothing but their innocence to defend them undauntedly looked the irate antagonist full in the face. Those who, then and two days later, saw the burning of that ancient town describe the awful scenes there witnessed and the wicked deeds performed, even now, in such a way as to make the simplest mind realize the meaning of "pompous war."

The Davis train dragged along the Danville Railroad at the rate of ten miles an hour, taking all day and the following night to traverse the distance which is now but a matter of three or four hours. The strain of this slow movement can be realized when it is remembered that Sheridan's cavalry were on the lookout for the escaping President and his cabinet. Every member of the anxious and disconsolate company expected at any time to be halted by a detachment from the army of Grant and forced to surrender at discretion. However, they reached Danville in safety and the new Executive Office was established in the house of Colonel Southerlin. For five days the fleeing Confederacy waited here to receive news from Lee. Davis issued a proclamation, the last of his public appeals, once so welcome and so effective. It bore the date of April 5th, and breathed a spirit of resolute defiance of fortune and the victorious enemy which, had it represented the feelings of the people of the South, must have proved an effective influence in rallying them to their cause. He called upon them not to yield their country to the "polluting foot" of the invader. The loss of Richmond he did not lament ; he would regain Virginia and every other state that had cast in its lot

with the South. He would "die in the last ditch,"
never yielding to despondency and relying upon the
"protecting arm of our God."   " Let us meet the foe,"
said he, "with firm defiance, with unconquered and
unconquerable hearts." [1]

But heroic words and resolute souls could not counteract the awful news which Lee's courier brought on
the afternoon of April 9th, that the Army of Northern
Virginia had surrendered. Seven hours later the
President's train started southward again, hastening
on now lest some of Sherman's cavalry cut the road
and make further retreat impossible. Next morning, Davis, with his cabinet reached Greensboro, to
find the snug houses of this comfortable town closed
against him. The latch-strings of his own people were
inside of their doors and he was compelled to live in
uncomfortable railway cars provided with none of
the conveniences which render a modern "Pullman"
a fairly pleasant place of residence in emergency.
Greensboro had recently held a Union mass-meeting
and she was now afraid that any courtesy shown the
President of the broken Confederacy might a little
later prove unprofitable. [2]

Davis and the members of his cabinet, except Tren-
holm who was quite ill and found a home with
Colonel John M. Morehead, spent the 10th and 11th
of April in their uncomfortable quarters, improvising
such necessities and comforts as their surroundings
would permit. On the morning of the 12th a conference was held in the house of Colonel J. Taylor Wood,

[1] *Messages and Papers*, Vol. I, p. 568.
[2] *McClure's Magazine*, December, 1900, Secretary Mallory's account of the stop in Greensboro.

fact that Davis had brought with him $500,000 (rumor estimated it at five or six millions), increased the zest of his pursuers. Dramatic interest attaches to the flight from Charlotte, because it was Joseph E. Johnston's act in giving up all his forces promptly after the first Sherman-Johnston agreement, that left Davis unprotected and without time to reach the coast. Wade Hampton, who was not present at the second conference of Johnston and Sherman, and who opposed the surrender, sought to detach his cavalry corps and escort Davis to the Mississippi, or cover his retreat and escape by manœuvring in front of Sherman's or other Union cavalry detachments; but Johnston declined to except Hampton's men from the capitulation. The brave and loyal South Carolinian refused to surrender in person and collecting what stragglers he could, offered his services to his chieftain at the risk of being declared an outlaw and public enemy. Davis appreciated the loyal spirit of Hampton and both he and Mrs. Davis regarded Johnston's conduct as treacherous.[1] They thought the general had purposely exposed them to capture, which was tantamount to the execution of Davis, if the sentiment of the North meant anything.

From Charlotte some $40,000 in silver was sent to Johnston's army to be distributed among the troops, whose pay was sadly in arrears; $230,000 of the specie was either returned to Richmond banks, to whom it belonged, or delivered to their agents. The party now hastened on to Abbeville, S. C., where Mrs. Davis was sojourning for a few days; but on receiving in-

[1] Letter of Mrs. Davis, undated, but written from Washington, Ga., a day or two later.

structions from her husband, she departed before his arrival on May 3d. She wrote him a letter from Washington, Ga., whither she had gone with Burton N. Harrison, the faithful private secretary. The letter was undated and unsigned. It read :

" My Dearest Barny : The young gentleman who will hand you this is just going by Abbeville, and I cannot refrain from expressing my intense grief at the treacherous surrender of this department. May God grant you a safe conduct out of this maze of events. I do believe you are safer without the country than within it, and I so dread their stealing a march and surprising you. I left Abbeville against my convictions but agreeable to Mr. ——'s and Mr. Harrison's opinion. Now the danger of being caught here by the enemy and of being deprived of our transportation, if we stay, is hurrying me out of Washington. I shall wait here this evening until I hear from the courier we have sent to Abbeville. I have given up the hope of seeing you but it is not for long. Mr. Harrison now proposes to go on a line between Macon and Augusta, and to avoid the Yankees by sending some of our picked escort on before, and to make toward Pensacola—and take a ship or what else I can. . . . We are short of funds and I do not see why these trains of specie should be given up to the Yankees, but still I think we will make out somehow. May the Lord have you in His holy keeping I constantly and earnestly pray. I look upon the precious little charge I have and wonder if I shall [unite ?] it with you soon again. The children are all well. Pie was vaccinated on the roadside. I heard there was smallpox on the road. She is well so far. The children have been

more than good and talk much of you. Oh, my
dearest, precious husband, the one absorbing love of
my whole life, may God keep you from harm." [1]

To this letter Davis replied, insisting on continued
separation as a means of safety. At this trying time
he was disposed to distrust every one. "I have the
bitterest disappointment in regard to the feeling of
our troops, and would not have any one I love dependent upon their resistance against an equal
force." [2] This was on May 3d; the next day they
crossed the Savannah River, hastening on to Washington. Benjamin and Mallory now left the President
to his fortunes; Breckinridge continued with him
until he reached the Georgia town, whence Davis
pursued a different route toward southern Florida. It
was here that the remnant of the troops who had followed the party from Charlotte were dismissed, each
being given a share of the gold and silver which had
thus far been a hindrance rather than an aid to all
concerned. Taking ten trusty men for his special escort, Davis with Reagan hurried on through Laurens,
Dodge, and Irwin Counties. He overtook Mrs.
Davis's party before they had gone far, and near Dublin they were sighted by United States troops.

Andrew Johnson, who had never been reconciled to
Davis since an ugly debate between them in the House
of Representatives in 1845, was now President. He
proclaimed Davis an outlaw for supposed connection
with the conspiracy to assassinate Lincoln and offered
a reward of $100,000 for his capture. It was a strange
fortune that made him dependent for protection upon

---

[1] Confederate Museum Papers.
[2] *Official Records*, Series I, Vol. XLIX, Part II, p. 1277.

Joseph E. Johnston in the last days of the Confederacy, and a still stranger one that elevated the shoemaker of Tennessee to the presidency of the United States at the time when the proud senator from Mississippi was a fugitive before the offended and enraged military power of that government.

Two miles northeast of Irwinsville, Ga., at early dawn on May 10th, Davis and his party were surprised by a troop of United States cavalry under the command of Colonel Benjamin D. Pritchard. Aroused by the mistaken firing of two parties of Union forces, the President was apprised of his danger. He dressed hurriedly and in the dark. Mrs. Davis aided him and undoubtedly caused him to put on one of her garments and, at the last moment, threw a shawl about his shoulders in the hope that the disguise might enable him to escape the vigilance of his pursuers. What woman would not have done so, and what husband thus pressed and under the full conviction that capture meant death would have refused a wife's tearful entreaties? And the ruse came near being successful. Davis had gone some distance from the tent and from the centre of the scene when in the gray dawn he was detected and captured. He was humiliated and ashamed of his garb as any other man would have been. For a moment he thought of fighting his way through the enemy's cordon or of giving up his life in the effort. Drawing a bowie-knife and moving toward his captors, he was nevertheless brought to give up his desperate resolve when a dozen revolvers sprang from the belts of Pritchard's men. A moment later he contemplated a sudden attack on a horseman standing near him. His aim was, thanks to the cav-

alry training of his young manhood, to throw his cap-
tor from the saddle quickly, mount the steed himself,
and hasten away to the southward as fast as horse-
flesh could take him. Mrs. Davis, however, seized
him fast around the arms and rendered the feat impossible. He was now conducted to Macon and there
turned over to General James H. Wilson, the highest
United States officer in this region. The career of
President Davis was at an end. Henceforth history
knows him only as a helpless prisoner or private
country gentleman.

CHAPTER XXII

AFTER THE WAR

THE journey to Macon was made unpleasant by the jeers of the captors and by the exhibition to the party of President Johnson's manifesto. Davis learned for the first time that a reward had been put upon his head and that the specific charge against him was that he had conspired with John Wilkes Booth to assassinate President Lincoln. He readily recognized the hand of Andrew Johnson in all this—the hand of him who had long been a bitter personal, as well as political, enemy.

With a few tried friends who still adhered to the fortunes of their fallen chieftain and with his family clinging to his skirts, all astonished that murder, not treason, was to be the plea of the United States for his trial and execution, he was led into the presence of General Wilson. The captive had known Wilson at West Point, where he had spent some time as a visitor in the summer of 1860, but this did not prevent the general from calling his prisoner's attention to the contents of the President's vindictive proclamation. Davis replied that none knew better than Johnson himself that he could not have desired the death of Lincoln, when this meant the elevation of a foe. This remark, which was reported to the White House, did not tend to ameliorate the conditions of the long prison life which followed.

From Macon, Davis was sent to Augusta, Ga., where Vice-President Stephens joined the party as a captive. Together these erstwhile Confederate rivals and opponents journeyed by sea to Norfolk, Va. Mrs. Davis and her little children had accompanied the prisoner; Mr. and Mrs. C. C. Clay of Alabama were also with them. After some days spent on the ship under the closest surveillance, Stephens was transferred to another boat and sent to prison in Fort Warren, in Boston harbor. Davis was placed in a casemate in Fortress Monroe. The light was bad, ventilation worse, and the atmosphere exceedingly damp. The bed on which he lay was below the water level in the bay. Four or five days after the arrival of "State Prisoner Davis," and after his family had been forbidden to remain with him or in Virginia or Maryland, General Nelson A. Miles, who had been given the custody of the distinguished captive, ordered irons to be riveted to his ankles. The officer of the day whose disagreeable duty it was to superintend this petty work on behalf of his own government, hesitated when he met with resistance, but soon resumed his task with the aid of half a dozen private soldiers. Davis was thrown down and held fast while the work was performed. The officer was ashamed of the deed; General Miles absented himself from the grounds, while the order of Secretary Stanton, a former Democrat who had coöperated with Davis in the Breckinridge campaign of 1860, was being executed. All books, except the Bible, were denied the prisoner; no one might visit him; no friendly voice was heard for many long weeks in this dismal dungeon. Letters from Mrs. Davis were not allowed to be delivered until after they had been inspected by General Miles, and no replies were permitted except on the same conditions. Boxes of appetizing food and of fresh underwear were retained by the order of the United States government and their contents doled out by the jailers as suited their convenience. In order that "treason might be made odious," the high-wrought Davis was forced thus to remain in close confinement, with a lighted lamp shedding its rays by day and by night, full on his face ; with the tramp of two sentinels falling incessantly on the stone floor of the cell, and with the eyes of a special guard peering at him. He soon fell ill, his appetite became poor, neuralgia appeared in his face and head, a carbuncle on his thigh, his eyesight began to fail, and his general vitality yielded daily to the torture he was undergoing. The physician, Dr. J. J. Craven, reported again and again that the life of his patient was in danger ; but the rigorous *régime* continued until late in the autumn when, after months of persuasion, such distinguished Northern men as Horace Greeley, Henry J. Raymond, and Charles O'Connor having taken up his cause, he was given new and more comfortable quarters. Late in November, when Dr. Craven seemed to become too intimate with his patient—for Davis was ill a large portion of the time—and ordered an overcoat for him from a Washington tailor, he was reprimanded and forbidden to talk to the prisoner except on professional matters. It was not long before he was removed. Dr. Cooper, his successor, second surgeon for this post, was of the same mind as his predecessor and soon began to recommend a change of *régime* and better treatment unless the government desired the captive to die under his sufferings.[1]

General Miles was transferred to another post in the early summer of 1866; opinion in Washington began to change and Davis's lot was made easier. Mrs. Davis called several times on the President and, despite her contempt for the Chief Executive of the nation, pleaded her husband's cause. She received the reply that public sentiment in the North and the bitter hostility of the Thaddeus Stevens group in Congress had been responsible for the rough treatment of the captive. As the summer of 1866 wore on, Davis and his family, now reunited, were allowed rooms in Carroll Hall, a commodious house within the bounds of the Fort, and life became more pleasant. The "State Prisoner" was allowed the freedom of the place. His friends came from Baltimore, Washington, and Richmond to pay their tribute of respect and devotion.

Meanwhile Secretary Stanton and Judge-Advocate-General Joseph Holt had planned to bring him to trial. They searched the departments for letters to Davis while he was Secretary of War; brought suborned witnesses to Washington to testify to his connection with the assassins of President Lincoln, but all to no purpose. The necessary evidence was not forthcoming and this ridiculous charge fell to the ground. Then the policy of proceeding on the charge of treason was taken up. Chief-Justice Chase, who was never quite satisfied with the outcome of the war, feared an acquittal, which would have put the government in a

[1] Letter to President Johnson, May 9, 1866. In Johnson Papers, Library of Congress.

serious predicament. Both the President and General Grant, now the most influential man in the country, opposed the plan of a trial on this charge. The latter had never desired severe measures to be inaugurated, and the President had repented of his former animus, though Davis was still kept under close surveillance.

According to American law, he had a case against the government, and it was time for *habeas corpus* proceedings to issue on his behalf. It was known that he could not be lawfully arraigned and tried in any other than the Richmond district of the Federal judicial system. To carry him to another, as was suggested by Stanton, would have subjected the administration to severe criticism. But no Virginia jury would find a true bill against their recent chieftain. In fact, a "satisfactory" jury in such a case would be impossible because of the certain publicity of the thing; not to pack it meant the release of the prisoner with every accusation of the Federal government pronounced false. The President and others sought, therefore, to procure from Davis an application for pardon. This the prisoner refused to the last, for, said he, "to ask pardon would be a confession of guilt." Finally, on May 4, 1867, Davis was conducted to Richmond, where his case was to be heard. When the ex-President reached the Spottswood Hotel, a greater concourse of people greeted him than that which had assembled at the same place in 1861 to pay their respect to their then newly chosen leader. On the morrow he appeared before District Judge Underwood in the building on Main Street where the Confederacy had made its headquarters during the war. He was set free on a bond signed by

Horace Greeley, Gerrit Smith, and other former opponents of the South. All Richmond donned gala attire on receipt of the good news, and wept for joy at the final release of their chieftain. The whole South rejoiced likewise at the liberation of him on whom the penalty for secession had been visited. George Davis wrote his son from Richmond, May 15, 1867 : "I have never seen this city in such a state of pleased excitement except upon the news of a Confederate victory. Men and women in tears was a common sight and the ladies say they are very much afraid they will have to love the Yankees a little. Mr. Davis, though looking better than I expected, is only the shadow of his former self, but with all his dignity and high, unquenchable manhood. As he entered the densely crowded court-room, with his proud step and lofty look, every head reverently bowed to him and a stranger would have sworn that he was the judge and Underwood the culprit." [1]

The released prisoner proceeded at once to Canada to meet his family and others, whom the fortunes of war had driven into exile. By the generosity of Southern towns and Southern citizens, Mrs. Davis had been able to make for him a modest home near Montreal where their four children were at school. Here James M. Mason visited "the President" to talk over the failure of their magnificent plans of a few years before. A colony of "Confederates" furnished him congenial company in this Northern land. In October Davis was summoned again to appear in the United States Court at Richmond. But his able attorney, Charles

[1] For this and other letters of Attorney-General George Davis, the author is indebted to Junius Davis, Esq., Wilmington, N. C.

O'Connor, brought news that the suit had been "quashed" and he felt free once again, though he had hoped to be tried for treason, so sure was he that he and his great cause would be vindicated.

As the Canadian winter proved too rigorous for his nervous, feeble frame, he journeyed to Cuba, there to receive the attentions of the leading citizens and officials of the island. Next he appeared in New Orleans, where the people crowded about his hotel as though he had been a hero of many battles returning to his native city. His vicarious sufferings had warmed the hearts of Southern men as nothing else could have done. Responsive always to popular applause, he felt deeply the returning gratitude of his people. From New Orleans he visited Vicksburg and the country around his beloved "Brierfield," to find his fertile lands overgrown with weeds and brambles, the houses burned to the ground and the former negro slaves scattered about the neighborhood "making a living" as best they could. No patriotic German of the seventeenth century could have visited a more forlorn and saddening region than that which greeted the eye of the returning Confederate chieftain as he looked upon the country around Davis Bend in the spring of 1868.

Overcome with the thought of his desolated Mississippi and receiving a severe injury from a fall, his health seemed about to break down permanently. He decided, on the advice of his physician, to spend a year in Europe where entire change of surroundings might restore his physical strength. Returning to Canada, he embarked with his family from Quebec. England loves to strew roses in the

paths of discrowned kings and Davis was hardly
an exception to the rule.   Noble lords invited him to
their country and town residences.   At Leamington
he was the fashion and in London the Houses of Parlia-
ment vied with each other to show him respect.
Crossing over to Paris, he renewed his long and intimate acquaintance with Slidell and A. Dudley Mann.
He was invited to the Imperial court, while Mrs.
Davis received attentions from the incomparable
Empress Eugenie.   Parades were held in his honor
and cards were sent him to attend mass in the Napoleonic chapel.   But Davis felt that the French monarch had played him false in the matter of Confederate
recognition and declined to see his Majesty.   The
dignity of the "Senator from Mississippi" still remained.

Returning to London, the cheerful countenance of
Secretary Benjamin, already risen to the rank of
Queen's counselor, was seen.   Together they talked
over the old Richmond days, without apparent regret
or bitterness on the part of the famous attorney.   His
health continuing poor, Davis went to Scotland, visited
that staunch friend of the South, James Smith, of
Glasgow, who had given a fine battery to the Confederate cause ; but he never found the vigor of which he
was in quest, though he was much improved by the
autumn of 1869.

He now received notice of his election to the presidency of an insurance company in Memphis, Tenn.
Leaving his family in London, he returned alone to
America, and after arranging business matters, he
went once again to England to bring them to their
new place of residence.   Putting the older children to

school in Maryland, Mr. and Mrs. Davis "settled" in Memphis as they thought for the remainder of their lives. The people of the city purchased a handsome residence for the distinguished newcomer, but the pride and sense of fitness so strongly rooted in Davis's nature forced him to decline the offer. He bought and furnished his own home and began with zest the new business of life insurance. He invested some of the meagre remains of his fortune in the venture, but in 1874 the company failed and with it went the much needed money of the ex-President—too old now to start afresh in life.

His troubles, as though fortune had not dealt hardly enough with him, now thickened. On the day he sailed from England to take up his new position, he received a message that his beloved brother, Joseph E. Davis, was dead. In 1874, just before the failure of his insurance company, his little son William was taken with diphtheria and died in a few days. Another son had fallen from a window of the mansion in Richmond during the war and was killed. There were now left to him one boy, Jefferson, and one girl, "Winnie," besides Mrs. J. A. Hayes, an older daughter who had settled in Memphis a few years earlier. The death of Joseph E. Davis caused both the "Hurricane" and the "Brierfield" estates to be thrown into courts, encumbered as they were with debt. After a protracted lawsuit, "Brierfield" was in part recovered, and from these lands Davis hoped to support his little family ; but again his health broke down and he was advised to go once more to Europe, where, as on his earlier visits, he received much attention. He saw Paris under the early Republic and, though displeased with the Emperor, sympathized with the fallen Bonapartes in their weary exile. The catastrophe of Sedan had been even greater than the collapse of the Confederacy.

Filled as of old with imperial notions on behalf of his beloved South, he strove on his return to Memphis to organize an international enterprise which should have for its end the upbuilding of New Orleans and the cities of the lower South. Two companies, bearing the name of the Mississippi Valley Society, one composed of English, the other of American capitalists, were formed. Then, as now, the rich trade of South America was monopolized by London and Liverpool merchants, and raw products of Brazil destined to be consumed in the United States were exchanged against English manufactures to be reshipped to New York. Nothing would seem more natural than a brisk trade between the two Americas. To bring about this proper and profitable state of affairs Davis bent his energies in 1876 and 1877. He visited England to stir up interest and coöperation and again turned his attention to New Orleans and the river and coast cities of the Gulf region. His elastic spirits and buoyant vigor warmed to the great undertaking; his health seemed restored and he looked forward, despite his seventy toilsome years, to a career of usefulness and possible financial independence.

But he was destined to fail again. The fatal protective tariff, rising after the close of the war rather than declining, made his beneficent scheme problematical. And the force of habit, too, kept ships of trade in their beaten paths. Besides, now as in the days of his magnificent fight for the Southern Pacific Railway, the combined energies of Northern capital and New England enterprise were against him. In the autumn of 1877 he saw all his projects come to naught and his own slender fortunes reminded him of the fact that the reasonable and the obvious are not always easily attainable. This was the last of his large plans in life ; he began now to look about him for a home in some secluded country retreat where he might spend the approaching evening of life in undisturbed repose, quietly collecting the threads of his eventful history, which he designed to weave into a solid fabric for the benefit of future students.

He turned to the Gulf coast between New Orleans and Mobile, where to-day so many beautiful suburban residences adorn the gently receding shores. A place called "Beauvoir," half-way between the two cities, was chosen. The house was large and well built, and only about half a hundred paces from the water's edge. There was no railway station and the neighboring post-office had only a dozen patrons. To the rear of the mansion lay a thousand acres of pine and cypress forest, and in front the gentle Gulf waves broke ceaselessly against the banks of shells on which the solid land had been built up. No more ideal asylum for the storm-tossed Confederate President could have been found. A prominent traveler has called it "the home of Jefferson Davis, the *chapelle expiatore* of the Southern Bourbon ; the modern rock of Prometheus to the Northern heart."

"Beauvoir" was the summer home of Mrs. Sarah A. Dorsey, a friend of Mrs. Davis and a writer of some fame. She sold the place to Davis to be paid for in easy instalments ; but she died a year or two later and

made him her executor.   When he qualified, he found
that the unpaid-for property had been bequeathed to
him, and in case of his refusal of the legacy to his little
daughter Winnie.   He accepted the gift, like the elder
Pitt, as a token of the love and esteem of one of his
devoted admirers.

Before the work of composing his account of the
Confederacy began, he was called upon by Mississippi
to represent her again in the United States Senate.
But he had steadily refused to ask the pardon of the
Federal government, which would have debarred him
from a seat in that body.   Realizing only too well what
a commotion his appearance at the bar of the Senate
would create, he declined this last political trust of his
much loved state.   The Northern theory of reconstruction was that all prominent Southerners who had participated in the war should be debarred from national
citizenship, and therefore from holding office, except
on condition of formal submission to and pardon by
the Federal authority.   Davis as the head and front
of secession, was not unnaturally excepted from these
conditions and he looked upon the intended stigma as
an honor.   However ably he might have served in the
United States Senate with Lamar, B. H. Hill, and
Wade Hampton, it would not have accorded with his
sense of the fitness of things to have taken his place in
Washington with Stephens, Vance, and Brown.

From 1878 to 1881, Davis labored on his great apology.   He had the assistance of his friend Major
W. T. Walthall and of Judge Tenney, an employee of
his publishers.   Mrs. Davis, who had spent the year
1877 in England, now returned and took up the
laborious task of amanuensis.   The greater portion

of the documents necessary for the work were in Washington, where they had been taken at the close of the war. An arrangement was made by which Davis received copies of the most important of these papers in return for copies of those he had collected from his friends. The product of these three years of toil was the well-known *Rise and Fall of the Confederate Government*—in two large volumes. As a justification of secession and the resulting civil war, it is the best in existence ; as an account of the military and civil events of the period, it is partisan and in some respects unreliable. Yet it is a monument to its author, containing many valuable documents, and in no way deserving the severe criticism which some Southern students have been wont of recent years to bestow upon it.

Disappointment and sorrow were not yet done with Jefferson Davis. In the summer of 1878 yellow fever broke out in the lower Mississippi states. It reached Memphis, where his son-in-law J. A. Hayes was engaged in a business to a share in which his only son, Jefferson, now twenty-one years old, had recently been admitted. The young man was stricken in October and died before either the father or mother could reach him. Without a son, and with only two of their large family of children remaining, it was with difficulty that the broken-hearted man controlled the will that had once been of iron ; but he kept diligently at his task.

The home at "Beauvoir," notwithstanding its out-of-the-way location, soon became the Mecca of "good Confederates." Generals of the armies of the Confederacy, governors of the Southern states, and old friends from the North, like George W. Jones of Iowa, visited him in his quiet retreat and reviewed the stirring scenes of earlier days. From all parts of the country came letters, bringing good wishes, addressing inquiry, or asking advice. One good lady, fallen into sore financial straits, wrings his heart with a request to cash her small bundle of Confederate notes. A Massachusetts Democrat of the Caleb Cushing *régime* writes to tell of the friendship of the chosen few in that Yankee commonwealth. Younger soldiers of the Confederacy want a line and an autograph from their great chieftain ; older ones desire his endorsement for political office, while ordinary voters ask his opinion on the merits of local campaigns. His house was full of guests every day and it would have taken all his time and that of a modern stenographer to answer his letters. Like Jefferson, his namesake at Monticello, he was about to be smothered by the kindness of his friends.

After the close of the war, men who had been his enemies began to forget their wrath ; invitations to speak at fairs and the unveiling of monuments began to come to him. Strangely enough, the first of these reached him from the authorities of the Winnebago County fair at Rockford, Ill. He unwillingly accepted the invitation, longing to visit again the places where he had "roughed it" in his young soldier days. Soon the news spread abroad that "Jeff" Davis would speak in Illinois, the state of Lincoln. The Chicago *Inter-Ocean* called upon the old soldiers of the state to behold the sacrilege. Smaller papers took up the chorus and the committee which had invited the ex-Confederate President was forced to annul its act. The Chicago

Tribune warned the people of the North not to repeat the blunder. Yet in September and October following, in the year 1875, Davis was cordially requested to address audiences at Jonesville, Wis., Des Moines, Ia., Danville and Lancaster, Pa., and several other places in the North. Having been humiliated in the first instance, he declined all further invitations outside the bounds of his "own country." Thus the first returning warmth of his arduous nature for his fellow citizens of the North was chilled.

Another invitation brought him even more annoyance. The people of Texas, for whom he always felt a peculiar attachment, were engaged in a hot contest over the question whether the liquor traffic should be prohibited by constitutional amendment. Ex-Governor Lubbock opposed the measure and wrote to ask Davis for his opinion which, if favorable to his side of the dispute, he desired to publish. Lubbock had been a faithful member of the President's staff during the war and a close friend ever since. Davis gave his dictum, as was to have been expected, in favor of the liquor traffic. His position was that of the individualist who reprobates state interference and believes absolutely in the doctrine that the "least government possible makes the best government." He had always been temperate in his habits and was least of all a friend of dram-drinking; yet he thought the state could not safely enter the field of moral and personal reform. The prohibition movement was to him another "higher law" campaign. His letter was made public and copies of it were circulated by the thousand. A storm was raised about the head of the venerable statesman; letters of protest as well as of approval poured in upon him. He soon regretted that he had given his opinion.

On the 10th of August, 1887, Bishop Galloway of the Methodist Episcopal Church, South, assailed the position of the "ex-President" and lamented that "the last words of a soldier, sage, or Christian, should become the shibboleth of the saloons." This able but rather caustic address stung Davis to the quick. He made reply which led to a newspaper discussion wherein the Bishop got the better of the argument. The young and vigorous dignitary of the Church was fighting for a reform which was steadily proving its reasonableness and value, whereas Davis defended the traditional individualism on which the American system had been built. The one looked to the future, the other to the past.[1]

While engaged in this controversy, he was tempted by a representative of the Louisiana Lottery Company to allow his name to be attached to a magazine intended to advertise that business. He was offered a salary of $10,000 a year to do for the new publication "what Curtis does for Harpers, only the opposite; namely, press the charter rights of the states again to the front."[2] The way was made very smooth and the assurance given that the lottery was only to have the right to advertise. The offer was rejected and the South was spared the necessity of apologizing for its Chief Executive's connection with what was regarded as an immoral enterprise.

[1] The discussion has been reprinted in pamphlet form and widely circulated in the lower Southern states.

[2] Letter, dated December 19, 1887, in Confederate Museum Papers.

After the publication of the *Rise and Fall* in 1881, Davis continued to grow in favor. The people of the South, realizing the benefits of the Union against which they had warred so heroically, were beginning to view the great struggle in the mellow light of history and to place statues of its leaders in their public parks. Lee and Jackson were gone forever ; Joseph E. Johnston and General Beauregard had compromised their popularity by connecting themselves with the Louisiana Lottery. Davis, the chief of them all, though once the most unpopular, came into his own.

In the autumn of 1886 he visited the capitals of Mississippi, Alabama, and Georgia and spoke to the people. He was received everywhere as no other American had been up to that date. In Atlanta the beloved Governor, John B. Gordon, presented Miss Winnie as "the daughter of the Confederacy"—a name which she bore until her death in 1898. That the South was true to her past, and determined to say so, was evidenced in these unprecedented gatherings. Davis, however, avoided all references that might give offense to other parts of the country or lead his hearers to believe that secession was still a "reserved right." He said it was best that the war had ended as it did ; but that nevertheless he should act the same way again with a repetition of the conditions of 1861.

His years were drawing to a close. The last of his great speeches, delivered at Macon, at the end of his tour, so exhausted him that his physician hastened him home, with the injunction to avoid all excitement in the future. Visiting his "Brierfield" estate in November, 1889, he was exposed to a cold rain on the 10th, and on the 11th Mrs. Davis received a telegram

saying that he was ill.   He started back at once but
was too much indisposed with something like bron-
chitis to proceed further than New Orleans.   There he
was taken to the house of his old friend, Mr. J. U.
Payne, and every assistance given him.   Mrs. Davis
had joined him on his way down the river.   After a
lingering illness, he died on December 6th, and all the
South sent representatives to participate in the last
rites over the remains of their historic leader.   The
people of New Orleans ceased their round of daily toil
to attend the funeral *en masse*.   Members of the Grand
Army of the Republic forgot for once their great
enemy and added their tears to the universal lament.
He was borne to his temporary tomb in Metairie Cemetery by the governors of nine states and during the
winter following, the legislatures of the South held
formal memorial sessions.   Never was more universal
homage rendered to a departed chieftain.   The North
looked on in mute astonishment at the loyalty of the
defeated South ;   for had not the Southern people
blamed Davis for their ruin !   In summing up a favorable review of his life, the New York *World* said
truly, "A great soul has passed away."

Four years later, by request of the people of Richmond, and of the South generally, his remains were
brought to Hollywood Cemetery and given their final
sepulture on the banks of the turbulent James, where
the conflict of his life had waged the hottest ; there
the visitor to the capital of the "lost cause" may
now stand by the grave of its most perfect representative.   The body passed from New Orleans through
the capitals of the Southern states, lying in state at
each stopping place long enough to be viewed by the

tens of thousands who desired to pay their final respects to the Confederate President. In Richmond
the people collected from all parts of the country and
listened to the fond eulogies of men who had known
him best. A fitting statue was erected to his memory
—representing him in the dress of a cavalry commander and in the full vigor of mature manhood.
The South's monument, however, stands at the west
end of Monument Avenue, Richmond, not less imposing than that to Lee at the east end. The work,
a memorial both to him and the cause for which
he fought, was unveiled in June, 1907, when the last
great assembly in honor of Jefferson Davis, the
South's "only President," attested in unqualified
terms the loyalty and devotion of this people to the
name of the man whom their fathers chose to lead them
in their heroic struggle for independence.

BIBLIOGRAPHY

Below will be found a list of the principal sources of information, both printed and in manuscript form used in the preparation of the *Life of Davis*. This is not, however, intended as an exhaustive bibliography or even a full list of all the sources consulted in the preparation of the preceding study.

ARCHIVES of the State Department, Washington. Letters to Davis from various friends and supporters during the period of 1852–1861. These papers have recently been transferred to the Bureau of Manuscripts of the Library of Congress.

BIOGRAPHICAL. Adams, C. F., *Life of Charles Francis Adams*, in American Statesmen Series. Alfriend, *Life of Jefferson Davis*. Du Bose, J. W., *Life of William L. Yancey*. Henderson, G. F. R., *Life of Stonewall Jackson*. Johnston and Browne, *Life of Alexander H. Stephens*. McLaughlin, A. C., *Life of Lewis Cass*, in American Statesmen Series. Nicolay and Hay, *Life of Abraham Lincoln*. Pollard, E. A., *Life of Jefferson Davis*, 1869. National Publishing Company. Curtis, Geo. T., *Life of James Buchanan*.

DAVIS, GEORGE. Letters, private correspondence between Jefferson Davis and George Davis of Wilmington, N. C., Attorney-General of the Confederacy.

DAVIS, JEFFERSON. Papers, letters, telegrams, newspaper clippings, etc., bearing mainly on the post bellum period—in the Confederate Museum, Richmond, Va. These papers are referred to in the footnotes as The Confederate Museum Papers.

DOCUMENTARY. *Official Records of the Union and Confederate Armies*, Series I, Vols. II, XIX, XLVI, and others not directly quoted. *Messages and Papers of the Presidents*, Vol. V, compiled by J. B. Richardson. *Messages and Papers of the Confederacy*, Vol. I, compiled by J. B. Richardson. *Reports of Secretary of War*, Jefferson Davis, to the 33d Congress, 1855–1856. *Report of the American Historical Association*, 1899, Vol. II—*the Calhoun correspondence*, by J. F. Jameson. *Proceedings of the Massachusetts Historical Society*, Second Series, Vol. XIX. Congressional *Globe*, 1845–1861. *Rebel War Clerk's Diary*, kept by J. B. Jones, a clerk in the Confederate War Department, 1861–1865. Trinity College (N. C.) *Historical Papers*, 1899 ; Southern Historical Society *Publications*, XXI ; *South Atlantic Quarterly*, Vol. II.

GENERAL ACCOUNTS OF THE PERIOD. Adams, C. F., *Constitutional Ethics of Secession*. Collins, W. H., *The Domestic Slave Trade*, 1904. Broadway Publishing Company. Davis, Jefferson, *Rise and Fall of the Confederate States*, 1881. Appleton. Garrison, George P., *Texas* in American Commonwealth Series. Rhodes, J. F., *History of the United States*, 1850–1877. The Macmillan Co. Schouler, James, *History of the United States*, Vol. V. Dodd, Mead & Co. Wood and Edmonds, *Civil War in the United States*, 1905. Putnam. Callahan, J. T., *Diplomatic History of the Southern Confederacy*. Hopkins Press.

MEMOIRS. Alexander, E. P., *Military Memoirs of a Confederate*, 1907. Scribner. Claiborne, J. H. C., *Reminiscences of Mississippi*, Vol. I. Davis, Mrs. Jefferson, *Memoir of Jefferson Davis*, 1890. Appleton. Davis, Reuben, *Recollections of a Mississippian*. Houghton, Mifflin & Co. Jones, J. W., *Memorial Volume on Jefferson Davis*, 1893. Lee, Captain Robert E., *Recollections and Letters of General Robert E. Lee*, 1904. Doubleday, Page & Co. Longstreet, General J. B., *From Manassas to Appamattox*. Johnson, Bradley T., *Life and Reminiscences of Joseph E. Johnston and Jefferson Davis;* General J. B. Gordon, *Reminiscences*. Scribner.

NEWSPAPERS. Washington *Union*, *National Intelligencer ;* Richmond *Enquirer*, *Examiner*, *Dispatch;* Raleigh (N. C.) *Standard*, *Progress;* Charleston *Mercury*, *Courier ;* Columbus (Ga.) *Times;* Augusta (Ga.) *Chronicle and Sentinel;* Montgomery (Ala.) *Advertiser;* Jackson (Miss.) *Mississippian*, the Mississippi *Weekly Independent*, Vicksburg *Sentinel;* New York *Herald*.

PERIODICALS. *American Historical Review*, Vol. X. *McClure's Magazine*, December, 1900. *Century Magazine*, Sept., 1899.

INDEX